Gifted by

A True Story of Cancer, Loss and Rebirth

by

Jane Duncan Rogers

Living Well
Publications

Published in 2015 by Living Well Publications

ISBN Paperback: 978-0-9537403-1-4

ISBN eBook: 978-0-9537403-2-1

Published with the help of Indie Authors World.

Praise for Gifted By Grief

"*Gifted by Grief* is, by turns, a raw memoir and uplifting companion that can be leaned on during one of the most challenging transitions we all face in life. Jane shares her journey through grief and out the other side with heart-rending honesty and humorous insights that will have you crying one minute, laughing out loud the next".

Andrea Gardner
Author of Change Your Words, Change Your World.

"*Gifted By Grief* is a courageous, wise and beautifully written book. Jane has my deep respect for her vulnerable and perceptive exploration of sadness, loss and integration, ultimately leading to true healing".

Malcolm Stern
Psychotherapist, author and co-founder of 'Alternatives' at St James's Church, London.

"A must-read for anyone just recently grieved. It will help you through the process and remind you that you are not the first or only to feel so wounded. The practical insights are right-on and helpful. But the very best aspect of this work is its unrelenting theme of love, always love. Love is present, love is the answer and love is all there is. I'm touched by Jane's raw, authentic and riveting voice. This is an important book for anyone looking inward to understand".

Diane Vasarkovy
Business Consultant

"A totally inspirational journey, both emotional and deeply spiritual, where life and death has no difference and the sacred hoop is complete. This is a read for us all, regardless of grief and loss - it is so full of humanity, growth and wisdom".

Julie Anne Hart
Intuitive Consultant and Spiritual Coach

"*Gifted by Grief* is a real, totally heartfelt and deeply moving human account of a married couple's journey through cancer, the dying process, loss and grief, and recovery. This may sound sad and not an attractive read, but believe me, you will want to read every word. To anyone who seeks a deeper context and meaning to life and death, this book will open your heart and mind further".

Delcia McNeil
Author of The A-Z of Channelled Wisdom and Guidance

"*Gifted by Grief* isn't just a story about cancer; it is an inspiring message of awakening. Through the honest and brave accounts of Jane and Philip, we discover how a truly painful experience can bring with it the gift of transformation. It is never easy to read about suffering or death but Jane has done an amazing job of bringing together their journal entries with her beautifully wise words to create a book that really helps you come to terms with a subject that so many fear to openly discuss. Reading *Gifted by Grief* was an honour and a privilege and I know that Jane's wisdom will stay with me and support me through my life, no matter how the path unfolds."

Tiffany Kay,
Author of From Pursuit to Presence

Dedication

To Philip

You were right; Love really is the answer.

Contents

Foreword by Robert Holden

Grief is an angel. Not everyone recognises her as such. Especially not in the early days after we have experienced our loss. We resist grief in the beginning. We don't want to know about her. She appears as an old hag and as a sinister character in a nightmare. We can't see her for who she is. The pain of our loss is too great. We are still in denial of what is. We are not ready to open our eyes.

We all experience loss. The form of every relationship has to end eventually. We know this is the deal here on earth. Even so, we are totally unprepared for loss. It comes as a shock. Life is impossible now, or so it seems. No one can survive grief alone. That is why grief appears at our door. She is an angel, I tell you. She is here to help us heal our loss.

Grief visits everyone. We have to be willing to let grief in and have her stay a while if we are to come to terms with what has happened. We will shut her out many times. Fortunately, she doesn't give up. She hovers over us, ready to catch us when we are off guard. She waits for us in the dark. She helps us to meet our anger, our pain, and the urge to die.

Grief teaches us to forgive. With her help, we forgive our losses in all their guises. We forgive the world for being only temporary. We forgive each other for leaving and for dying. Through forgiveness, we see that some things can't be lost. Form changes, but love is constant. Bodies do die, but souls still keep each other company. Relationships are forever in the Oneness of things. Forgiveness gives us life after death.

Grief takes us on a journey. She helps us to forgive our past and heal our future. She introduces us to new friends. Chance meetings happen as soon as we're ready. Invitations appear from nowhere. Extraordinary encounters are arranged. Books land on our lap – books like this one that you're reading now. Each day we take another step into a new world. We are not alone and synchronicity is the new reality now.

Jane Duncan Rogers is my friend. We first met when we were both living in Oxford, some twenty years ago. I remember my first visit to Jane and Philip's house. Philip gave me a copy of his book *Do You Feel Loved By Me?* It's a beautiful book written by a loving and kind man. I see Jane each time I visit Findhorn with my family. Mostly we don't plan our meetings. They just happen, as if they are arranged for us.

I smiled when I read Jane's email asking me to write the Foreword for *Gifted by Grief*. My own angel of grief must have had a hand in this. Just a few weeks ago, my mother died. The loss is hard to bear. I miss her physical presence. My father died many years ago. He was born on December 1st, which is the date that Jane's husband Philip died. Another synchronicity.

Reading *Gifted by Grief* is a healing experience. Jane has written a raw memoir, as her friend Andrea Gardner says, that is intimate and spacious, private and revealing, and honest and wise. In sharing her journey with grief, Jane helps us with our journey too. I feel lighter each time I read another bit of her manuscript. In witnessing her healing, I am experiencing my own. I trust that you will experience something like this too.

Thank you Jane for your courage, for your loving presence in this world, and for the gift of your beautiful book.

Robert Holden

London, May 2015

Preface

This book is divided into three sections: Cancer, Loss, and Rebirth.

Part 1: Cancer

My husband Philip was motivated to write a blog during the final year of his life, and this section includes excerpts from that blog, and also my own journal entries, as we embark on the 'cancer journey'. It also introduces quotes from 'The Listening', a series of messages I received during meditation, which was a huge source of support for us both. These different writings are identified with their headings, but also in different styles. I also share about our relationship – how we met, what was important to us in 20 years of adventurous being together, and how we learnt to live with cancer as part of our relationship.

Part 2: Loss

Philip's death catapulted me into a journey of grief and discovery in that first year, and selected journal entries express this in an honest and in-the-moment manner. Further losses and unexplained joy found me asking, at the deepest level, 'who am I?' This section contains my explorations into this subject, my thoughts and feelings on the matter, as well as all the practical and physical aspects of being a newly bereaved woman.

Part 3: Rebirth

About 15 months after Philip died, it became clear I was a very different person. As with all births, this one took many months to come to fruition, and showed up in many ways. It included a completely new understanding of what is real and what is not, who I am now, and how that translated into a physical level. The amazing revelations during this time, including what it is that is within an alive body, underpinned everything, and continues to do so in my life now.

Jane Duncan Rogers, May 2015

Part 1: Cancer

Prologue

October 2010

Philip didn't soften the blow. "It's stomach cancer."

"What?" I felt my body go cold all over, and sat down suddenly. I wished I was with him at home, instead of on the end of a phone, miles away in London. "No. Really?"

"Yes. The consultant told me they found traces of it in the lining of my stomach."

"Oh, God. What happens next then?" Immediately, I was into trying to get the problem solved, even though I was so shocked that I didn't really take it all in. This kind of announcement is one of those things you think only ever happens to other people. But, devastatingly, here it was now, in our own lives.

Later that night, I came through the gate at Inverness airport, and saw Philip waiting for me. "Is it really true?" I whispered, nestling into his tall, strong body. It didn't seem possible.

"I'm afraid so."

"I can't believe it." Somewhere, on that plane trip, I'd been desperately hoping it was all a dream. Philip told me he knew, really, when he got a letter from the hospital earlier that week, saying he should contact them immediately. He'd spoken right away to his daughter, Jackie, a nurse. The hospital simply confirmed his worst fear.

It confirmed my worst fear, too; that he would die and abandon me, leaving me all alone in the world with no husband and no children.

Summer 1990

"I know I'm not sure about having children, but I'd at least like to have the *choice* to have them," I confided to my friend, as we sat together on the beach, looking out over the turquoise Aegean sea, waves gently rolling in. "To do that, though, I want to have a man to have them with, and my track record isn't great in that department. After three months we always break up, mainly because I'm so terrified. What about if I commit to someone and then they leave me? How would I cope?" This fear had clearly been a dominating influence in my relationships.

"Jane..." she murmured sympathetically, "it sounds like you need some help. How about getting some counselling?" I felt the warm sand underneath the soles of my feet. My gaze shifted to the far away horizon; in that moment I began to feel a sense of possibility.

That short conversation was the precursor to several months of therapy during which I pronounced I would commit to the next man I met who was suitable, to whom I was attracted, and who was attracted to me. Rash, but bold, and it would need to be, to counteract the three-month-break-up pattern and my fears.

One autumn morning, sitting in the counsellor's attractive room at her house, I pronounced:

"I think I'm ready to meet a man now; the thing is, there's no decent ones out there." We had a back and forth conversation about this, and at the end of the session she surprised me by saying something that would change my life forever.

"I have a friend staying with me who's going to your office today, and can give you a lift there. His name's Pradeep, although he calls himself Philip for his work." Pradeep was an unusual name for a white, middle-class Englishman, but my counsellor had an odd name too, Viyog. I knew it meant they were both sannyasins, followers of spiritual master Osho, then known as Bhagwan Sri Rajneesh. After the end of the session, Viyog called Pradeep's name and a friendly head appeared at the door. Within a few minutes, I was sitting next to him in his car.

I was captivated by the air of still presence surrounding this man. I simply wanted to be near him, and soak up some of that stillness for myself. Taken aback by this desire, and to cover my nervousness, I chattered the whole of the half hour drive to the office. There, we continued to talk until I protested, "I really have to get on with some work now, you must go," and shepherded Pradeep to the door.

"Will you have lunch with me today?" he asked.

"No, no, I've already taken my lunch break by having my therapy session." I felt disappointed, but touched by the invitation. Bidding him goodbye at the door, I went to shake his hand; he reached out and hugged me. I felt a bit taken aback.

"That's a bit forward," I thought, "is this what all sannyasins are like?" Still, the hug was lovely; warm and affectionate, and I felt sad saying goodbye, and spent the next couple of hours focusing on work as best I could.

Later that afternoon, he rang to invite me to dinner on the following Monday, when he would next be in London. 'Yes!' burst out of me, and I scampered down the office corridor, shouting "I've got a date, I've got a date!"

The three month relationship test came. I knew from previous experience this would be a watershed moment. Despite a week of shouting, arguments, and stomping off on both our parts, I held to my resolve. Sure enough, the pattern was broken, and after that week, we had made a commitment to each other. I rang my Mum in France. "I think I've met the man I want to marry," I announced with excitement.

"Isn't that a bit soon?" she sounded worried.

"It's all right Mum, it'll all be fine," I waved away her fears cheerily.

October 2010

When we found out about the cancer, I was catapulted back into that moment with Mum. Now, it wasn't all fine. I was terrified; Philip, too. My worst fear – of being without the fabric of belonging; a husband, children, a family – seemed like it actually might happen. Was I really going to be all alone in this world? It seemed possible, and yet I had no idea at all that even if I was alone, I would also find myself having received a gift and being grateful for it.

1
An Unusual Man

Philip, or Pradeep, was an adventurer. He'd been self-employed since his late teens, married young when a baby was on the way, and had a mixture of jobs to support his growing family, including mini-cabbing and working in London's Smithfield Market.

One of the most fascinating things about him, though, was the seventeen or so years he had lived in the Rajneesh ashram in Poona, India, since the breakup of his marriage. The ashram, now known as The Osho International Meditation Resort, was a hotspot for all kinds of different therapies and personal growth workshops. Pradeep was a man who would understand why I'd lived and worked in a London-based spiritual community for five years in my twenties. He would recognise, and understand, what was so attractive about living such a very different lifestyle. From that very first date, in a vegetarian restaurant in Hampstead, London, and a moonlit walk on Hampstead Heath afterwards, we became best friends. He was a deep thinker, he offered radically different perspectives on life and was unpredictable. In all of the years we spent together, I was never once bored.

*

Early on in our relationship, on a long car journey from South Wales to my family's holiday cottage on the shores of the Solway Firth in Scotland, I heard many of the intimate details of the years he spent in the ashram in the seventies and eighties.

"What did you do all the time?" As I sat next to him in the passenger seat, I glanced across at him, curious as to his reply.

"The emphasis was on all kinds of meditation, first and foremost. For instance, Dynamic Meditation goes through five stages: the first is quick, heavy breathing; the second you let yourself go completely, screaming, dancing about wildly, whatever you want to do. It's kind of chaos, really."

"That doesn't sound like traditional meditation at all!" I was intrigued.

"No, it's not, but I found it wonderful. The third stage is jumping up and down with your arms above your head shouting "*Hoo! Hoo! Hoo!*"

This was unlike anything I had come across before. "The fourth stage is freezing – wherever you are when the music ends, you simply stop and hold that position. Finally, you sit still." I was curious and critical all at the same time. This sounded even weirder than some of the things I'd got up to in my community. "For a while I was working in the kitchen. That was hard work, very hard, and in a boiling hot environment too. I had to learn to cut bread, 2000 slices per day, and get it right. That took some doing, I tell you!" he laughed. "And then I was in the carpentry workshop a lot, making some fine furniture for Bhagwan's house. That's when my joinery skills came in really handy."

"But you told me you also worked as a psychotherapist there, how did that happen?"

"I learned on the job, so to speak, by being an assistant on several year-long trainings; holding groups, leading meditations, and learning all about group process. When Bhagwan left India for Oregon, USA, I didn't have enough money to join him, so I returned to an off-shoot of the ashram, the Medina Community in England, and co-led several therapy workshops and trainings there. It was in a beautiful old building in Suffolk. Can you imagine us, the place overflowing with young people and children, all wearing orange robes?"

"Why orange?"

"It's the traditional Indian garb of the devotee. You see it all the time on the streets in India."

"Not so much in England, though," I pondered, "much too chilly."

Before the breakup of his first marriage in the sixties, Philip and his then wife had been attending encounter groups, one of the many radical offerings of the new personal growth movement. His explorations after the divorce had led him to visit Bhagwan, who at that time was simply giving discourses in what was then Bombay. That balmy, Indian night, Philip walked to a house following directions given by a friend he had met in London. Climbing the stairs, he arrived in a small room in which a crowded forty or so people were sitting cross-legged on the floor, waiting to listen to Bhagwan's words. It was an opportunity for new people to sit in front of Bhagwan and receive 'sannyas', a commitment to Bhagwan's philosophy and teachings, marked by being given a new (Indian) name, the wearing of the orange clothes, and being known as a sannyasin. Philip stepped through between other bodies, and sat down before Bhagwan. Looking into his eyes, he saw something so utterly beautiful, so peaceful, so unlike anything else he had ever experienced, that in that moment he dedicated the rest of his life to discovering what that was for himself. He received his new name, Swami Anand Pradeep, meaning 'light of bliss,' and started to work in the ashram, beginning his journey of discovering what enlightenment was about. This was irresistible for him, but it came at a huge cost – not being able to see his children back in England easily. Even when he did manage to see them, on irregular visits back home, it was something he found so painful, that he concluded it would be easier for him, and perhaps for them, if he kept his visits to a minimum. Balancing the compelling need to be with his spiritual master and trying to find a role in the family when he did visit, were two elements that proved impossible for him to reconcile. This he later regretted and, sadly, found it impossible to forgive himself for.

In 1990, Philip had just recently returned from the ashram as a result of developing what turned out to be his first bout of chronic fatigue syndrome. The previous six months had been spent lying in his bed with friends bringing him food to break the monotony of the days. Slowly, with rest, he recovered enough to be able to come back to England, where he could be under the wings of the National Health Service. The cause of this illness later turned out to be immune system poisoning by pesticides commonly used in India at the time, although it took many years before this was discovered, and it considerably affected his day-to-day living. However, while he had all those months in bed he discovered his writing talents, and produced his first manuscript, albeit very slowly. This was a personalised description of life in the ashram in the seventies, before Bhagwan abandoned India and moved to America.[1] If he'd written it now, it probably would have been a blog.

Back in England, having fully recovered, Philip had started work again as a psychotherapist, with individuals and couples, as well as groups. He founded *Green Events* in Oxford in 1990, a monthly broadsheet advertising all things green and holistic, which in those days was very definitely alternative. *Green Events* was later sold and became the highly successful London-based magazine, also titled *Green Events*, with an offshoot in Devon. His motivation for starting this had been to help him advertise his therapy practice, and as he was a great one for getting things going, this really suited him. Although he used his original name, Philip Rogers, for work, he still called himself Pradeep with his friends, and it was at this stage that we met.

The Monday evening of our first date turned out to be the beginning of one twenty-year long conversation, about life, love, the universe and everything. We sparked each other off, had our challenges, and found each other inspiring and enthusiastic about our many shared interests. Neither of us were easy to live with, which made for a lot of learning about how to share our lives and space together happily. He dropped the name Pradeep shortly after we started living together, having found using two names too cumbersome, and insisted on being called Philip – no shortening to 'Phil' was ever allowed.

The man I had now committed to caused me a big challenge. He had already had a vasectomy. So what about children? I wasn't

1.Philip's forthcoming e-book of this will be available at www.giftedbygrief.com/the-book/other

prepared to let a good man go just in case I wanted children; I still felt ambivalent about them and had never had the broody feeling that many women experience. But I was keen on something else.

"Let's get married," I enthused, while lying in bed one morning.

"No, no, we're fine as we are," Philip replied.

"Why not, though?" I persisted. "I think it's a great idea. We know we love each other; we like living together. So let's do it."

"Sorry, darling. I just don't want to. I've been married, done that. I don't want to do it again." Philip's previous marriage had produced the three children he had loved and missed so much, and he was now a grandfather to a delightful little boy, Daniel. I didn't leave it there, though. Insistent, I continued, until one day he exasperatedly shouted:

"Okay then – do you promise to look after me in sickness and in health?"

"No." The word suddenly popped out of my mouth, and my excitement died in the shock of what I'd uttered. It was as if something else was speaking through me, giving my conscious mind no time at all to compose a more reasonable answer. Why was I shocked? In the early days of our relationship in Oxford, whenever Philip had so much as a bad headache, I'd run away home to London. So though what he said may have surprised me, my own answer shouldn't have. His question worked, though: it shut me up. Marriage was no longer mentioned as I digested the meaning of my 'no.'

About eighteen months later, Philip casually suggested dressing up and going out for a meal. This was very unusual, especially the dressing up bit. I remember leaning against the fridge in the kitchen as the thought he might propose crossed my mind. It was scary, because getting married really did mean I would be unlikely to have a child. Not to mention how I felt about looking after him in sickness and in health. But I pushed the thought from my mind, in case I was mistaken, and end up disappointed.

Later that evening, towards the end of a beautiful, candlelit Thai meal, alongside champagne and red roses, Philip did indeed propose, and I burst into tears.

"But Jane, I want to double check with you," Philip held my hand and looked at me lovingly across the table. "Getting married almost definitely means no babies."

Tearfully, I looked into his blue eyes.

"Yes, I know, but I'm still not sure I want a baby. Let's cross that bridge when we come to it." I was 38 – if the bridge was going to be crossed, it would be happening soon. However, my previous 'no' had changed so completely, that all I could do was utter a 'yes' to his proposal. In fact, we had both changed, and were able to make a real commitment to each other, regardless of sickness, health, children or anything else.

The years after our marriage were full of adventures. Philip had encouraged me to become self-employed when I first met him, and as I had already trained in California with Louise L. Hay, founder of Hay House publishers, I became the first woman to lead study groups of her famous book *You Can Heal Your Life* ® in the UK and Europe. Together, Philip and I also ran various other personal growth groups around the UK, as well as having our own private practices as a counsellor and psychotherapist.

The 'babies bridge' did emerge to be crossed, not surprisingly, about two years later. I was in therapy again, rather unsuccessfully trying to come to terms with feeling ambivalent about being a mother. Philip was clear on the subject though.

"Jane, I don't want any more children. But if you really do, if you're 100% clear, then I am willing to try." Eventually we decided he would undergo a vasectomy reversal, which all went smoothly, and we had a couple of months of lovemaking where we knew the result might change our relationship forever. Our lives did change, but not how I thought they would. In the tests after the operation, no sperm were found. Not even weak ones. None at all. I was devastated. Choosing not to have a child and not being physically able to have one were very different propositions. I would never be part of the Mothers Club. That was my first experience of how debilitating grief can be. Later, I gave birth to my first book[2] instead of a baby.

When you don't have children, there's a lot of time available for all sorts of other things. Alongside everything else we were already engaged in, including renovating our house, we ran a large alternative health clinic in Oxford for several years. Philip became ill again with chronic fatigue, and yet, despite that, we had a six week camper van trip through California down to Mexico (me driving) to see the grey whales and their babies: the warm waters there are perfect for giving birth.

After selling the clinic in 2004, we lived on a yacht in Auckland harbour, New Zealand, for the best part of the next year, fulfilling one of Philip's dreams to island-hop in warm weather. Although I wasn't as keen on sailing as Philip was, I wasn't exactly averse to swimming in warm waters, diving off the side of the yacht, and generally enjoying myself for a few months after all the hard work of running the clinic.

2. Choose Your Thoughts, Change Your Life. Now out of print but available through www.giftedbygrief.com/the-book/other

We were drawn back to living in the UK when we heard my sister was pregnant, and moved to Belfast, Northern Ireland, to be near her. This was very important to me, as I imagined it would be the closest I would get to having a baby myself. Living just twenty minutes walk from both my sister and my parents was wonderful, and I delighted in looking after my nephew regularly. However, I discovered, as all new parents do, how exhausting and all-consuming it is to look after a child. I loved looking after him, but I breathed a sigh of relief when I could give him back at 6pm every night.

It seemed as though our lives were all planned out for the next couple of decades, being with family. I felt happy, even though we weren't really connected to a community of spiritual friends.

However, plans changed for my sister and her husband, and two years later they moved back to London. I felt devastated. Neither Philip nor I wanted to live in London, so instead we decided to seek a community where we could feel at home. We were clearly still looking for a 'family' to belong to. We tried out an eco-community in the south of Ireland, but six months there proved it wasn't the right place for us, and we moved back to Belfast again. My parents only lived in Ireland half the year, spending the rest of their time in France, so when they were away we felt as if we were in limbo, with no real reason to be in Ireland.

One day, feeling at a bit of a loss about what to do, I read about a course called *Communicating with God and Nature*, led by Dorothy McLean of the Findhorn Foundation in Scotland. My spirits perked up as I completed the booking form. Unwittingly, this action was to set us on the next step of another adventure. I loved being on the course; during that week I had an intense experience of coming alive, and when I told Philip about it he got on the next plane. The next thing we knew, we were looking for a house to buy in the vicinity of the Findhorn Foundation, and within 3 months had bought and moved into a house, feeling immediately at home. After all these years of searching, I especially found a place where I felt I belonged.

When we looked back one day on this whole story of how we came finally to rest at Findhorn, we realised what a rich and adventurous life we had led. Before Philip contracted chronic fatigue, we had climbed up and down mountains together, travelled widely, and he had been a strong and vibrant man, fully engaged with life at all levels. While his illness had robbed him of much of that, we still managed to pack in quite a lot, and enjoy ourselves.

"You know, Jane," Philip remarked one day, while lying on the sofa in our new cottage in Forres. "In many ways, this chronic fatigue has been a blessing. It's given me opportunities I'd never otherwise have taken. It would have been very hard for me to stop seeing my long-term clients, in particular; or to go off on our camper-van trips, and I would never have travelled to New Zealand. I wouldn't have been able to justify it, would have thought I needed to earn money, to work, to create a living for us. Instead, all these opportunities arose and we've found a way to take them, despite me not being very well. I would never have chosen this, mind you, but sometimes I can almost feel grateful for the illness."

I wasn't entirely sure about this. The chronic fatigue totally floored him for the best part of two years; at his worst, he'd walk up one flight of stairs to the bedroom and have to lie down again for the rest of the afternoon. Of course he had given up work, and I'd learned to cope by myself with our businesses and with day-today living. I found this very hard, but just got on with it, one step at a time. He did improve somewhat over the years, but always had to manage his energy levels very carefully. It was not an easy time for us, to put it mildly. Given how I used to abandon him when he had so much as a headache, I'd been severely tested with his inability to do very much at all. I was about to be tested again.

2
Diagnosis Day

You know how easy it is to live thinking nothing bad will ever happen to you? We were both like that: didn't have life insurance, not much in savings, took opportunities as they came up. No game plan; just trusting all would be well. Nothing really bad *had* ever happened in my life.

So it was a sobering few hours, the first night cancer became part of our lives. I'd come home from London determined to address some of the recent marital challenges we'd been having. Now this news put those things into even sharper perspective. I knew we both had to be willing to tell the truth about our relationship, because the stakes were so much higher.

"I was going to tell you we had to do something radically different to change things between us, because we haven't been very happy these last few months. I realise now that's not going to happen, is it? But I still want you to hear how very desperate I've been lately." I spoke softly and firmly.

Philip's head was hanging as I continued. He said nothing for quite a while, just listened. "Well, I have to stop being so stubborn, and look at all sorts of things differently now," he murmured. "I know it's been difficult; I know how hard it's been for you, with me having chronic fatigue for so long – it's nine years now, you know." He paused. "I'm willing to do something different now, though. I have to."

"What about the chronic fatigue?" I asked.

"I haven't got time for that now."

I nearly hit him. For the last decade in our marriage, I had lived with a man who had been unable to participate fully in life with me. He'd stubbornly shown little interest in exploring the emotional or spiritual aspects of his illness, and this refusal had exasperated me. Now, he was willing to address this new condition, cancer, at all levels. Chronic fatigue mysteriously disappeared, and the greater challenge of cancer took his attention.

Despite a rocky start after that last comment, we talked long into that night. Long and lovingly. Finding a good, connected place together once again, something that had been part of our marriage often previously, and yet had been missing in the past few months. It was a huge relief to me, even in the face of cancer.

"I'm going to write a blog about this," he announced.

"That's great!" I felt so pleased. Philip had been a good writer in the past, self-publishing two books before the internet days, and writing many stories of his time aboard various yachts with his sailing buddy, Cap'n Kabba. To me, one of his strengths had always been his ability to write. Sadly, he hadn't written anything for years, and that was one of my frustrations with him. So I was very encouraging, and proud, of him starting a blog.

Blog Post: C – Day

Posted on 12th October 2010 by Philip

Jane and I go to the hospital for the scan. I have to dress in one of those back-to-front gowns. I keep my socks on, my feet are cold. I look and feel ridiculous. The machine is huge, like a 10 foot doughnut and I am passed through the hole, being instructed by a disembodied recording. "Breathe in and hold your breath for a few seconds. Try not to move."

I don't feel anything. It is like something out of Star Trek. White plastic technology, a little red light whirring round the doughnut so quickly it becomes a line, then disappears altogether. It is soon done and I have to wait while they check to see they have got it done right.

I sit in the corridor with Jane. We do a Sudoku puzzle together, which is Jane being nice to me. She has never done one before. She is not impressed by my dressing gown and socks. Nor am I, but I don't have to look at me and anyway, I've still got cold feet. Not surprising really. I am scared. I say "All is well," to myself, but I don't really feel it.

Meanwhile, it took time for the real impact of the diagnosis to land in me.

My journal, Sunday 10th October:

Today while singing in the Taize[3] group, it really hit me that my worst fear might be about to happen: I would be 'abandoned' by Philip, and worse, without any children. This is in response to seeing P, sitting chanting with our singing

3. Taize singing originated in a monastery in Taize, France, when the monks (both Catholic and Protestant) sought to reach out to people and traditions through their singing of chants and canons in many languages. Mostly sung in 4-part harmonies, thousands of people still visit Taize today, to sing and pray together. In the Findhorn Foundation Community, there are opportunities to sing every morning, and we also include many songs from the world music tradition.

group, and me wondering about him not being here. Very emotional. I thought about interrupting and going over to sit at his feet. I almost didn't do it, wondering what the other singers would think, but then I remembered how important it is to actually act on my intuition, and I did go over. So glad I did. It felt absolutely right. I want to open my heart to him in full, despite what might happen.

Reading *Love, Medicine and Miracles* by Bernie Siegel, I felt soothed by a quote: 'In the face of uncertainty, there is always hope.' Though I found some comfort from these kinds of words, I wrote in a letter to God in my journal.

24th November, 2010:

Hi, God. I want a miracle for Philip and me. Please have it happen. I want him to have no sign of cancer when they do a scan after the chemo has finished, and then not have to operate. Or if they do operate, for it to be a complete success. In short, I want him to survive and thrive for many years yet. I want us to have a new revolutionary relationship, one that encompasses sheer love through and through. In even shorter terms, please send a miracle! Thank you for this in advance. Thank you for the miracle of his total healing on all levels, of how sweetly this has affected my life and our relationship.

Feeling desperate, I was reaching out in every way I knew, affirming the miracle I wanted. Philip was also wanting a miracle, in his own way. While at the hospital one day for tests, he blogged:

Tuesday 19th October 2010

I am sitting in the chapel in the Royal Infirmary in Aberdeen, Scotland, two hours drive from where we live. It's large and empty. I set my alarm for twenty minutes and sit. Towards the end of the time I start affirming:

"All is well and I am safe."

I don't feel safe, so I change it to: "I am feeling safer every day." Then I affirm: "I am open to the messages these cancer cells have for me. I invite any message in whatever form to come to me, that I may understand the reason for this visit."

I have previously realised the attitude I want to adopt in this situation is to treat the cancer as a welcome guest. To ask respectfully to hear and understand any message it has for me, and having heard that and acted on it as best I can, to then ask this guest to leave.

As I sit, I ask to hear whatever I need to hear, and the words 'Heal your wounds, my son' appear in my mind. They feel loving, and I respond with "How do I do this?"

What comes is not so much words as a sense that the first step is to know I am wounded. To see it more clearly, to acknowledge it in a new and deeper way. Also, that this is the foundation of healing. A clarity arises in me that is hard to articulate, and is already slipping away as I write. I get the message, though:

"Keep healing yourself. Do whatever you need that will help this to happen."

Philip hearing a voice was a miracle in and of itself. He had been envious of others' abilities in this capacity, and so this message whilst in the chapel was of huge importance to him. More miracles did happen, but not quite in the way Philip had wanted, nor in the way I had laid out in my letter to God.

3
Facing Realities

Our twenty year long conversation took a new twist when we had to admit to the starkness of what we were told by the doctors in early November, 2010. I wrote in my journal:

> *We were sitting in a hospital room about 6 p.m. when the registrar came in with three other students. They had found the original cancer cells seen before, plus a thickening of the stomach wall somewhere else. The upshot is that if P doesn't get chemo and surgery done, he will likely be dead within one to two years. Not that we were thinking not to get it done. Ha! But then he said 30-40% of patients survive to five years – and if they do, it's considered cured. That happens if they manage to get all the cancer cells out, and they don't know if they do that or not; it's just a matter of waiting and seeing. Blimey. That, along with discovering that the operation takes five hours, was a big shock. For some reason, I have been denying the seriousness of this, assuming he would have the operation and all would be well. Not as simple as that, though, it seems.*

We really were dealing with a biggie here, just in case we thought we already had enough on our plates, what with being on the brink of likely bankruptcy as a result of our land investments in Ireland going belly-up. Not surprisingly, it all felt a bit much. After the Macmillan nurse, a specialist in cancer care, visited one day, I wrote:

> *She gave us some printed information sheets from the Macmillan website. I notice I'm rather reluctant to read them. I will have to, as we have to be very clear about what is involved in this chemotherapy business. But I am OBJECTING! I DO NOT WANT THIS TO BE HAPPENING! Fuck! Fuck! Fuck!*

Whether we liked it or not, though, our cancer journey had begun, with both of us as reluctant travellers. Of course, it included many more people on the journey too. Ringing my parents to break the news, my Mum, as usual, was positive.

"Well, darling, it's treatable, and you know Joan had that kind of cancer and look, she is fine." I knew this was her way of coping with the impossible thought of impending death, so I was gentle in my reply to her.

"It's really serious, Mum. Of course we hope he will come through okay but the stats aren't that great." She heard me that time. A sobering call in the end, and a bit different to when I called one of my brothers who, just before ringing off, commented,

"Just think of it this way – at least the food bills will go down."

I laughed; when I told Philip, he laughed too. That's how we began to discover the black humour that is available when death comes knocking at the door.

Philip had to tell his children. Jackie, his eldest, had had the heads-up of course, and had already told her sister and other members of their family. Much more difficult was the conversation Philip had with his son.

Philip's blog

5th October 2010

We now have a lot of people to tell about the cancer. How do you do this? "Hi, Matt" (he's my son) "just calling to tell you I've got cancer." No, that won't do. "Hi Matt. I've got some bad news. I've got cancer." No, that won't do either. I settle on, "I've got some bad news. I've just come from the hospital. They did an endoscopy last week and found some cancer cells." Short and not sweet, but there it is. The awful thing is that Matt is getting it from two directions. His eldest daughter, Becky who is 13, has got cancer too.

We'd been on the receiving end of cancer news earlier that year when Matt rang to say that dear Becky, his eldest daughter, had non-Hodgkins lymphoma. A very shocking call, and so having to make this one to Matt was particularly difficult.

In the meantime, I was feeling confused.

Journal: Sunday 6th November 2010

I wrote to someone last night that I was grateful for this cancer. Amazing! How can I be grateful? I've even had thoughts that if he died, I would still be grateful for this time and therefore for the disease that is causing this massive shift in Philip, and us feeling so close again.

This is weird. Maybe not so weird, though. Am I grateful to the credit crunch? I certainly have written in my journal about being grateful that our financial circumstances have propelled me into a deeper place of peace within. It might never have happened without that, so yes, I am grateful, though it's easy to be grateful when you think it might all be coming to a resolution.

With this cancer, though, it hasn't even started happening yet! Will I be able to continue feeling grateful while he deals with chemo side effects and goes through an operation – if he has to go through it? Who knows? Does it matter? No.

What matters is just right now. Right now I feel back in love with my husband, and it's just wonderful. In fact, not back in love. Loving afresh someone whom I have always known could truly flower and blossom, and yet was sitting on it. He ain't sitting anymore, though! My God. He's jumped off his position and has embraced all kinds of things that are allowing him to shine, and it's really coming out through his blog. He's getting wonderful responses, and I'm not surprised because he's a great writer and storyteller. I feel so proud of him, and it is wonderful to be able to say that.

So thank you, cancer.

Another reality we faced up to was the predominant way of thinking about cancer in the West, which is that whether you like it or not, you've entered into a battle. Hence words like overcome, beat, fight against, conquer, and book titles like *Anti-Cancer, Understand, Prevent and Overcome Cancer* and *Foods to Fight Cancer.* It is all about a war. Philip felt very strongly about this, as he'd written in previous blog posts.

Respected Visitor

Posted on 6 December 2010 by Philip

I'm thinking of changing the title of the blog from 'Cancer – A Welcome Guest?' to 'Cancer – A Respected Visitor.' I feel the first is not really true. Maybe in some ideal world I would be able to say that genuinely; or at some point in the future, but not right now. I want to reach for that, a bit over the top. Whereas, 'respected visitor' feels a better place to stand.

Philip wanted to find the message this respected visitor had for him, and then ask it to leave. I created a short healing visualisation for him along these lines which he listened to only occasionally, but it emphasised the acknowledgment of the presence of cancer cells, while asking them to leave with the power of love.[4]

The final reality check was how to fit in taking care of Philip around my work. Just before the diagnosis, we had rented out our cottage and moved into Newbold House, a small community in Forres. Currently living in two high-ceilinged rooms in the huge and rather gorgeous Victorian building, set in lovely gardens, we were to be there for six months on a trial basis. It would be an experiment as to whether I could continue my own work – being self-employed as a life and small business coach – while also contributing to the running of Newbold House and being part of a highly-structured community. In the usual hectic run up to Christmas of that year though, I was focusing on sending

4. Copies of this visualization, 'Healing Love', are available from www.giftedbygrief.com/the-book/meditations

in a book proposal for a competition. I felt a bit overwhelmed by the work to be done for that, on top of normal client work, and chemo support on top too. It's amazing what you can get done, though, when you have to.

Living in a community like this wasn't an easy option. We were twelve people at the time, and just like any family, you get on with some members better than others. One major lesson was learnt at this time for both Philip and myself.

"I can't believe Mary did that! How could she say what she said?" exclaimed Philip to me one morning, after our regular community meeting. "It's so unfair, what on earth was she thinking of?" Mary was a community member whom Philip was regularly challenged by; she pressed his buttons just by being around, even without saying anything. On this occasion, though, Philip had lost his temper with her, and there was a bit of a cold war going on for a couple of days. One morning he told me, "I've just realised I've been blaming Mary for what happened. I've been thinking all kinds of negative, judgmental things about her, furious she hasn't apologised to me, determined she should. That's not all right, though, because it's *me* that's feeling terrible. So I'm going to apologise to her for thinking all these horrible things about her. At least I'll feel better about that." Later, he brought me up to date. "I bumped into Mary in the corridor, and told her what had happened for me. I apologised. She looked a bit taken aback, but she smiled and thanked me. It really feels like the air has cleared between us. I'm so glad I said sorry."

I hugged him. "You are amazing. I love how you've been able to turn this situation around. If only everyone could practice forgiveness like this, what a different place the world would be."

4
Self-Importance

Philip was an entertaining writer with a dry sense of humour and, around this time, he wrote a blog post about the self-importance involved in having cancer.

Self-importance

Posted on 12 November 2010 by Philip

There are some uncomfortable aspects to having cancer. One might die is the first. I'm afraid of that. I tell myself, "You have to die sometime. It's going to happen one day. OK, but not yet. I'm not ready. Get ready, then."

Hmm, what do I do to get ready? First, deal with these old issues – that's clear. Which will make living a lot more enjoyable, I imagine. Already is, in fact. I am enjoying dealing with these things, going for healing. Diana, my therapist, comes with lots of good recommendations, and she seems to know what she is doing. I can see writing this that I am not exactly enthusing about her. Sorry, Diana, if you should be reading this. We've only met twice, so it's early days. I am probably a bit guarded in relating to psychotherapists. I wonder what that says about me, as that was my work for so long. I don't know, and as Kate, my nutritional and herbal medicine advisor wisely stated,

"You don't need to understand everything."

She and I are discussing the 'vibrational medicine' side of her work, which is the part of it I am least comfortable with.

"I haven't got a clue what you are doing."

She's using a pendulum, dowsing for answers to questions about my cell function, and then for which remedies to dab me with. Hocus pocus comes to mind. I've been given flower remedies and other vibrational essences before with no noticeable effect. I know from my reading about the placebo effect that it if I don't have confidence in a treatment it will lessen its impact so it's better if I speak up. This is a bit uncomfortable.

"This is the bit I didn't do as consistently as the other things you told me to do. I've been taking the Slippery Elm powder religiously, I have cut out all wheat and dairy products, no sugar. However, the dabbing on of this stuff from the little vial I have missed a few times. I have tried these kind of things before without seeing any benefit."

"There are other things that you trust and don't understand, I expect. Is that so?" She's right. I'm not consistent. "My own experience with these methods is they are extraordinarily effective," she continues. "I have seen people heal long-standing ailments very quickly. It's had a very positive effect on me too."

"Well, that's a good start," I smile. "At least one of us trusts it. I read about a study where doctors were given medicines to prescribe and some of them were placebos and some the real McCoy, or so the doctors thought. In fact, all the pills were placebos. However, the doctors who thought they were prescribing real medicine had better results than the control group. How can we understand that? All we can say is that it happens. It's observable. It's a powerful effect."

As she continues with her dowsing I sit and think about it. I say to myself,

"I can and do get healing from things I don't understand. I can be open to healing from things that are unfamiliar. I don't need to understand something to trust in it."

The truth is that most medicine of all kinds is beyond me. I've never studied it and, in my opinion, lots of people who have are still in the dark. The best people for me are the ones that are willing to admit that. This actually increases my respect for them and then also my trust.

I affirm again, "I am open to healing in ways that I don't understand." Saying this helps.

She works away with her lists and pendulum and I glance at the clock. This is taking longer than I expected. Am I talking too much? Is what I'm saying relevant? I'm telling her all sorts of things. She wants to know about the sessions with Diana. Maybe I should tell her to read this blog!

"I'm worrying about you again," I tell her.

She looks up and smiles. She's got a faint Australian twang and a warm way of speaking. Her hair is starting to grey – at least she doesn't look young, like Diana, who is definitely younger than my daughter – which I find reassuring. I appear to be more than a little ageist. She looks over her glasses at and me and smiles.

"We went through this last time. I'm fine, I am enjoying this and enjoying our work together. Relax."

"Well, it's all on my blog, you know, at www.philiprogers.co.uk*. I'm enjoying writing about it all. I think it's good for me and I hope it may help other people, too."*

I feel a little frisson of self-importance. This is not the first time I've noticed this, and I don't like it.

"I've got cancer, you know." Certainly gets people's attention.

"I've got cancer, you know." You can jump queues, I expect. Get all sorts of advantages and benefits and special attention. I've never had so much attention in my life.

My friend Alan, the plumber and Alexander Technique teacher offered reiki healing, at no charge. "I'd be happy to do it for you." I thanked him and the next day called and set up an appointment.

"Thank you," he said, surprising me, "thank you for letting me help you." I felt really touched and amazed. I was helping him, it seems!

Another friend offered to pay for some therapy and wrote me a large cheque. When he gave it to me he seemed a bit embarrassed. I was very touched again.

Someone emailed me and offered to bless me.

A friend who does distant healing has arranged for a group of thirty healers to 'hold me in the light.'

I have never received so much loving attention in my life. Messages, cards, phone calls.

I'm seeing a healer, getting reiki sessions, seeing Kate for her nutritional advice etc (don't mention the little vials) Diana for psychotherapy. I'm meditating, I'm singing Taize songs.

I've become positively virtuous. But there's also this feeling of self-importance. Being in the centre of so much love and attention makes me more than a little uncomfortable and feels special in an odd kind of a way. It's hard to describe. It's ego, I suppose, just the old ego rearing its head again. Hard to not have one I have found, though I have tried, but who was trying? Which 'I'? And will I become one of those beacons of hope and inspiration? At last I'll be special!

There is even an excitement in me at this new adventure. Am I weird, or what?

Onco Man (the Oncology specialist) asked me today:

"Do you feel more tired?"

"No, I feel energised. Given a massive kick up the bum!" He looked a bit surprised.

Kate finishes her dowsing and we talk about using herbal medicine to help reduce the downside effects of the chemo. She uses her pendulum again.

"We could ask your father to help with the formulation. What do you think? He's willing."

Whoa! Here we go again, off into the realms of the unknown. My dad is a dead herbalist. Kate is sincere about this, I can see.

"Well, I suppose so. Do you think it will help?"

"Yes, I do."

"OK then. Are you going to ask him?" I'd prefer that.

"Yes, I'll get out my reference books and pharmacopia and go through them with him using the pendulum and I'll let you know what we come up with."

Relief.

"Well, thank you very much. I suppose I should say thank you both very much. I certainly think I can support my body in this way, and I've been taking his remedies since I was little. We used to have a little song we sang about the tissue salts."

I hum and sing,

"Ferrum Phos and Kali Mur
They will cure your cold for sure."

I stop, a bit embarrassed. "There's more." Kate smiles.

"Actually, I always thought we were a bit odd: living above our health food shop in the 50s, baking whole-meal bread every day, selling herbs, fresh fruit and vegetable juices made on the spot, being vegetarian, not going to doctors. I never, ever invited anyone to our house. I was afraid of being ridiculed."

"Maybe he was a bit ahead of his time," she smiles again.

"Just a bit." I smile too. "One of my tendencies, as well."

5

Chemo, Pills and Mistletoe

When we moved to this part of Scotland, it was because of the nearby Findhorn Foundation, a spiritual community, learning centre and eco-village of over fifty years standing. Having both been interested and lived in communities before, we knew we didn't want to make the full-time commitment to doing that again, but we were interested in being around like-minded people, and the area around the Foundation is full of them.

Belonging to a large community like this was a big blessing, and a lesson for us in learning to receive help.

"Let's make a list of who might be able to drive you to Aberdeen for the mistletoe," I showed Philip our community address list. "I can't do it every time; a minimum 6 hour round trip is just too much time away from my work." Some weeks he was going twice or three times.

"Good idea. It'll have to be people I can have a great conversation with in the car, though," he sounded slightly anxious.

"Yes, of course, and people who don't mind waiting in Aberdeen while you're being treated."

It felt like a lot to ask of friends, but we made a short list, and to our delight found many people were willing to do this, in fact found it to be a privilege. It turned out this was just the beginning of many and varied forms of support available to us, so long as we were willing to ask. Not always an easy thing to do, but we learned fast; and it was particularly necessary for me, given my various other commitments, and the recent move into Newbold House.

Journal: 27.11.10 Philip's 65th birthday

Oh God. How can it be I have spent from 9 a.m. to 1:15 p.m. today just tending to Philip's needs? I just am not getting the time to write this book proposal. Maybe I need to give it up? But I would be so disappointed and so would he.

How could all that time be taken up? What on earth was I doing?

8 a.m. Slipped out of bed without waking him, had my own breakfast and met with the other community members for the usual morning meeting downstairs.

Got upstairs again just as my phone rang. He was awake and feeling awful. Not just a bit of nausea but also a clenching heartburn type of pain. I settled him, got him to take the slippery elm powder. That meant a trip down all those stairs again to the kitchen to get a banana to take it with; forgot to take the rubbish with me.

Worried about the amount of medicines he is taking, and what he should be taking when. There is so much, and so easy to get it all muddled up.

Rang NHS 24 (National Health Service) to get hold of doctor. Waited for doctor to call me back. Spoke to her. Now 11 a.m. Rang chemist to see if they had the prescription in yet. Six inches of snow outside and still snowing hard. I asked

James to take me down to the pharmacy – I'm afraid of going in the snow. The darling did so even though he has a deadline to meet.

Got the prescription and more of the anti-sickness drugs and some other stuff to help stop the reflux. He's like a walking pill bottle.

District Nurse arrived while on phone to Jackie. Managed a quick cup of coffee with the others downstairs at tea-break time. Spoke to nurse. She gave him an injection. Time for slippery elm again, went downstairs to get prunes to mix it up with this time. Need to make up list for kitchen for what he can eat – when will I ever get to do that? Thank God I am not in the cottage and having to do all this myself. Blessings to the cooks in the kitchen. (Last night did my toilet community shift while he had a bath, as he was feeling a bit better).

Back upstairs – at least I am getting exercise – with prunes; back down again to see what has been cooked for lunch. No good for P, it's got spices in. Put some beans on to boil, along with heated up rice. Bring it up again. I am knackered.

Still, maybe he is beginning to feel a bit better. I come through to my own room and burst into tears. Then ring a friend, Candy, who has been through this. She was wonderful, calm and reassuring. It was great. Now maybe I can take another look at the book proposal. What a way to spend his birthday.

Philip's treatment plan was three rounds of chemotherapy over nine weeks, then an operation to remove part of his stomach. Then a further bout of chemo recommended, even if all the cancer cells had been taken out. It sounded horrific. It *was* pretty horrible, but we made the best of it, which for us included trying to think differently about the poison being put into his body – a drip for about ten hours in the hospital once every three weeks, and then pills to be taken regularly.

Philip wrote after the first treatment of this kind:

Shock

4th December 2010:

I am shocked by how little I've been able to share in ten days, since I had my first chemo drip. I've been wanting to tell you about my new mate, Lanky, ever since I met him. We became inseparable straight away. You know how it is with some people you meet? You just click, fit together smoothly. So it was with Lanky. We went everywhere together for the following twelve hours, couldn't be parted.

Sometimes, I had to go somewhere he could get refreshment, recharge his batteries, but apart from that we were free to roam about together. Thank God for Lanky! Because of him I could escape the ubiquitous televisions blaring in every room and get some semblance of peace. If you're not well, I wouldn't recommend a hospital for rest and recuperation. It was noisy, mostly because of the TVs. I retreated to the comfortable, well-appointed day room, but unfortunately one of it's major furnishings was an enormous TV. Not long sitting there before two visitors came in, and without so much as a 'by your leave', switched the damn the thing on. Lanky and I left. He doesn't like them either. We went and sulked on a chair at the end of the corridor, as far away from everyone as we could get.

I suppose I should mention that all this time Lanky was supporting me in a specific way, that is, carrying the bags of various liquids that were dripping into me through the IV. Sometimes, he managed to get a bit tangled up with cables and drip lines, but mostly he did a great job. He was very discreet in the loo; he turned the other way.

So, thanks, mate, but I have to say I feel a bit ambivalent about you, looking back. Now I've had a bit of space, I'm not so sure you were a good influence. The days after we were together were like the worst hangover I've ever had. Sick as a dog, and never a drop or dram had passed my lips. Not even any drunken, half-remembered carousing to regret to balance it out a bit. We'll be together again for the day quite soon again, too. I shall be polite, of course, but definitely hold a bit of English reserve this time around. I let myself go a bit, looking back; got too familiar, too trusting, let you a bit close for comfort, in truth. You carry some powerful medicine, man, but you're not what you seem. I'm going to be a bit more careful second time around.

Today is the beginning of the second week of chemo, one down, eight more to go. If the other eight aren't better than this first one, I don't think I'll make it, but today there's a bit of hope. Last night I slept for five or six hours continuously for the first time. I wasn't woken up by pain, and now I'm not in pain and haven't taken any pain killers, either. This is good.

When I woke up, I felt much, much worse, in a way: free of pain, but almost free of everything. I could hardly move, and now I'm thinking maybe my body had been fighting the drugs. And I had been fighting the drugs, because, as you know (if you've read the other bits), being against drugs is one of my positions in life, and here I am – extreme irony – taking so many pills I can't keep track of them. In fact, neither can Jane; we have to write it all down. She's become like a proper nurse, doing 'obs'.

He had some other mates also, collectively known as The Pills.

"It's really strange, having to take these pills I know are going to poison me," complained Philip.

"Yeah, I don't blame you. But you have to take them. I wonder what we could do to make that easier." I was back in being positive mode, and thinking along the lines of the 'welcome guest' idea. "I know. Let's give them names; we could call them Tom, Dick and Harry. Tom can be saying hallo to the cancer cells, Dick can be saying goodbye, and Harry can say thank you."

"I like it!" replied Philip. "My Dad's name was Harry; it feels just right he would be saying thank you." So we began the regular monitoring of when Tom, Dick and Harry came to visit – it wasn't always all three of them – and how Philip was feeling about them.

There was another vital treatment that Philip embraced in a big way. Here's his full blog post about it:

Mistletoe

29 January 2011 by Philip

A friend called Auriol has been encouraging me to take mistletoe therapy. She's been receiving it for about two years and her cancer is in remission. She hasn't had any chemotherapy. The other day she was talking to me about it; I was speaking about the side effects of chemo, and asked her if there were any side effects from the mistletoe.

"Oh, yes", she spoke enthusiastically, "Hope, courage, and joy!"

"Wow!" I was amazed. Not what I had expected to hear at all. "That sounds really good. I could do with some of that!"

I was still being polite, though, and feeling ambivalent about doing it. There are so many different things I could be trying, and so many people telling me things, and offering me information. I don't know how to choose between them except on the basis of some inner prompting.

"Why don't you give Dr. Geider a ring?" she suggested. "He's the mistletoe doctor."

"Yes. I could do that, couldn't I?" I was still being polite.

"Yes, you could. When will you do it?" Ah, ha! She'd got me! So I either had to say no, I'm not going to, or carry on being polite.

She committed me to ring his secretary tomorrow, and I spoke to the doctor later in the week. I felt he was very experienced and knowledgeable, and that his knowledge made him very flexible, because he knew the kinds of pressures I'm under, particularly from time.

I liked that. So I arranged to see him in Aberdeen after the next appointment with Onco Man.

The same evening after this conversation with Dr. Geider (aka Mistletoe Man), I got a phone call from an acquaintance.

"Hi, this is .... I don't want people to know I've got cancer, I've kept it to myself, but I wanted to tell you about my experience with mistletoe therapy."

"Wow. That's extraordinary, because I just had a conversation today with Dr. Geider about doing it, and I've been very ambivalent about it. What's it like?"

"I would totally recommend it; that's why I'm ringing you up."

He told me in some detail about his experience, which was fundamentally very good, and as I listened I felt this was a very clear 'agreement from the world,' a synchronicity. This feeling gave the whole prospect of using this therapy a deep power, which is what I need in order to engage with whatever it is I am going to do. I was very grateful to him for calling, and also grateful to some other - what shall I call it . . . higher power? for arranging it. It didn't feel like coincidence.

So I went to the meeting with Mistletoe Man essentially committed to doing it, even before I'd got all the information. Meeting him and talking with him just confirmed my feeling.

"We will give you an initial dose here in the clinic, and then you go home, and either on this first occasion or

the next, after a day or two, the mistletoe will induce a fever," explained Dr Geider. "The mistletoe toxins can attach themselves directly to the cancer cells and, with the fever, stimulate and alert the immune system to act against these cells because of their excessive proliferation. We all have cancer cells present in our bodies, all of the time. It's the job of the immune system to not let them proliferate. In your case, and in the case of people with cancer generally, the immune system has not done this. The mistletoe aims to re-educate this function. It's mostly paid for by the NHS, and we have a charity here that makes up the difference. This means you don't have to pay anything unless you wish to contribute, by making a donation to the charity."

"Auriol told me the side effects were very positive."

He laughed. "That's true. Over 95% of my patients report various things like relief from pain, a lifting of spirits if they're depressed, more motivation, more courage, more hope, more physical energy. The treatment protocol goes alongside the chemotherapy, and ameliorates its effects on the body. You will be taking it for up to five years, slowly reducing the dose and the frequency." I'm surprised by this. I didn't know it would have this type of time frame, but it all sounds good. "The treatment keeps the immune system alert, and helps the body deal with any leftover presence of cancer, and we have very good results with the large majority of our patients."

"Gosh, what an amazing thing," says Jane.

Yes, it is an amazing thing, and we leave together, both of us feeling really blessed. The only downside is it means several more 150 mile round trips to Aberdeen. I'll probably take the train.

6
The Web of Light

For a while, after the initial chemotherapy and mistletoe treatment, and before the scheduled date of the operation, Philip was quite well; funnily enough, stronger than he had been for ages. We decided to take advantage of this.

"Let's go on holiday, a real one," he said, enthusiastically.

"What, you mean where we spend money, someone else looks after us, and we have a great time?" I looked at him enquiringly.

We were used to going to the family holiday cottage, to visit my parents in France or taking long trips, not a package deal or, as we called it, a 'real' holiday.

"I know exactly where to go!" I exclaimed, "Years ago, Mum took me and my sister on holiday to Tarouddant in Morocco; it was through Holidays with Heart, at a place called La Maison Anglaise. There were so few English speaking visitors at that time, that the locals gave the guest house that name, but it's actually traditional Moroccan. They've similar values to us, and we had a really wonderful time. I always wanted to go back again. Let's go there. I'd love to show you it, and we can take a week with them, and then another week in the Palais Salaam."

This was a rather ancient-looking hotel in Tarouddant, very beautiful in its slightly decaying splendour, and I'd promised myself a stay there if I ever visited Morocco again. We looked it up on the internet. La Maison Anglaise offered a booking service where they would organise it all, including the stay at the hotel, which sounded like heaven to me. It was going to cost about £2,500 altogether, and we'd never spent that amount on a holiday before. But this was a different situation entirely, and called for us to behave completely differently. The appeal of going to a place I knew and loved, to share with Philip, was wonderful. Meeting some like-minded people, and being able to visit interesting places was a bonus. So I booked it.

Next morning, I woke with a start. "Oh no! That money we just spent last night on the holiday, we were supposed to be saving to pay the bank! Now what are we going to do?"

It was too late, there was nothing to be done. Philip, having had more of a cavalier attitude to money, wasn't bothered. He was right of course; the money was not our major issue, ill-health was. So off we went on a trip that was perfect; everything was organised, we met interesting people, ate delicious Moroccan food especially prepared for us by a chef in our own guest lodge, and explored the exotic, colourful souks. It was the first time we had ever been so beautifully taken care of.

One day in particular stands out, when we went walking in the Tizi n' Test mountains, part of the Atlas range. Philip would not normally have been able to walk far, due to the chronic fatigue. But during those two weeks, he managed to walk more than he'd done for years, and one day, surprisingly, on a two hour guided trek in the mountains. In the minibus, on the way to the pass, he said, "I would love to be able to walk amongst these mountains.

They are incredible." Having been a great fan of fell walking and mountain climbing in the past, he was wistful. We headed for a cafe at the top, and our guide led us up a small path from there, with magnificent views over more mountains, dry scrub land, and a heat haze in the far distance. We stopped about half way, under the shade of a tree.

"Look at me!" he exclaimed, "I'm managing just fine; it's wonderful!" I was hesitant, knowing he was seriously ill and about to undergo an operation, but I didn't want to take his delight away from him.

"Darling, isn't it great? I'm so glad you're feeling good about it." Was he secretly thinking that somehow the cancer had miraculously gone away, or had never even been there in the first place? Who knows? I was worried he was deluding himself. For his sake, I didn't voice my fears.

Later that year, when it became apparent just how serious the whole situation was, we were so very, very grateful we'd taken this holiday, spent the money and enjoyed ourselves so much. It gave us beautiful memories – stunning scenery, delightful new friends, and moments of utter bliss and contentment.

On arriving home, we moved house two days later. Living in a community with a seriously ill person was just not practical. Trying to find a balance between my own work and contributing to the life of the community had not worked as well as I'd hoped, either.

We were very practiced in moving home, having lived in ten different houses throughout our marriage. However, it was daunting for us to be uprooted again with everything else going on, and yet, moving provided another opportunity to practice reaching out for help. Our wonderful friends rallied round yet again, and in the few weeks' gap between Philip's last chemo and the operation, when he was relatively well, we moved out of the community and into a sunny, spacious, rented bungalow in town, with a garden that was very special. Somebody had planted it with love, care and forethought, and I was going to benefit from it. It had been one of my dreams to have a garden like this, and I couldn't wait to get into it. We settled in there, preparing for the next upheaval: the operation.

Philip was very nervous about this. He found support by coming with me to our local Course in Miracles group. He posted:

More Thoughts on Weakness and Vulnerability

Posted on 8 March 2011 by Philip

Last night I was asking for support from some friends in a small meditation group I won't see until after I get back from having had the operation.

"I'm happy to sit and meditate and send healing that day," says K. There's a chorus of agreement. It's a loving atmosphere, and I feel grateful.

"Thank you all very much. Thank you." We sit quietly for a few moments, and I take it in. I feel supported.

"I feel scared," I tell them. "It feels kind of cold-blooded to have an appointment at 8 a.m. one morning; basically, you just show up, lie down and they cut you open. I'm not looking forward to it. I'm trying to replace my fear thoughts with positive ones."

"All is well; out of this only good will come," someone says.

This is interesting: the last time I was saying this to myself was after the diagnosis, and the last phrase that Jane suggested then was to add, "I am safe." I wasn't able to say that honestly then, and now it feels a bit different. There is more of a possibility of saying that to myself and believing it. That's good to see.

"It's good to admit you're scared," says B. "It's much better than hiding it from yourself or us. You can hold yourself, hug yourself. Be like a mother, gentle and loving." She puts her arms around herself. "There's nothing wrong with being afraid."

"You're right, though I'd rather be more accepting of it than I am. I have a part of me that judges myself as being weak."

"It's not weak," says R. "Saying you're afraid is honest."

So, this is me being vulnerable, not weak, and it's clear the thoughts about weakness are judgments. I have some foolish notions about strength and courage, and probably some rubbish ideas about manliness hiding away in there too. Several people have commented on me being brave, being courageous. I don't feel either, and it's obvious I don't really know what courage is. I think the root of the meaning is from the Latin, 'cor', which means speaking from the heart. Well, I'm focusing on my heart these days, hoping I can feel more connected to love. As for courage; it's nice that people say things like that, but the truth is I'm doing it the way I'm doing it because I think that's the best way for me, not only as I go through this ordeal, day by day, but also because I think it makes it more likely I'll survive.

I read this to Jane.

"That's lovely, darling, but you can't feel brave or courageous because they're not feelings. What you usually feel when you're being brave or courageous is fear or worry or anxiety; terror even, any of those. Despite the feelings, though, you're taking action. That's what courage is."

"Ah," I say, "Of course, thank you."

Philip decided he wanted to have the operation in Coventry, near to where his daughter, Jackie, lived. From a practical point of view this was more sensible – if I'd been staying in Aberdeen, I wouldn't have had as much support. Even though it would be an upheaval, this seemed the best solution. In March, we drove down to England, having ascertained the nearest place to Coventry that could do this kind of operation was in Birmingham. One big benefit was this would mean keyhole surgery, minimally invasive as it's carried out through a very small incision, and they don't have the instruments available to do this in Aberdeen.

We set up camp in Jackie's back bedroom, buying a bigger bed, organising our belongings, and generally making ourselves comfortable. It was like a mini-project, complete with visits to Ikea and another DIY shop. Just like the old days of renovating our house. That helped, given how I was feeling.

"Philip, I'm very nervous about this. It's a huge operation; what if you die on the operating table?" Nothing like facing the facts square on. "Sorry, darling, I didn't mean it like that. All the same, I'm really scared. Are you?"

Philip nodded. "Yes, I am. Let's ask for support from everyone. I want to buy a map of the world, and put dots everywhere there is someone praying for me or thinking of me. It will really help me to know there are others out there who care." The map completely covered the chimneybreast in the bedroom, and we linked all the dots with white wool, to create a web of light representing everyone we knew throughout the world. We both blogged about it; I posted on Facebook, and we told everyone else whom we knew. It looked amazing, literally a web of light, and worked wonders in our minds.

"There's nothing like knowing you are loved to make you feel better," Philip sighed, and hugged me.

"Yes," I pondered. "I wish getting a healthy body was as simple as putting the map up." I spoke in sombre tones, one of the few times I was not able to access my store of positivity. It was not surprising, as earlier that week we'd heard some bad news. Becky, having had successful treatment for her cancer, had been readmitted with signs of it in her bones.

Becky

Wednesday 15th March 2011

Becky, my grand-daughter, is going back into hospital next Monday. This is not good news. What do I call this? A synchronicity? A ghastly coincidence? Surely not an agreement from the world? The cancer has reappeared. We thought she was okay. The previous scan was clear, but not the latest one. It's come back, in her spine. She starts a new and more severe course of chemo next Monday. She has to stay in the hospital for a week while this is started, and the course is for six months.

Here IS something I can agree with, though – the level of care she and I will both receive. The vast majority of people alive today do not have anything close to the level of care that Becky and I get, and it is easy to take for granted. We are both probably going to be in one of the top hospitals in the world. Hers is just down the road, a new children's hospital. I can't get over the weird coincidence of her going back in on the same day. As her Dad, my son Matthew, joked,

"At least that's eco-friendly: I won't have to drive so far to visit you both."

Good for you, Matt. It wasn't exactly a good joke, but it's important to laugh, even if it's difficult to find something to laugh about. Black humour it may be, but it's still humour. I can't imagine what it is like for my son to have both his Dad and his eldest daughter in the same boat, the cancer boat, at the same time. This coincidence certainly brings it into focus. My heart goes out to him and there is so little I can do. When he told me this morning about Becky, I responded with, "I am so helpless; we are so helpless. All I can offer you is my love, and to her too. It doesn't seem enough." So we cried. A long silence on the phone.

"I wish I could hug you. I'm so glad I'm going to be there this week. I'll come and see you as soon as I can."

So, my friends, we need a double vision on Monday.

Energy, light, healing in two places at once, both in Birmingham; Becky is in the Children's Hospital and I will be up the road in Heartlands. How do we send light to two places at once, I wonder? Will there be enough to go around? I'm joking. If there is one thing in the universe there is plenty of, it's light.

In the meantime, I set myself up to do Skype coaching sessions and classes from my laptop in Jackie's box room. One of the advantages of my work is it can be done from anywhere, and this was now proving very helpful. I found it a relief, and healthy, for me to have to focus on clients, update my website and run online classes – it took my mind off everything else. Besides, I was busily blogging at least once a week to my mailing list about what I was learning, and how that related to life and business, which it sometimes did. If you're self-employed, running a small business, or running a project, whatever goes on in your personal life can affect your work dramatically. Ever practical, I used the challenges we were faced with to demonstrate learning and education to those subscribed to my mailing list. Meanwhile, the date of the operation drew ever closer.

7
The Operation

Journal: Monday 21st March

We got up at 6 a.m. to meditate. Arrived at the hospital by 8 a.m. no problem, P driving. Yesterday, we received lots of lovely messages, texts and emails of support, love, and light. So nice to know that others out there are thinking of us.

Very impressive action happening in hospital – within a short space of time he had blood pressure checked, been administrated, saw the anaesthetist (not a great bedside manner), met by the registrar (Sri Lankan, very nice and friendly), met briefly by the surgeon (I asked him to ring me when it is over), and fitted with surgical stockings and two gowns (because of no dressing gown of his own). All in an hour!

It was because he was first on the list. Such a relief; no waiting around time. I hugged him, and watched him walking off down the corridor with a nurse to the theatre. As I write this, he will still be there. Hopefully, all will be going well: keyhole surgery will have happened smoothly, nothing untoward found, and back straight onto a surgical ward.

Downstairs, Jackie and I ate breakfast in the hospital cafeteria – teacake and tea. Life continues even with major operations going on. Now we are home; bumped into Jackie's daughter-in-law who had cooked us some lasagne for our dinner tonight. Really very loving of her. We were touched; Jackie was in tears.

Just waiting now. Noise of the washing machine in the background, the ordinary things of every day. This afternoon we'll go into town to get P some homoeopathic remedy and a dressing gown. Hopefully see him later during visiting hour. How do I feel? A bit bemused by the whole system. Will be able to focus better when he is out of theatre.

Later – 2:30 p.m. in fact.

NO. NO. NO! This is taking far longer than we have been told. I can't believe it. I now don't trust the Doc to call me. Dear Jackie has called the wards only to find that they think he has only just gone into theatre – surely not?

This waiting is really horrible, horrible. I'm going try to meditate for a bit. I need some help.

I'm so scared I'm going to get a call telling me he has died. Don't know what to do. I'm just scared. Ah, right, though. Yesterday I posted a blog all about scared and sacred, and the juxtaposition of just two letters, so I need to go in that direction. I will try to meditate.

Just read some lovely emails from people. It's very nice to receive them. And I am still scared. Maybe that's all right. Perhaps it would be odd if I wasn't scared. Not much room to think about Becky though. Perhaps that's all right too.

3:05 p.m.

Oh, my God. The surgeon just called and he is okay! He's okay!

Thank you, thank you, thank you. The surgeon told me technical equipment difficulties meant he had only just come out of the theatre. It was straightforward, there was no more cancer found anywhere, they took out what they had said they were going to take out, and now he just has to have a safe recovery and all will be well. (Actually, he didn't say that – he said the recovery period was still to happen and they would be monitoring him closely and that he was in the High Dependency Unit). I am so relieved. The first stage is past. Thank God, thank God, thank God. Jackie and I will go to visit tonight. What a relief.

10:30 p.m.

Just back from visiting. Seeing him was great, even with all the tubes and things, and looking as if he wasn't quite here because of the effects of the anaesthetic. I feel HUGELY relieved. So good to see him. We looked at each other with great love, just at the end; nice to see past the anaesthetic into his real eyes. Beautiful. So I might sleep now.

Not such good news about Becky though; her blood count was so low, they couldn't start the treatment. She needs a transfusion before beginning the chemo, and they'll do that tomorrow. Will send many blessings to her, too.

Saturday 25 March 2011

Unbelievable. I am sitting in Jackie's front room, and Philip is opposite me on the sofa. He is out. Released. Freed. Having had the fastest recovery ever, as noted by the nurses and doctor. All that light and love must have been doing some-

> *thing! This afternoon I felt completely wiped out. Just lay on the bed, sort of dozing, but mostly just feeling exhausted. I guess this whole process has taken more out of me than I realised.*

Given it seemed the operation had been a huge success, and the mantle of imminent death lifted, we were quite excited when the after-op appointment was brought forward a week. That must be a good sign. We (including Jackie) walked into the consultant's office, me with a big smile on my face.

"Hallo, to our favourite man!" I greeted him cheerfully.

"Hm," he looked sombre. "I may not be your favourite much longer." We sat down in a line in front of his desk. "I am terribly sorry. Despite the fact we left a nine centimetre margin of tissue around the site of the cancer, the biopsy has shown microscopic signs of cancer within this margin. So although it looked like in the operation we had got everything out, there are still traces of it left. We also found it in six lymph nodes, and there is no way of telling how much further it may have gone into your body. I wish it could be better news, and I'm really so sorry to have to tell you this." He looked almost embarrassed.

A shocked silence pervaded the small room. I felt stunned, and going straight into management mode, I asked for more information.

"The only thing that is possible, and I wouldn't recommend it, is a further operation to take out the remaining stomach."

"Why don't you recommend that?" asked Philip.

"Because I can't guarantee it would get out all traces of cancer, and the impact on the body of such an operation so soon after this one would be extremely high."

"So the next step is the second round of chemo?" I questioned.

"Yes, and as soon as possible", replied the surgeon. Clearly, the appointment had been brought forward not because he was doing well, but because of the seriousness of the situation.

Daily Delusions of Immortality

Posted on 9 April 2011 by Philip

I refer to the delusion of immortality I normally persist in on a daily basis. Today I am thrust out of this comfortable, but unreal, padded room, and into the bright light of another world. Today, I am faced with thoughts of my mortality, rather than the usual streams of thought that simply don't include it. Along with these thoughts there is fear. I've been told the cancer may spread, and that it is 'aggressive'. Also, that there is no way to detect the spread until I get symptoms. This was a big shock to us all.

Today, three days later, I am still in shock, having had my daily immortality delusion snatched away, rather like Lucy whipping away Charlie Brown's football in the Peanuts cartoon. We are now 'living with cancer' in a new, more intense way. It seems both Jane and I preferred not to think about this option, and thought the operation would succeed. By this I mean we would have heard some more comforting words that would have put me in a category that has 'a better chance.' Now, I have to make my own chances. Somehow, I was relying on the doctor to reassure me I had a good chance of recovery.

I feel scared. I am working on it. I feel knocked back. I hope I recover soon. My main aim now is to take care of my body and do everything I can to increase my strength. Jane and I will create another visualisation to support the mistletoe and the chemo and all the healing energy in helping my immune system to seek out the cancer and ask it to leave, to stop multiplying. In the meantime, we are facing mortality. Perhaps this is a good thing. All the sages say so. "Meditate on death," I've been told. "Face death and live life to the full today." I like the theory; I'm a bit lacking in the practice as yet!

Journal: Saturday 9th April 2012

Oh, God.

6:15 a.m. and the reality of yesterday has sunk in. I can't believe we were so silly as to forget what that very first registrar told us:

"For those people where we manage to get all the cancer out, they continue to lead a normal life and we consider them cured." I remember that, because I remember focusing immediately on the second part of the sentence only – the fact that all the cancer in P's case would of course be cut out. But it hasn't been. There is still cancer left in his stomach. Worse, possibly in his lymphatic system, which means it could go anywhere. My biggest fear, of Philip dying and me being left behind, all alone, is a distinct possibility, if not immediately, then in the nearer rather than distant future.

Oh, God.

Did I make a mistake marrying Philip and not having a child? Even though you can't guarantee a child will look after you, I'm scared of being left alone when I'm old and no-one is around to take care of me. I'm scared of being old, lonely, cold and poor. Well, I can take care of the poor stuff, which will affect the cold bit, but I can't do anything about getting old (I will); nor can I do anything about being lonely if everyone else around me has died off. So, back to the unknown again. For whatever reason, we still need to be here, I suppose.

David, a close friend sent a nice email today: 'Living with the unknown! This can be a sweet or terrifying place, depending upon your mood on the day. I love you both and wish you the strength to take each day's offering for what it is, remembering that what reactions pass through the mind and emotions are of momentary consequence.'

Very wise words. The unknown can be a sweet or terrifying place; I never thought that before. Please can we have it be a sweet place?

8

His last summer?

Even though you know death is very likely, when you're actually still living, you just get on with it. You can't help it; that's just what you do. Getting on with it included the next round of chemo, although that looked increasingly mad. In fact, after just two days of the chemo pills at home, let alone any transfusion in hospital, with Philip looking and behaving like a zombie, he quietly murmured,

"I'm not sure I want to do this anymore."

"What? What do you mean?"

"I mean, take the chemo pills." He looked at me with both love and fear in his eyes, in equal measure. We both knew what this meant. "It's only a five percent chance of a longer life, anyway," he continued, glumly. Secretly, I felt relieved. Not so secretly, he was, too, despite the probable consequences. The ravages of the first round of chemo had been so difficult on a relatively healthy body, that I couldn't see how he would cope with a second round, having been through the stress of the operation, and having lost so much weight. He wasn't putting any on again, either.

"Darling," I took his hand, "I think you're right. I will back you in whatever you decide, but actually, I think you should stop them."

Together, we made the decision to stop the second round of chemo, in our lovely sunny dining room, overlooking the chirping birds on the bird table and the woods at the back of the house. In the moment, any moment, there is beauty to be found. Especially when a truth has been told.

Sometime during the summer, a book, *Enlightenment Is Not What You Think*, had arrived by post from our friends in America. They had been going to listen to talks by the author in Los Angeles, where they all lived. Philip, intrigued by the pun in the title, was positively devouring it, and getting a lot from it.

"Can I read you something, Jane?" he asked me. We'd got good at asking permission for things like this, as both of us were perpetually finding interesting things we wanted to share with each other. We had learned the hard way that we needed first to find out if the other person was open to listening at that moment.

"Sure," I replied, and put down my paper.

"*'In humans, at around the age of two-and-a-half, a profound shift occurs in which we change from spontaneous, free-flowing beings, to creatures in which everything is about Me! and Mine! and how to get what I want and think I need. It is the moment that a false sense of personal authorship starts. It happens to virtually every human being. It is the false sense that I, as this body-mind organism, am the source that makes things happen. It is this false sense of authorship that creates suffering, because the new perception is that I am in control of things. Yet there is continuous evidence to the contrary – that I am not in control. So a powerful tension is established.'* "

"Well," I mused, "I don't know what he means exactly by *I*, but it's certainly true that neither you nor I were in control of you getting cancer – or rather, you were not in control of getting it, and I was not in control of becoming a care-giver for someone with cancer. In fact, I've never felt more out of control."

"Yes," replied Philip, "this is why it's so interesting to me. I always did have a challenge with the idea you can manifest what you want . . . how on earth could it be said I manifested cancer, as if it were my fault I had it?"

"I know, I know." I bowed my head. Certainly in the past I'd strongly believed in the powers of personal manifestation, had even taught it, and yet now I was questioning that. In fact, it felt like every single belief I had about health and well-being was up for grabs. We were both in completely unknown territory. Nothing like that for making you turn to all kinds of things to help you in the search for some sense – any sense at all – of safety.

Philip posted:

I Kneel and Pray

Posted on 11 July 2011 by Philip

The other day I knelt before our little meditation altar and prayed. This is the first time in my adult life I have done this. As a child, I was in a choir and was taken occasionally to church, but that's different: it was not coming from me. Praying the other day was different. I think the big difference is in me. These days, I am asking for something I never knew of before. I am asking to be connected. The other day I wanted to ask humbly, so I knelt before our little altar and spoke these words:

"Please help me to be connected, or to accept the absence of connection."

I have no idea who or what I was addressing. I have some scanty ideas about what I want to be connected to. Light is part of it. Consciousness beyond this small spark that is within me is another.

Looking back, I can see this is always what I was wanting in my seeking. Finding a spiritual master actually got in the way of this because I focused on him. Of course, I don't really know what the benefits of that relationship may be, and don't want to discount them. Bhagwan regularly would say:

"I am a finger pointing to the moon. Don't worship the finger."

This was impossible for me to do. I failed dismally at it. I found him too beautiful. He was unlike anyone else I ever met. I can hear people talking about charisma when I express these sentiments. They have never met such a being. Charisma was a tiny part of him, the word itself a critical view that arises from ignorance or fear. It is a belittling that is common in the media, mostly from people who have never met him.

Asking to be connected now is different, partly because I am afraid. I was not in fear of losing my life when I was a disciple. I find this is wonderfully focusing of my attention. I really don't want to die feeling this sense of disconnection. I have heard that dying may lead to connection – many people say this – but I don't know it myself. Not truly KNOW it.

I am aware I'm asking for something which I may actually be obstructing. I have been told this too.

"It's your ego, Swami. Just drop your ego."

Yes, yes, this may be what I need to do, but I have tried and dismally failed at this too. So my prayer includes,

"Please help me, guide me on the right path because I am deeply unknowing, deeply ignorant."

It felt appropriate to say this, and feel this, on my knees. I still felt a bit self-conscious; I hope that didn't ruin it.

Later that month, Philip decided to go to the famous Penny Brohn Cancer Help Centre in Bristol, England, to join in one of their courses. While he was away, I wrote:

Journal: 11th July 2011

I'm sitting now in the sunroom, all alone in the house, feeling very blah. Don't want to do anything. Not even eat. It's very quiet. Too quiet. Is this what it would be like if P dies soon? (I nearly wrote 'when' – shit). Oh dear.

And now I can't get the printer cartridge to go in. Aaagh! Typical that something that he has been in charge of goes wrong like this. Or that I can't do it. Or that I am just proving myself right that I need him to do it. (That's probably more like it, actually).

Scared I will slope off down into depression. Actually, I AM afraid. Really afraid. Can't see the point in living myself if I'm not sharing it with someone. And right now I can't imagine living with someone else.

My fear of being left alone was playing itself out, in terms of not allowing the concept of being alone to even enter my mind. It was so big, that even while he was still alive I was thinking about the possibility – or not – of being with another man! Mad.

We talked on the phone every day, of course, and then one day he told me, "It's no good. I feel like there is something in the way, stopping the food going in. I'm having real difficulty in swallowing." This was distressing, because by this time he'd already become really thin.

Journal: Monday 25th July 2011

> *Picked P up from airport yesterday. Leaning up against him in bed last night, my head was on his shoulder bone – nothing of any other substance there. He is having considerable trouble eating without pain.*
>
> *It is lovely to have him back. I drove him to Aberdeen today for his infusion of mistletoe. Later, I was just in tears; tears, tears, and more tears. About him possibly dying. I told him last night, in the middle of the night, that I had been working out how much money I needed to pay off all the mortgages and be okay if I was on my own. He says he has been thinking about how I would manage financially, too, if I am on my own, and he has deep regrets he didn't take out life insurance with the money we got originally when we sold our clinic. So do I! Hindsight is a wonderful thing, though, and I had no idea he was thinking about how it would be for me financially after he dies. See, I am speaking as if it IS going to happen, and the truth is we just don't know. Shit! I REALLY DO NOT LIKE NOT KNOWING.*

That's the thing with dying: even when you know you are dying, you don't know when death will actually happen. So no matter what way it happens, you have to be comfortable with living in the moment. Even if the moments are very uncomfortable.

Journal: 4.15am 27th July 27, 2011

I was awake with a sore back, not fully awake but sort of, and P got up. He has heartburn. He took some anti-acid pills. I cuddled him. So warm, even if so bony.

"What are you thinking about, darling?" I asked him this, because I was thinking about him dying.

"I'm doing the Ho'opono'pono."

So I started, too. Ho'opono'pono is an ancient Hawaiian practice where you say, over and over again, "I love you. I'm sorry. Please forgive me. Thank you."

Had to leave him though, and go to the other bedroom, because I got overtaken with the fear of him dying. Imagining how it would be, and what on earth I would do. What really got to me, though, was yesterday, when he said he wanted to go to America for a holiday, and he didn't want to go in the winter. That means going very soon. He said if we put it off to the spring or the summer, that meant taking a risk we couldn't go. That means he thinks, if he is going to die, it would be very soon indeed.

No. Surely not? Now feeling very sober. Low. Sad. And I want to be fine, because right now he is HERE! Warm and soft next door (well, not that soft); and I am in a fearful future. I need help here, please give me help – and please, I beg you, if he is to die soon, please let him experience you, God, or whatever you're called, before he goes. Please let him feel connected, at last. I do so want that for him, as it is all he really wants. Has ever wanted. I told you, while I was in the shower the other day, that I would let him go to you if it

meant he felt that connection. I know that's trying to bargain with you, but I do mean it.
Later: At breakfast I asked him, had he spoke about wanting to go to America soon because he thought he might not be here next spring? He replied yes.
Crying. Me crying, not him. I am finding this very hard to face up to.

9
Inner Listening

Feeling Low

Posted on 2 August 2011 by Philip

Went to Aberdeen for mistletoe last Monday, to the hospital for a scan Wednesday, and back again Friday to see Onco Girl, a new consultant, the youngest one yet.

"There is nothing we can see in the scan," she says.

"I'm having a lot of trouble eating. I'm losing weight," I tell her. "It hurts in my stomach and my intestines. Could this be the result of the chemo, even two months later?"

"Yes, it could," she replies. "The effects can last a long time for some people. There is nothing in the scan that would relate to that."

This is good news, of course, though not unexpected. They can't see microscopic spread, and it is a bit soon for any new tumour to have grown. My experiment with the second round of chemo is looking, increasingly, a poor decision. It's hard to eat when it hurts. Even drinking hurts sometimes. Losing weight is a worry, though since I got home, I haven't lost more. I'm awfully thin and bony; I need to change this around. It's depressing.

The basic situation is we now are in the next phase, called 'Living with Uncertainty.' Will write more soon. I've just read this over and it seems pretty depressing. I'm sorry about that, but that is how it is at the moment.

It was a good thing that, around about this time, I gave up working. My latest online coaching programme, which showed such promise earlier in the year, and on which I'd worked very hard, just didn't take off. Even with all the right marketing pieces in place, it hadn't translated into many sales. I ran an excellent course anyway, with just a handful of people, and then, after the last lesson, I simply stopped. I had tried so hard, and it wasn't working, so something else had to happen. That something else was handing my business over to a new CEO.

For many years, since I'd moved through the grief about not being able to have children with Philip, I'd had access to the 'still, small voice within.' I'd been introduced to this back in 2003, when I was exploring my psychic abilities. Out walking one day, I'd been railing against not having a family of my own, and out of the blue came the words, 'You were not meant to have children this time round. Your path is purely a spiritual one.' The words were so clear, I almost looked round to see who had spoken. They brought with them immense relief, peace, and a relaxing into what my life actually was in that moment. I wasn't shocked, just intrigued. Over time, and with practice, this 'voice' spoke many, many wise words – most often when I sat down with a pen and paper in hand.

We came to refer to this voice as 'The Listening.' I didn't tell anyone about it other than Philip, who was delighted for me – and for him, because we had access to a seemingly external wisdom. For these words were always, never-endingly, loving, supportive, and clear – sometimes truthfully hard-hitting, too. Always in the context of love, though.

However, I felt somewhat embarrassed if I thought about telling anyone else. Was this the 'channelling' that others talked about, and about which I had all sorts of negative judgments? Channelling is a word used to describe a particular kind of intuitive connected communication which covers many forms, including expressions or words that seem to just 'come to you.' It is not mediumship, where contact with the dead is made, although some channellers do report receiving help from a deceased loved one, or feel their presence.

How did I know it wasn't my imagination? Was I just making it up? All sorts of questions posed themselves, and so I simply kept this to myself, gaining soothing and sustenance from a source that felt different from whom I thought I was.[5]

When I thought about what on earth to do regarding working, what came to mind was handing over the running of the business to The Listening/The Universe/God . . . whatever I wanted to call it. Here's the letter I wrote:

4th August 2011

To: God/Source/Light/Love, whoever/whatever you are

I hereby resign from my position of RichThinkers CEO, and humbly await your instructions.

My ego has been sent out to grass, to do its new job of eating grass. Should it creep in again via the back door, I hereby

5. You can read an example of The Listening from this time in Appendix 2.

commit to notice it as soon as possible, take it back out to the field, or return to you, and await further instructions.

I understand you are the new CEO of RichThinkers Coaching, and I humbly accept this fact. I will do my best to serve you, by standing in your light, listening to your instructions and carrying them out to the best of my abilities.

Yours in full faith,

Jane Duncan Rogers

After writing this, in the playing field at the back of the house, I experimented with being my ego. I stomped around the field, like a horse, pretending I was my ego put out to grass. It was a huge relief, despite the ego objecting with all sorts of mind chatter going on. Ego always needs a role, but it didn't like the role of eating grass much. However, all I had to do now was obey instructions. Easier said than done, of course.

The relief continued for a few days - but I soon realised my instructions were simply to do nothing at all on the business. To do nothing was anathema for me. It was inconceivable. And yet the guidance was clear. I was to continue seeing clients who already existed, and respond if any came towards me, but otherwise I was only to do basic administration, and answer emails. No promotion or marketing, or learning, of any kind. This was completely opposite to how I'd been living my life over the previous five years. It was a blessing, as it turned out, because Philip needed me much more now, but it was also a challenge; I wasn't used to full time care-giving.

It was quite something for me to finally manage to accept I was doing this job. It was from this understanding that I applied for a care-giver's allowance from the government. I hadn't ever wanted to be a care-giver, a fact brought to light in my reaction to the 'sickness and health' promise when I wanted to get married. Here I was, though, admitting it to myself and the world, and being given money for care-giving. It was sobering, but I was certainly doing an enormous amount of caring. Admitting to this, instead of struggling away on my own was yet another step in accepting our situation. If I'd been willing to embrace the situation earlier, I would have received quite a lot more money. Ah, well, that's life. Death too, I suppose.

Later that month we visited our holiday cottage in the south of Scotland. It's a 7 hour drive down there, but we made it, me driving, of course. Several of his family were also up in the area from England, including Jackie. She was horrified at how thin he was.

"Dad," she smiled, but was concerned. "You've got to eat something. You'll waste away otherwise. Here, what about this?" She offered him a sliver of boiled egg and a bit of toast and butter.

"I know, I know," he replied. "I am trying, you know!" Poor man, he now had two of us offering him tempting morsels, saying how important it was to eat. As if he didn't know. The weight was dropping off so fast, I was worried he was going to die of starvation, not cancer – which seemed all wrong. I couldn't understand when he said he wanted to eat, but then wouldn't – or rather, couldn't.

Later that week, after all the children, dogs and adults departed down south, it was very quiet, something we normally loved.

We were staying on for another week, looking forward to simply sitting enjoying the sunshine, pottering about on the beach, and playing Scrabble together in the evenings. The tiny wooden cottage, built by my grandfather in 1937 right on the beach in Dumfries and Galloway, had many beautiful memories for us. We loved it – we'd had our honeymoon here, with lots of present-opening, champagne, and sunshine in May, 1994. Every year since then we had visited, sometimes for as long as three weeks in a row. It was where I'd got clear about writing my first book. Where we both could relax, unwind, and relax some more, and where we lived a much simpler life without TV's and computers. This time, though, it was different. We were both really worried about him not being able to eat, so two days later we got in the car and returned, a trip that included a hotel stay and a restaurant dinner, me eating too much, and Philip not eating a thing.

10
The List

Journal: Late August 2011

It is so bloody scary seeing him so unbelievably thin. Deep hollows in between his thumb and forefinger. Even bigger hollows at his shoulders – I simply cannot lean my head on him comfortably any longer. Fuck. Maybe I need to be glad he is still alive, even if he is thin. Oh, God, I don't know. I just do not know anymore.

I am finding it almost impossible to do any work. I do not know what to do. I am not receiving any instructions from the new CEO, other than being kind to myself, and I am going bonkers!

Sunday 4th September 2011

More of the same. I manage by letting the tears fall whenever they are there, and going out into the garden before trying to do anything remotely like work. I went to the Sunday Taize singing this morning at the Findhorn Foundation. It was in the Universal Hall with masses of people, maybe 70 or more, and almost immediately I was in tears. These songs are so touching.

Have been crying on and off all day though. I am very scared for him. He is not eating or drinking enough, and I'm terrified. Going to see Onco Man on Tuesday, but it doesn't feel soon enough. I wonder if they will want to have him in hospital. In the meantime I am still distressed because I can hardly do any work. I have a proposal to write, other people to contact and I just do not want to do it. Actually, I cannot do it, for I will be out of integrity with myself if I do.

Clearly, I wasn't following the instructions of the CEO to the letter. I think that's called both avoidance and denial.

At the beginning of September, I spoke to Onco Man privately.

"How long has he got?"

"Well, it's difficult to be sure," he wavered. "However, I would say, at this stage, it will be months rather than years." He looked sympathetically at me. I didn't say anything else, other than thanking him. What could I say? I took in the information without really realising what it meant. I had wanted to know, rather than not; at least it was something I felt I could know, rather than being in this state of uncertainty all the time.

I didn't tell Philip. It didn't feel like there was any point. He hadn't asked, didn't want to know, had never read anything on the internet about his condition. I guess he was just too scared to face up to it.

That's another thing about death. Even though it's the one thing we know is going to happen to us, so many of us just don't want to admit that. I've always been interested in death as a concept – have read a lot, been fascinated by it, really. I've thought of death as another adventure in the experience of life. Philip was different

– he was very scared indeed. He never wanted to die, never even wanted to have an intellectual conversation about the idea.

Towards the end of September he posted:

> *I am seeing myself as a failure a lot at the moment. Dying of this cancer looks like that to me often. That I am letting myself down, and letting Jane down, and Jackie, my family and friends. At the same time, I am trying so hard. It is pretty clear to me I can never satisfy this critical voice, whatever I do. I will never be able to do enough. I even feel conflicted about writing this, because I am not being positive, not able to share stuff that might inspire people. Blah, blah.*
>
> *This is in great contrast to another thing I want to share, which is positive, or at least I think it is (I feel confused about it). One afternoon this week, I spontaneously sat silently in the sunroom, and felt a deep sense of peace for quite a long time. This was along with not much thinking that I was aware of. It felt the oddest experience.*
>
> *For so many years I have sought this, yearned for it, felt that it would be the biggest possible change in my being that could arise, and here it was – and no big deal. I am still feeling puzzled by it. I have touched upon it a bit at night sometimes, too, when awake in the dark. Content to just be there. I don't know what else to say, which seems a bit lame!*

In early October, we were visited by Barbara and Michael, Philip's oldest friends from sannyasin days, and the ones who had sent the book *Enlightenment Is Not What You Think*. Having flown over from Los Angeles, they had booked their flights months ago, and now were here, staying in a local bed and breakfast for a week. It was so good to see them; I could share the burden and the worries.

Barbara was a nurse specialist in an LA hospital, and was instrumental in getting us to do what became known as The List. Months ago, she'd mentioned it, but we still hadn't done anything about it. In an earlier email, she'd written down a long list of all the questions that might be useful to be answered in the event of death. Questions such as 'Do you want to be buried or cremated?' 'Does your partner know your user names and passwords?' and 'Who would you like around you as you die?' No wonder it wasn't easy to do. Fortunately, she was a persistent person, and I knew she was right. Now she was on our doorstep, no doubt going to make sure we completed The List.

In the first week in October, I wrote in my journal:

4am: Jackie thinks he is going to die soon. I think she thinks weeks rather than months. If he is not 'in charge,' as he says, he could die at any minute. I watched him for ages tonight to hear a sign of breathing. And I need to sort out practicalities:

- *How I will cope financially when he dies?*
- *Phone contract*
- *How TV works*
- *British Telecom arrangement*
- *His will*
- *What kind of funeral does he want?*
- *Get Natural Death Handbook*
- *How to pay off mortgages?*
- *What to do with any money from the outstanding legal challenge in Ireland?*
- *His computer*

It's strange how the mind copes in situations like this; I veered dramatically between terror he was about to die on me, and a concern with practicalities. Obviously, I was already thinking, and acting, about things that might need to go on The List.

"I need to know about the car, darling," I spoke gently one day over breakfast. Well, my breakfast, not so much his.

"Oh." He sounded glum. "I suppose so." Our eyes met. I was being practical; I knew it was information I needed. I knew it would be much easier for me to cope with this if I asked now, as opposed to waiting until after he died. I persevered. "Yes – when does it get a service, how often should it happen, what are the tyre pressures, how often do I do those, when should I sell it – those kinds of things." The roles in our marriage had been divided up, as is common for many couples. Philip was, in theory, the person who cared more about the car than I, so he did what needed to be done in that area. Having been a mini-cab driver for some years in his twenties, he knew about cars. He was also brilliant at DIY, doing whatever I asked him. My role was more in the garden, planting and weeding, and endeavouring to keep the house tidy.

The week with Barbara and Michael was taken up with an unexpected visit to the local hospital, due to Philip being dehydrated. We still had visits to the beach, though, and talks about the world, life, projects, computers – all the things we usually did, when life was normal. I felt more relaxed having them there because we were sharing the burden, and we didn't talk about The List at all. However, I pestered Philip about it one Saturday morning after they left.

"Come on, we're going to do The List properly now." He was still reluctant, but, lying in bed, with me and the laptop next to him, he didn't have a chance. "It's going to make a huge difference to me in the future, darling, and besides, Barbara will just nag us if we don't."

"Yeah, all right then."

Poor Philip – for a man afraid of dying, this was an amazing act of courage, another step in the acceptance of what was happening. We began at the beginning, and continued on until the end, referring to it later as our final project together. In those two hours, I asked him the questions, and he gave me his answers. There were all kinds of questions, from the most basic such as "What kind of coffin do you want?" to which he replied, "Any old box will do," to more sensitive ones, such as "Are there any of your personal items you would like to leave to anyone in particular?". This one we discussed in much more detail. It was tough; these are difficult questions to ask of somebody who knows he is going to be dying sooner than later. Feeling a great sense of achievement afterwards, we were very close, connected and loving for the rest of that weekend. Who would have thought that? It ended up being a couple of hours of slightly macabre enjoyment.

Once again, the strange thing about dying/living in the face of death is that while you're alive, you're alive, and you keep on doing as many of the things you usually do, because – why not? In fact, this kind of living is more intense, it was enhanced for us by the fact we knew this time was special because it was all we had.

This kept on hitting me. Just because you think you might die sooner than you expected or wanted, doesn't mean to say that life stops. On the contrary, life continues right up until the moment there is no breath left.

Journal: 15th October 2011

This is a time of great pain, when I fall into tears and sobbing – such loss. And yet also great intimacy, as I realise – as we realise – the Love that is present. How I wish I could take away his pain, and yet would he be as open without it?

More than that, though, is his fear, apparently ever-present and difficult to have it not take him over. Such fear, especially in the middle of the night – pain, morphine, rapid heart-beating, nightmares, bewilderment, confusion, and little peace. And yet he does respond to my varying relaxation methods. I find myself in a mix of frustration that he won't or can't deal with this fear himself and needs me to do it. I feel guilty, of course about this, but my guilt is tempered with this intimate closeness.

Oh, God. Oh, God, indeed. Where is my own sense of peace? I feel it behind me, but I am rarely in it these days. Is he dying? Just not wanting to admit it? Is he dying and just fighting it? Is he not dying at all, but just not eating? I cannot reconcile this not eating with wanting to live – and yet he does try, tries hard sometimes, and just cannot get it down. God. What a shitty way to go.

One of the questions on The List had been: "Who would you like around you as you are dying?" Not an easy one, unless you are dealing with it in the abstract. Even then, it's not that easy. Philip listed several people, until I mentioned the room might be a bit crowded. However, Barbara was top of the list. She must have realised something like this, because before she left she told us, "I'll come over any time, just let me know and I'll be there with you as soon as possible." We didn't think she would be coming back over again so soon.

11
Visions and Visitations

After coming back early from our holiday cottage, when a scan had showed nothing abnormal, we were confused. Was he dying of cancer, or starvation, or was something else going on? Suggestions were made it could be scar tissue, or the pain being pressure on a nerve, but the doctors were not clear. Radiotherapy was an option to relieve the symptoms, so Philip agreed, dubbing the specialist 'Gamma Ray Man.' This was not easy; it would mean travelling to Aberdeen, staying over 3 nights, receiving the radiotherapy each day, returning home at weekends, and on top of that, trying to fit in mistletoe appointments.

By the second week of radiotherapy, in mid-October, Philip's weight was nine stone only, at least three stone underweight. For a man over 6 feet tall, this was serious. I was genuinely worrying now that he would die of starvation before cancer, not realising it was most likely the cancer that was actually killing him, being the probable cause of him not eating. I guess we didn't want to think that – and because the doctors were baffled, this supported us in thinking along these lines.

"I suggest we admit you now, pause the radiotherapy for a bit, and get you hooked up on a drip. You're dehydrated anyway, and we obviously need to get some intravenous food into you." Gamma Ray Man spoke decisively. Philip was taken to a chemo ward of 4 beds, with his nearest to the toilet in the corner. A TV was on, but nobody was watching it. This was one of Philip's bugbears; he hated a TV being on in the background, even while in great health. So I turned it off. None of the other three men in the ward uttered a word. Maybe they were secretly glad.

One day, in that first week in hospital, I pulled the curtains around Philip's bed. I wanted to lie on the bed with him, and we needed some privacy.

"I can see some people at the end of the bed," he suddenly announced. My ears pricked up. It was distinctly unusual for this kind of thing to happen to him. "They are four sannyasins I used to know. Two of them are dead, though." He was speaking in a very matter-of-fact voice, as though they really were there. "They're asking me to come and join them, but I told them I'm not ready."

I was amazed. Amazed that Philip was experiencing this so calmly, and had spoken back to them so clearly. He was very definite his time was not yet. I'd heard of this kind of experience before, as I'd read a lot of books about death and dying, and also studied it professionally as part of my counselling training. But I was surprised that Philip, who was averse to thinking about the end of life, took it all so very calmly. Instead, we both felt blessed, and lay there together in a state of peace and love. It was a very beautiful half hour or so, despite being surrounded by three other men in a cancer ward, with all its attendant noise, bustle and interruptions.

Meanwhile, food was finally being given intravenously.

Food helps

Posted on 28 October 2011 (typed by Jane)

I had a better night last night. A combination of fear, unpleasant hallucinations, pain, and lack of sleep for the last week has meant I haven't been able to write a post; it has all been pretty grim. It is moving in the right direction now it seems, as I've been getting this intravenous food and drink.

I have not had any extra painkillers, either, for at least 24 (if not 36) hours now. A good sign. Perhaps the radiotherapy has helped. I am being encouraged now to live a bit, get out in the wheelchair to the dayroom, sit in a chair, stand a little. Basically, come back into the land of the living.

The plan is that, on Monday, Gamma Ray Man will talk to the gastroenterologist specialist, who has got X-ray eyes, apparently. This means he can see both with the camera, and also with ultra-sound at the same time. This man comes highly recommended in terms of his years of experience.

At the end of the first week, Philip was moved to a single room. It was such a relief, no more unnecessary TV on. A bit cramped, especially when we moved a reclining chair in, but at least he was on his own. Our good friend River arrived from the south of England to help me keep Philip company each night, by sleeping on the recliner which we had moved into his room. Philip was having horrible, frightening hallucinations from the morphine. It was proving difficult to get the right type and dosage, and often he needed someone there just to hold his hand. Meanwhile, I was having my own fears.

Journal: Friday 21st October 4am

> *This is my greatest fear: Philip dying and me no longer able to have children. What on earth is the meaning in this for me? Is there any? How do I feel about this? I think it is very ironic. It is as if Life itself has made jolly sure I have no one of immediate connection. Feels unfair. Am I angry? Not at this precise moment, although I have been. I am curious, though, and understand I was clearly not supposed to have a child. I do feel very sad about that. Even though I can't quite imagine having a child, it doesn't stop the sadness being there. But was I supposed to not have a husband too? That's definitely not fair.*

My perceptions at this time were all mixed up together; hearing the whirr and beep of the machines, experiencing the small irritations of hospital life, and yet feeling gratitude for being taken care of. It was confusing because we didn't want to be there at all; despite that, we were so relieved he was in hospital.

River and I were staying in the newly-decorated suite of rooms provided by the Camphill Wellbeing Trust on the outskirts of Aberdeen, next to the clinic where Philip had been receiving the mistletoe treatments. The building was in a very beautiful, wooded setting that both he and I had become used to. It was available for us at a reasonable rate, and we were there so often that it had begun to feel like a second home.

More friends began to visit. My sister came up from England, relieved from her duties of being the mother of two young children for a couple of days, and my parents booked to come over from their home in France towards the end of November. I'd been putting them off, hoping they could come when Philip was home again.

Carrie, River's wife, came up for a week, and took her turn at staying overnight with Philip, massaging his legs and feet, listening to him, reading and doing crosswords. Every day, I battled with hospital protocol around the various options that were open to him – not a lot – and started to learn very fast about how to 'cause trouble,' standing up for myself and Philip in the face of bureaucracy.

"My husband has been given an appointment for an endoscopy," I spoke politely to a receptionist.

"Fine. He'll be seen sometime today, probably. You can wait here if you want."

"Thank you; but actually, I want to go in with him, so can you arrange that please?"

"Oh, I don't think so. That's not what normally happens."

"Well, it is what I would like to do. Can you find out if that is possible, please?"

I was being politely insistent, aware this was not like me, but much more aware of Philip's distress at a very invasive procedure, and his desire to have me there with him. The receptionist looked at me. She must have sensed how serious I was.

"The thing is, my husband is really ill. He's got stomach cancer; he can't eat anything, and they need to find out what is causing that. He's terrified and really wants me with him, and I want that too. So if you can possibly find out when he will be seen, and where I should go, I would appreciate it a lot."

"Well – okay, then. Hold on a moment," and off she went. A few minutes later, she returned, and looked at me conspiratorially. "We're not supposed to do this, but if you come through that door over there and turn right, you'll see your husband in his bed on that holding ward, and you can then go in with him when he's called for the procedure."

"Thank you so much!" Relief caused me to give her a big smile.

When he saw me, Philip's face was also full of relief, and it wasn't long before he was called into an operating theatre, with me alongside him. That's how I saw the state of the inside of Philip's stomach on a screen. It was shocking. You couldn't see anything, there was so much fluid and gunk in it. They were investigating to explore the possibility of feeding him through a tube directly into his stomach, but even I could see there was no way this could happen. The doctor had to position it very carefully, and how could he do that if he couldn't see anything?

I was so glad I'd followed my intuition to be in the theatre, had stood in the face of authority, and not had to live with the guilt of knowing what I needed to do, but not doing it. Back we went to his single room, hoping, somehow, for a miracle. A miracle of sorts did happen, but not in the way we wanted.

Journal: Friday 11th November (11/11/11)

Might be an auspicious day for some, but not for us. Gamma Ray Man did the 'I can't do any more for you' speech. I didn't think it would happen so soon.

How can this be happening? Philip got me, Jackie and River together tonight and thanked us, and spoke very eloquently about moving into the next stage. He is amazing. I do love him so much.

Feeling very raw tonight. I imagined my own death, and how horrible I would feel departing the party, so to speak, and leaving everyone behind. Mind you, I need to be able to accept this for P, as it is happening to him. Secretly, I hope he doesn't have long left – or, rather, that what he does have is of good quality, where he can be pain free, mobile and able to do his book. That doesn't seem very likely at the moment.

In fact, there was a reprise from imminent death, due to the operating doctor saying he was willing to try to position a feeding tube for a second time. Philip grasped at this opportunity.

"Are you sure, darling?" I was worried. It felt to me like he was just prolonging the inevitable.

"Yes. I want to try everything possible." He spoke so definitely I could not argue, nor did I want to. What I wanted was for him to not be in pain, but the only way now for him to be pain-free was to die. It was a terrible paradox.

Then, out of the blue, another kind of 'visitation' happened – this time to me. I couldn't wait to tell Philip when I arrived by his bedside the next morning.

"I've had an amazing vision!" I was really excited to be telling him. " I'd woken up, and I was lying on my back in bed. My hands felt very big and tingly. There was no apparent reason for this, and I knew I wasn't dreaming, but I was awake in a different sort of way. You and I had come to somewhere. It was golden and glowing, some sort of mountain type thing in the distance, but otherwise just this gorgeous, golden, loving glow everywhere. It was time for you to continue walking and for me to stop. I watched you walking, walking just like you used to, with those very steady, sure steps, and your back upright, tall and lovely. You were going towards a glow, and surrounded by it at the same time. It was so very beautiful. An incredibly loving feeling. The thing is, it was perfect for you to continue walking, and for me not to. And I knew that you knew it was perfect, and that you knew that I knew it was perfect. It was just so loving. So much love. Very, very beautiful." I spoke with great enthusiasm, really wanting him to feel the joy that I felt.

Philip looked at me with bleak, sad eyes. "I'd like one of those visions, please."

12
More from the CEO

Philip had continued to read Wayne Liquorman's book *Enlightenment is Not What You Think* since the summer. Not that he was doing any reading himself at this stage –his arms were too weak to hold a book. However, he'd found the book very useful; I'd read a bit of it, too, so we were able to discuss the ideas in it together. One of these ideas was about the function of the human mind.

I believe the mind always wants to know the answer to *why?* because it likes to be in control of life, which makes it feel safe. However, when things just happen which the mind didn't apparently decide to do – like getting cancer – it likes to put meaning to the event, so the experience can neatly fall into a category and be filed thus. It's very soothing to the mind to find meaning in any situation.

It seems to me that humans are wired this way, with some of us desiring more meaning than others. Philip and I definitely belonged to this category. So when he had a long sleep one night in the first half of November, and neither of us woke when the machine beeped for the changeover of the food supply – one of the bugbears of intravenous drips – I wrote in the early morning:

Journal: 10th November 2011

I am tempted to ask why we didn't wake up. There are several reasons I can attribute not waking to: River and P's exploration of P's dream the night before; understanding what causes occlusions of P's tube and why; attention to angelic presence; the light being on; practical info re what to do if he wakes.

Nonetheless, underneath all this is a further more seismic shift and it is to do with having had a Skype conversation with Wayne, and our own resultant conversation.

The real truth about P is that no one knows.

No one actually, really, knows what is going to happen to Philip.

Just because X, does not necessarily mean Y. As in, just because he appears to be going to die, doesn't mean he actually will. Just because he has cancer, doesn't necessarily mean he will die from it. He might die from something else. Just because the doctor says one thing, does not mean it will indeed happen. There are too many outside influences in all situations to be able to state this categorically, even though it appears that way. I don't think this is denial, I think it's just being willing to be here now, with what is happening, and not projecting into the future about what the mind thinks will happen.

Really there are only a series of moments to be experienced, without meaning or interpretation, rather to be enjoyed with the inclusion of what is happening in that moment. If this moment, now, is fully experienced, instead of being pushed away (which is what we do most of the time with our insis-

tence on thinking about the future or the past), then there is simply an acceptance of what is.

With this recognition, right now there is a warm glow. It feels lovely. Peaceful. Loving. Perhaps it is Love.

P just woke. "What's happening?"

"Nothing; you're asleep and I'm awake."

"Just wanted to connect." I reached out from the reclining chair at the bottom of his bed and touched his hand. "Sleep well."

Lovely.

Earlier that day, we'd had a conversation about me.

"Darling, I'm afraid of what it's going to be like when I'm on my own." I carefully avoided saying the word 'dead.' "I'm afraid I won't want to do my coaching anymore, that RichThinkers will just become pointless, that I won't want to live where we are anymore." I was just plain terrified of being on my own without him. It might have seemed selfish, me talking like this, but I needed him to hear me. And he did, sort of.

"You'll be all right, Jane. You're a very strong woman, and anyway, you have The Listening to help you. Just follow the instructions, and you'll be fine." Clearly he was comforted by this idea – much more so than I was. Later, however, I wrote:

Journal: 10th November 2011

I've just realised that the CEO is for life, not just the business. It's the CEO of Everything. Chief Executive Officer of All. Ah. Perhaps it was 'him', then, who said 'Everything will be all right,' which I heard when I was driving into the hospital yesterday – and then the peace and calm just descended on me. And when I asked about P , I heard: 'Everything is going to be MORE than all right for him.' It was wonderful.

So that IS the CEO speaking. I felt it so strongly too – a real dropping away from the superficial and down into the sea of peace and calm. It was lovely. Okay, the CEO is running the show. It's not got a lot to do with me really. In fact, all I have to do is obey instructions, which means I have to listen for them, of course. Once again, despite appearances, there is something deeper. It's not about the form, it's about the ESSENCE. Oh, this is kind of exciting!

The Listening said:

"I am indeed the CEO of all Life. You can turn to Me for anything and everything. Welcome. I am the peace and the calm. Do not worry about the future: there is no need for that, as it is My job. It is affected by the choices you make. But if you turn to Me first, the choices you make will always come out of Me and will bring you growth, learning, peace, calm, joy and utter satisfaction."

Question: Is Philip dying right now?

"Philip is struggling with some sense of heralding a new vision. This requires a putting down of the old first. Ask him to adorn himself with Me, as this will help him to see."

Question: What are all his negative and anxiety thoughts about?

"This is representative of him holding onto a branch that will no longer bear his weight. It will break eventually, or he can let go of it gradually. He can do this by singing out to Me, and knowing the peace that comes with that. The branch will then become less and less necessary,

for his feet will have touched the mossy grass of the next part of his journey."

Question: Will he continue to live and live well for some months?

"It is not My job to interfere in decisions made at a human level, so this information cannot be given. What can be given is an assurance that I am present, whether you be in a bodily form or not."

Philip continued to hang onto the branch desperately. He could not let himself drop to the mossy ground.

This conversation was just more evidence for me about how crucial it is to be able to face our own death, so we can embrace the process of dying with ease and grace, rather than resistance and fear. My dear, sweet man made it there in the end, but the run-up to that was extremely painful for him, and could have been easier if he'd been able to admit death was actually happening.

My journal for this time is full of The Listening – that, and a combination of *I Ching* readings. The *I Ching* is an ancient Chinese form of divination, providing inspiration through readings based on your current situation. Both this and The Listening brought me considerable solace and peace during a roller coaster ride of highs and lows, as further attempts were made to feed Philip via a tube down his throat, each one of them being unsuccessful.

It became obvious to me that he was indeed dying, and I wanted him to come home. He wanted to be home too. However, because for various reasons he couldn't be fed in any manner at home, this would have meant him facing up to the fact of dying. He couldn't do that, not until every possible avenue of feeding him had been explored. I had to respect this; and so had to bear witness to his pain, both physical and mental, and trust we were both in this position to learn yet more about the journey we were on.

Journal: 15th November 2011

> *Shit. Fuck. Shit. It didn't bloody work. One last chance. Looks like his opportunities really have run out. Can this actually be happening? It's a nightmare. Can it really be true? Tonight I'm at Camphill on my own, and it's lonely. And pointless. Pointless. How am I going to manage without him? I can't believe this is happening. I can't believe he is – very likely – to die. How did that happen? It's not fair. What will I do without him? Who will I talk to? I'm afraid I won't be able to get him home and he'll die in hospital. Shit. Please don't let that happen. Not yet.*

A few days later, sitting on the side of the bed, I turned towards Philip.

"I love you," I spoke directly to him, looking lovingly into his eyes, him looking lovingly back, "but it doesn't feel quite right to say that any more, somehow."

"No", he replied. "I know what you mean; it's as if there is no 'you' or 'I' to say it. Perhaps it's more true to say, 'Love is present.'"

"Love is always present, it's just that, sometimes, we're more open to it than not."

"We're definitely open to it now," responded Philip.

Yes, in its full splendour: we looked at each other and felt we were basking in Love's presence. We knew then what was really happening – just Love showing its full colours in those moments when, to the mind, the words 'I love you' wanted to be expressed, and yet the simple essence was just – Love is here, right now.

At this point, Philip was no longer able to write or even dictate, but I realised his blog readers would want to know what was happening, and so I posted the following:

Things are unpredictable...

Posted on 18 November 2011 by Jane

Things didn't go entirely to plan today. The doctor has had two emergencies to deal with apparently, and so of course he has run out of time. Therefore the feeding tube will not go down today. It's 4 p.m. on a Friday, that means a lot in a hospital, as nothing will happen over the weekend. Unbelievable.

Obviously, we have to learn about not being attached to a) the timing of a particular event, and b) the outcome of an event.

Difficult when it is a life or death situation. This is not the first time we have been presented with this lesson to be learnt, mind you. Nor the first time we have to see that we are not 'special cases,' able to bump up the queue, or that just because we think in a certain way, it will happen.

In fact, it is the third time. I see that my mind got caught up in believing and thinking that a particular event was going to happen. The endoscopy the first time, when the actual result was they couldn't see to do it because of the amount of gunge in Philip's stomach; it happened again last Friday afternoon when I forgot the first lesson (completely) and was given another outcome I hadn't imagined (the opportunity to do the procedure again) –

and now it has happened for a third time, and I STILL fell for it! Amazing! I believed that something will happen just because it was scheduled in a calendar; just because someone in authority had told me it will happen; and just because I wanted it to happen.

It's true that this is often what does happen of course, but events conspire to interfere often enough for me to question all of this.

It must be the same for outcomes, too. How do I know what the outcome of these procedures will be? It looks like there are only two options: get a tube down and have successful feeding, or not get a tube down and die – eventually. But how do I know there aren't other options my mind has not thought of?

I don't.

So the real truth is: we have no clue what is going to happen, or when. The only thing that is sure is what is happening right now, in the moment. That is all. As many wise sages have said, "What is, is."

The good thing is that time does not exist in the spiritual realm, and so everyone's thoughts, prayers and love are still entirely relevant. It's just the mind that thinks that's not the case.

13
An Auspicious Star

A beautiful gift had arrived for Philip a couple of weeks before his 66th birthday. Jackie, his eldest daughter, flew up from Coventry. Standing by his bedside, she dropped a kiss onto his forehead, and smiled. Holding out a piece of paper, she said,

"Here you are, Dad: it's a star." Philip read the paper and was amazed. It invited him to complete the online details necessary to name a star. Neither of us knew this was even possible. It was a lovely thought and, pragmatic as she is, Jackie had decided to give him an early birthday present, in case he wasn't around for his birthday. We were both hugely touched at her thoughtfulness and originality. It was a very loving action. Philip would be able to name the star anything he wanted. I assumed he would call it 'Philip Rogers'. But no; he announced the name a bit later on that day.

On a lighter note

Posted on 14 November 2011, typed by Jane

I'm going to call the star 'Love is the Answer.' So next time you're out in the night sky and you can see Orion, if you move slightly to the west and north, in the direction of Gemini, and point about half way between them, you'll be looking at a star called 'Love is the Answer'. Just behind another, Betelgeuse.

"How lovely!" Jane and Jackie chorus.

According to the fact sheet, most stars are not like our sun, which is a singleton star, but are known as binary stars, which means they are one of a pair circling each other. So in fact, the star that's known as 'Love is the Answer' is most likely to be like that. The stars in the night sky are catalogued, and have been being catalogued for millennia now, and most of them are designated by a combination of numbers and letters. Only the large, easily-recognised and famous ones have names, and there are many of those that don't. So this is an opportunity to change the registration in these star catalogues, from the given one to a new one of your own choice. And this is what I've done.

Tears rolled down my face as I witnessed another example of the transformation that was happening in Philip. He may have looked physically dreadful, but his soul was shining brightly, still offering to the world a gift of Love, and that still presence to which I had been so attracted when we first met. The details were completed via the website, and a certificate naming this star was received. (It hangs in my office as I type this. Often, when the stars are visible, I look for 'Love Is the Answer').

Later that day, Philip said to me, "You know, Jane, I've always been keen on knowing things."

"That's one way of putting it!" I laughed. He had been a fount of knowledge, a collector of all kinds of weird and wonderful pieces of information. In fact, sometimes I'd had to ban him from telling me about something I was learning about, as I wanted to discover it for myself.

"Well," he continued, "it's been really hard to know in this situation I'm in now. The good news is I actually think I am beginning to come to terms with not knowing, and with that being okay."

"That's wonderful!" I looked deeply into his eyes, gazing up at me from his bed with such innocence and love. Hearing him say this, and be at peace with not knowing, was a huge relief to me. Perhaps it was this acceptance of not knowing that led to him naming the star 'Love Is The Answer.'

During the morning of Friday 25th November, I had been Listening. From my journal:

> **Q: The next procedure is supposed to be happening today, this morning. Oh, God. How to be?**
>
> **The Listening:**
>
> *"Patience is a quality of Love, where each moment brings a connection or a disconnection. Choose to stay with Me, stay connected, for then you are in the land of what you call miracles, and I call ordinariness.*
>
> *"You do not know until you do" is something I spoke of yesterday, and it is true. It still applies. So bring your connected moments with Me here, right now, and rest in My arms knowing this is always here for you, regardless of what the state of affairs is.*

Of course, at a human level, it is natural to be afraid. Do not dismiss this. Rather, acknowledge it, and have fear be present, too, so it can also be warmed by the blanket of love so succinctly described by your sister Anna.

Be with Me here, now, dear one. There is no separation between us – you are in my arms now as fully as ever, as always – and I am always available to you. Love is present, for Love is Me and Love is you, and in the presence of Love, everything is seen differently."

For Philip:

"You are blessed dear One, no matter what happens today. As a conduit for My Love you are shining; a shining light serves to emphasise the dark corners, hence the fear. But the Light is always here in the presence of Love, and fear is welcome here, too. Step into My quiet arms and be held. I am always here for you."

Late on in the afternoon, after the last attempt to insert a tube into Philip's stomach had failed, Gamma Ray Man finally acknowledged there was nothing more he could offer. This time it really was true.

Philip looked at me glumly. "Bar a miracle, this is the end, then." I felt a mixture of feelings, and one of them was relief. But still, I felt unable to really believe that Philip's life could actually end and that one day very soon, he just wouldn't be there.

We agreed he would be moved to Dr Gray's hospital in Elgin, but everything goes quiet in hospitals during weekends, and when Monday came, we were told there were no rooms available. However, we had another decision to take before any moves could happen. Gamma Ray Man asked Philip, "While in the ambulance, if necessary, would you want to be resuscitated?" I held my breath, waiting for Philip's answer. With tears in his eyes, he looked at me.

"No. Is that all right?"

I had tried to talk to Philip about this before we left home for the hospital, but he wasn't having any of it then; and I was hugely relieved to hear his answer. I looked at him lovingly and agreed. I knew this was another step towards him accepting his death. I rang Barbara in Los Angeles and asked her to come over.

On Philip's blog I posted about all this and ended with:

> *What more can I say? Have the implications of this really hit me (or Philip) yet? I don't know. What I do know is I have waves of disbelief that this is happening at all. He, believe it or not, has cracked two jokes today. :-) What an amazing man I have married!*

But then I wrote in my journal:

> *I can't believe this is happening. A move to Elgin and hopefully home – to die. How can he die when he is a few days into being 66 and I am only 54? It's not fair.*
>
> *Later: Philip is dying. Dying. Dying? It is very hard to believe. But he doesn't look very well and is very thin. And has cancer and a lung infection. Oh dear.*

On Tuesday, when we were hoping to move, there were still no rooms available in Elgin. We geared ourselves up for a move on Wednesday, when we were assured there was a single room. In the meantime, poor Philip was trying to cope with increasing amounts of black bile being regurgitated, from the pneumonia he had contracted. Very distressing. Barbara's arrival brought some compensation, and although he didn't say this to me, he must have known what this meant. She had been so instrumental in his life.

"Philip, we might not get home, you know." I spoke very gently to him. He looked wiped out. "But really, home is wherever you and I are, and here we are, now." He nodded. We had talked about this before; so many times in our lives we'd been apart for various reasons, and home was always in the moment when we were connecting, talking, or writing to each other. Once again, we were being given the message: the form is not important, only the essence is.

On the morning of Wednesday 30th November, a nurse visited. "I'm really sorry, but because of the strike there are no ambulances available to take you to Elgin." The nurse looked apologetic. Later in the morning, Gamma Ray Man visited.

"I'm sorry, Philip, but actually I can't recommend you move now. You are too ill. You've gone down fast in the last few days." Philip couldn't talk much because it easily activated the coughing reflex which was painful, so he tried to avoid that. He sighed and looked resigned.

"Oh. So my body is giving up." At this point we both knew the end was near.

Journal: Wednesday 30 November

My poor man. His body is beginning to break down. When I told him his kidneys and liver were not working properly, I knew he would know what that meant. I don't want to have to talk about these things with him. I don't want him to die. I just want to be with him. Sad. So sad.

*

In the wee small hours of Thursday 1st December, a text from Barbara, who was staying overnight with Philip, woke me.

"P. is having a difficult night. Can you come in?"

I shot out of bed, putting clothes on over my pyjamas, and was up there within ten minutes, to discover Philip in considerable distress. With further medication, he calmed down, began more regular breathing, and was out of pain. I stayed with him while he slept, his breathing hampered by the liquid in his gullet, making a rattling, raspy sound. Horrible to hear. Barbara told me,

"You know, something odd happened. About midnight, he asked for the remote control."

"But he's never yet watched telly in hospital!" I looked at her, astonished.

"I know. But I asked him if he wanted to watch the telly, and he said yes. So I got him the remote and asked what channel he wanted."

"Channel 4 – I want to see Countdown," he replied.

Countdown used to be one of his favourite TV programmes. He would pit his wits against two teams on the TV as they tried to make the longest word possible out of a series of letters. He loved that sort of stuff. When I heard this, I knew he was telling us the end was near: he was literally counting down. I called Jackie, and told her to get on an earlier plane than she had intended.

All Thursday during the day, he was more or less sedated: various medications to manage the pain, and others to help dry up the secretions.

"I want you to take him off the intravenous feeding. And please: can you do whatever you have to do so he's not conscious of what is happening anymore?" I asked the consultant who was visiting.

We had rarely seen her before and she seemed not to know the whole story. She looked at me, alarm in her eyes. "Have you said all you want to say to him?"

"I've had lots of opportunities to say everything. I don't mind if he never opens his eyes again; I just want him to be out of this agony." I was very clear. During that day, Philip was aware of conversations: we could tell because occasionally he would murmur or grunt, and even more occasionally would come round from the drugs enough to speak a little. Good friend Christopher Raymont visited, and together he and I softly sang some of Philip's favourite Taize songs, particularly 'In manus tuas pater, commendo spiritum meum, meaning ' *Into thy hands God I commend my spirit.* Although it appeared he didn't know we were there, I'm sure he did. Old friend Wyon arrived, and sat with him too.

Later still, while I was alone with him he softly murmured to me, "I love you." Then he put his shaking hands into the prayer position.

"Take me." With that, I knew he'd let go; he was giving himself up. My dear, lovely, brave man.

Later that afternoon, leaving Jackie and Daniel, his eldest grandson, at Philip's bedside, I returned to where I was staying to get out of my pyjamas from the early morning start and have a shower. I was supposed to sleep, but not much of that happened. Returning a couple of hours later, I found River and Barbara by the bedside, and saw Philip was lucid once more.

"Help me."

Even with slurred words, we could understand this plea. More medication was given, and I spoke again of the angels waiting for him, telling him my vision once more. River suggested having the nurses move his body, as it looked as though he was falling out of bed. I left the room in tears; I couldn't bear to see him suffering so much. The nurse returned. "We've moved him, and his breathing has changed."

Barbara and I went back in to be with him and River. His breathing was no longer a rattling sound in the back of his throat. I sat down and held his hand. His eyes were shut, and he occasionally took a big breath, and then there would be a long gap. Within a few minutes, he stopped taking these breaths. At one point, his face seemed to change colour, just subtly. That was when he left his body, and it was clear he was no longer there.

Looking upwards towards the ceiling, we each took turns to speak to his spirit, telling him what had happened, reassuring him he was loved, blessing him. It was very beautiful.

Journal: Thursday 1st December 2011, 8.19pm

My dear, darling, beautiful, courageous and conscious husband died tonight. So brave, so brave.

Barbara, River, Jackie, Daniel and I finally left the hospital to go back to bed. At 4am I was awoken from sleep and sat bolt upright. I felt a cold circular spot on the back of my neck and a huge urge to write and post it on the blog. I just knew this was Philip visiting and encouraging me.

Leaving the body:

Posted on 2 December 2011 by Jane

Last night, 1st December, dear Philip left his body peacefully at 8.19 pm. I say left his body, because it became very obvious there was no longer an inhabitant in that body at that time. One moment he was there, the next moment, gone. And that is death. That moment.

Philip struggled in the last few days of being in the body. I have to say 'the' body instead of 'his' body, because it sounds too odd now to refer to him as having a body when it was so clear that the body was just the packaging for his spirit. Who Philip is was simply flowing through that particular form, for that particular time. Now he is elsewhere, but very close. Can I feel him? I feel immensely loved, immensely. So, yes, I think I can say I feel him.

Philip did not want to die, not one little bit. "Why are you afraid of dying, sweetheart?" I'd asked him some weeks previously.

"I want to give more," was his simple reply.

Well, he had given more. Given in the manner in which he approached the impending death of his body, which was in full consciousness. Never for one minute was he not present in his mind's abilities during his stay in hospital, even through all the drugs. He was clear and conscious about everything: what the doctors were prescribing and why, and the amount he was taking. He knew what was going on around him: his body's needs, the meaning of his hallucinations. He was even aware of my needs to the last moment, and the presence of Love itself. He has been an amazing example of conscious dying.

Thank you, my dearest one, thank you.

Part 2: Loss

Introduction to Part 2

It's two and a half years on as I write this, and for the first time I have begun re-reading my journals and diary, of those awful days, weeks and months right after he died. In tears, I've been shocked at how utterly dreadful it was. If I hadn't written it down, I wouldn't have remembered how horrible it was. Even when I knew he was going to die, even when I was with him, watching it happen, it was all so unbelievable. What on earth can it be like when death is sudden? The grief I felt over not being able to have children was minimal compared to this. Despite knowing quite a lot in theory about grief, despite the enormous amount of support I received, it was absolutely awful. Just stark, raw pain.

I'm also heartened, though, as I read my writings. There, in my journal, are the moments of bliss and joy, and they grew steadily – little bit by very little bit, over the next months.

It really was true what everyone told me: the gap between the horror and ordinary life does grow. Grief comes to visit, as opposed to being a permanent presence. I began to know grief's hallmarks well: fatigue of a kind that drains the bones; headaches; the inability to find any point in whatever I was supposed to be doing; sudden rage; and many, many tears. Tears with a cleanliness to them; tears of deep, deep sadness; and tears of pain. I discovered that if I allow the tears – and the rage, as well – to simply flow, then, just like a river changes in the course of its life, the feelings change. Eventually, they flow less. And, after a longer period of time, they stop. I may or may not feel better afterwards – that was a surprise at first. I was used to crying and then feeling a bit better, or even a lot better. Sometimes in my life, I could recognise I needed a cry, about goodness knows what, just to relieve tension.

However, these tears were different, very different. Many times, I did not feel any better afterwards. The tears were just an expression of the seemingly never-ending grief. Then I would eventually go and do something, or someone would call, or I'd go to bed.

I know not all people experience grief in the way I've done and have written about; it can take many different forms. A friend of mine whose brother, mum and cousin died in the space of two years found herself incapacitated by fear, and found C.S. Lewis's recognition of this immensely useful, but when I read Lewis's *A Grief Observed*, I didn't find it helpful at all.

What did help was knowing that feelings always change. So, even in the midst of the worst times, I knew it would pass. 'What you feel, you can heal' and 'This too shall pass' became great consolations. Not always, but often.

I also could sometimes receive comfort from the sentence, 'I cannot know that this is not the next step towards my liberation.' I've lived long enough now to look back and see that what appears to be the most dreadful episode, has often turned out to have a blessing in it. I didn't have even a glimpse, at this time, of the full nature of what the next seven months would bring.

14

Coming Home Alone

It never occurred to us that I would be coming home without Philip. We never imagined it. Not until right at the end, when it became obvious he wasn't going to get home, and then my mind had been taken up with other things; Philip's comfort, his pain, last visitors, and not knowing when he would actually die. Suddenly all this had gone, and I was faced with empty, stark reality. Barbara, River and I all checked out of our rooms. We packed into the car and drove home without him, River in the front seat, instead of Philip. Surreal.

Journal: Friday December 2nd 2011

10 p.m. River staying, thank God.

I dread being alone in this house, and I will have to face it sometime. I dreaded coming home, actually, and it was horrible, but I cried, hard, and got through it. Many loving comments on Philip's blog, and over 1000 views today. I was very touched. I hope he knows. Perhaps he doesn't care now, though.

A funeral director had previously been recommended to me; River had asked him to come over on the Saturday morning.

River, Barbara and I sat in the sitting room with him, as he described what was to happen next.

"We'll drive to Aberdeen and bring Philip back from the hospital to our funeral home."

"It's not Philip!" burst out of me. "It's just a body. That's not him, that's not who he was!"

He was good, that funeral director. Took it all in his stride, and adjusted how he was talking by referring to 'the body.' He must be used to people behaving oddly after death. I imagined the body being delivered in the back of a white van – Philip would definitely have thought that funny. I've no idea how they did it; I never did find out, nor did I care. My detachment from the body had been complete in the hospital, when I went back into his room to double-check it really had all actually happened. The nurses had laid the body down flat, and that's all it was: a dead body, lying flat on the bed, covers up over the chest. Could almost have been any old dead body. Nothing to do with the man I had known and loved so well.

The funeral director listed the procedures that needed to happen. I'd no idea; we hadn't gone into this amount of detail on The List. The only thing I knew we'd agreed on was a fairly ordinary service with an inexpensive, cardboard-box type of coffin, and then to have a Celebration of Life in the Universal Hall, in the Findhorn Foundation.

Just after we'd joined the Findhorn Foundation Community in 2007, a member of the community died suddenly, and there was a service for him in the Hall.

"I'm going to go to the service," Philip announced one morning over the breakfast table.

"What? You can't do that; you didn't know him!" I exclaimed.

"Yes, but it says here in the Rainbow Bridge (the community weekly newsletter) that everyone is invited. It'll be fine; and I really feel drawn to go." I didn't agree. I was caught in a place of worrying about what other people might think of me. So Philip went alone, and experienced a lovely outpouring of appreciation for the life of Andrew Murray, which is why Philip later stated on The List his desire for something similar. Ideally, he would have been here to join in . . . but too late for that now. However, I could organise it for him. I'd pressed him in the hospital for who he wanted to hold the ceremony.

"Duncan will be great. He was so good when he stayed over with me that night in the hospital. Do you think he'd be able to do it?"

"I'm sure he'd be delighted. Well, maybe not delighted. But if he can, he will."

I was remembering all this as I listened to the undertaker in the sitting room. He wanted to know about dates of a funeral service. We had learned that the Universal Hall was only available on 9th December or in early January. I couldn't bear to wait until January, which felt too far off in time, so we arranged to have a cremation service on 8th December in nearby Lossiemouth Funeral Home, and then the service in the Hall the following day. All this fitted in with my parents, who'd already booked to come over from France, hoping to see Philip again before he died. So many practical things to think about. Thank God for The List.

How would you like the body to be dressed?" asked the undertaker. I knew the answer to this one: it was on The List.

"In the dressing gown I made for him. He really loved it. Also, can we put in the pockets the two little clay sculptures he made?"

"I'm not sure about whether they will burn successfully; I'd have to check," he replied doubtfully.

I smiled. "Well, you decide. I will imagine them in there, and if you have to take them out, just don't tell me about it. Philip won't care. So – what will all this cost?" He'd been speaking not only of cremating the body, but of transporting it, holding a service, and probably some other things too, which I've forgotten.

"£2,600."

"What! That's a huge amount for something I don't even want!" I shouted at him again, through a big burst of tears.

Once again, he just sat there silently. No one said anything. There was nothing to be said. It was true. I didn't want it to have happened, and I certainly didn't want to pay that kind of money for something I didn't want. However, I had no choice.

Eventually, he murmured, "You'll be able to claim back the £200 for transporting the body from the hospital to Lossiemouth." Later, I discovered this was a very good deal for a funeral. So that's why people have funeral insurance.

Journal: Sunday 4th December 2011

> *4:30 a.m. I'm having six hours sleep a night but I'm sure it's not enough. What can I do? I've been lying here for over an hour, crying, worrying about money, the future, where to live, how it'll be when everyone is gone, what to do.*
>
> *Right now, I cannot imagine doing any coaching, ever again. I suppose that will change. Wish I didn't have the pressure of earning an income though.*

I used the *I Ching* after making the above entry in my journal. Throwing three coins in the air 6 times, a hexagram was constructed according to how they landed. Then I referred to the

I Ching guide itself for a reading. I was given the hexagram that meant 'Disbelief in the power of non-action, or in the power of just being'.

After this reading, I wrote: *"I recognise this. When I was made redundant so long ago, I didn't 'do'; I was just waiting. And it really worked. I need to 'do' that now – just wait and see what happens."*

I've used the *I Ching* for so long because there's nearly always one sentence or a paragraph that rings true, and relaxes me enough to go back to sleep, and so it proved that night.

Several days later, Mum and Dad arrived; I collected them from Aviemore train station. Although they had missed seeing Philip alive, I think they didn't mind that, preferring to remember him in good health when they had last seen him the year before. It was a bit of a hair-raising journey through the snow on the Dava Moor, and then we had to come back the long way, via Inverness, as by now there was too much snow on the moor. My neighbour Alison had offered her house opposite ours for them to stay in.

Mum and Dad took the few steps over to my house the following day to join me with some other friends. I sat and listened to them all talking, social chit-chat.

"That's an interesting painting."

"Oh, you're living in France. Whereabouts?"

"The weather's really bad, even for here, at the moment." I screamed inside: *"What are they all DOING, talking about these inane, ordinary things when Philip has just died?"* The scream came out in a burst of sobbing as I shouted,

"I want you to talk about Philip! It's too awful, pretending this is just an ordinary social occasion. *It's not!* You're all here because he died, and it's *not all right* to *not* talk about him!"

There was a hint of a hush, and then someone broke the silence, "Of course. You're absolutely right," and someone else started to talk about Philip.

Clearly this journey was going to be not just full of ups and downs, but round and round and upside down too. I didn't care though; I didn't care about anything, because he was dead and I was alive, and it was all wrong.

Journal: Tuesday 6th December 2011

Nearly a week now. I can't believe he is actually DEAD. Can that really have happened to him? I'm so afraid of being on my own, rattling around in this house, terrified of the emptiness. Maybe that's how P felt about death. He didn't have a choice; I have lots of choices. So if he can do it, so can I.

Have you really gone away, Philip? Have you really gone away?

River came with me to register the death in the local council office in Forres. Again, it felt so surreal. So many things to tidy up after a death, the remains of a life in all its messiness. Over coffee afterwards in my favourite coffee shop, I turned towards him, touching his arm.

"Thank you so much, River." Our eyes met and he nodded.

"I've been thinking . . . I may not stay for the funeral service. Would that be okay with you?"

"Of course!" I was so very grateful for his support; he'd arrived in the third week of October, thinking he was coming just to help out for maybe a couple of weeks at most, perhaps seeing Philip for the last time. He'd ended up staying the whole 7 weeks we were in Aberdeen, and then at our house with me afterwards. The least I could do was honour his desire to leave when he wanted to.

Besides, Barbara was staying a while longer, and could move into the house with me. I had the support, too, of all my local friends, and all the rest of my family would be coming up as well.

Philip and I would have had a very different experience without this special man, such a good friend, who had supported several of his other friends through the dying process previously.

The funeral service at Lossiemouth a couple of days later was another surreal experience. A modern, low building in amongst factories and other industrial buildings down by the sea. I hadn't been there before – River had checked it out, and said it was nice. The cardboard box with Philip's body in it lay at the head of the room adorned with a few wild flowers from our garden. On the wall behind was a beautiful mosaic of the bay with a sailing boat. Philip would have appreciated that, being a lover of both sailing and creating mosaics. Margie McCallum, the celebrant, held a beautiful service in which several friends spoke of him lovingly. We sang *Morning Has Broken* by Cat Stevens, which had been sung at our wedding, and I drifted through the whole thing. I had no tears, and, unexpectedly, a feeling of complete detachment.

After the short service ended, the coffin was wheeled by two kilt-clad funeral home gentlemen to another side room, where my three year old niece piped up,

"Is that Uncle Philip in there?"

"Well, not exactly, darling. His body's in there, but he's gone away up into the stars."

She and her seven-year-old brother looked as though they wanted to see inside, but that was definitely not on the cards. Not having wanted to see the body even five minutes after he'd died, why would I want to see it now, or have it be seen?

Besides, you have to pay more to have the coffin open.

Journal: Thursday 8th December 2011:

Actually, Philip, I think it's time you came back now. Well, sort of. I don't want you to come back, because you were so very ill. So you can only come back if you are healthy. And I do so want to be able to talk to you. I'll just have to write to you instead.

Hi Philip,

It was very strange today. I cannot equate the words death, cremation, coffin, or body with your name at all. I'm looking right now at the photo of you on the mantelpiece. It looks so much you, such very loving eyes. It was a great ceremony, you would have loved it – but it was about you! How weird is that? Then afterwards at home, it was just like another party, and honestly, you could have been in the bedroom, like you were when we had my birthday party in September. It was great to have so many lovely, loving people around, but why are they here? Because you are dead? Dead? What on earth is that, and how on earth can it apply to you?

It amazed me at the time, and it still amazes me, how much of a state of shock I was in, even though I'd known he was going to die. Even though I had been there when he died. All the things one thinks are supposed to be 'good.' None of it made a blind bit of difference; I still couldn't believe he was dead and never coming back again. It took a long, long time before I began to fully realise it.

15
Celebration of A Life

The morning after the service in Lossiemouth, the phone rang. It was the undertaker.

"I'm very sorry to tell you, we couldn't get a slot in the crematorium for Philip's body right after the service. In fact, there won't be one available until a few days away, on the 13th." He spoke in very sombre tones.

"Oh. Well, never mind. I suppose you'll keep it there and then deliver it. Will you?"

"Yes, of course." He sounded rather surprised; perhaps he'd been expecting me to object, or shout at him again.

"Everyone will think it's happening immediately, so I won't say anything. It'll be all right," I was very prosaic.

I really didn't mind; in fact I thought it was funny, and I knew Philip would have laughed at the irony of it. Imagine something so practical as a queue at the crematorium interfering in the whole solemn process. Black humour indeed.

*

In the Findhorn Foundation Community, we are very good at acknowledging and marking transitions. Whether they be weddings, births, deaths, or anything in between, there is an honouring in a very beautiful way of these occasions, and Philip's Celebration of Life the following day was indeed lovely. Particularly beautiful were the few minutes of Taize singing, which he had loved so much. Flocking from their seats to the centre of the hall, people separated themselves into 4 different voice parts and sang three of Philip's favourite songs in beautiful, haunting harmonies.

Barbara, sitting next to me, leaned over and whispered,

"They are singing him home." I burst into tears. It was so true, and I so wished he was with me to share it.

Afterwards, over tea and cakes in the community centre, the Memories Book that I'd instigated was passed around. My friend Deborah had suggested it a few days previously.

"In the Jewish tradition, we have a Memories Book when someone dies. Have you thought of that? It gives everyone a chance to express their wishes to you, or memories of Philip. It can be a very beautiful thing to do."

"That sounds really great!" I immediately knew how important this was, and I'd bought a book that very day, covering it in material from a sewing project I'd been doing when we had lived on our yacht in Auckland Harbour. The book was an immense source of solace and comfort at the time, and in the months to come. Many people wrote in it during the tea and cakes, about which I remember hardly anything, other than being hugely touched by the presence of a colleague from my local Toastmasters group. I didn't know him that well, but it meant a lot that he was there for that very reason. I was also hugely grateful to those people in the community who had organised the baking and tea pouring. I still don't know exactly who they were. In fact, it was only many months later that I wondered about something else.

"Hi, I'm Jane Duncan Rogers; you printed the service sheet for my husband's funeral service." I was visiting Big Sky Printers, based in The Park, the main campus of the Findhorn Foundation. "I was wondering whether the bill ever got paid, as I don't remember paying it."

The man replied in a gruff Scottish accent. "Och, that was taken care of by someone else."

Tears bubbled over again. I felt so nourished and cared for.

At the actual celebration, our community had come out in force to acknowledge one of its members passing on, and to be there for me who had been left behind. This kind of support continued in many different ways; it had been happening during Philip's illness, and it was still there for me now. I never knew before how very important a card, email, text or phone call could be; or a hug without words, or just someone's presence. I was surprised by who sent cards: some were from people I hadn't known knew Philip, or from those whose our lives had only briefly touched. I was also surprised by who didn't send cards, or acknowledge his death in any way at all. This was my first introduction to how odd some people are around death. I quickly learnt how much I appreciated it when someone we had known said something to acknowledge what had happened. It didn't matter what, even if it was, "I don't know what to say." It's true: it IS hard to know what to say, especially if you're just an acquaintance.

Someone shook my hand. "Please accept my condolences." Very formal. Fine on a card but it sounded very odd spoken out loud.

"So sorry you have lost Philip," said someone else. I thought, "Thank you, but it's me who's lost, not him."

Another acquaintance approached, and expressed how sorry he was – and then went on to tell me how he knew how I felt as his father had just died. Inside my head, I screamed, *"Your father?! And you liken that to losing my husband? For God's sake!"* On the outside, though, I just nodded my thanks.

Then someone else announced,

"You're very accident-prone, you know."

"What? What have I done?" I was shocked; had I caused an accident somehow and not even realised it?

"""No, no, I mean you're likely to have an accident; it's well-known that people who are bereaved are accident-prone, so be very careful driving; better not to drive at all, actually."

This was someone I hardly knew. By now, though, I understood that people do say odd things when all they are really wanting to do is help in some way. So I politely accepted what he was saying – and then ignored it. How could he know how utterly unhelpful it was to be told this, and on top of it, not to drive? How could he know it would make me feel like punching him? I listened politely to him expound his views, while all the time paying no attention in my head. It was almost laughable.

Later, I told this story to a trusted friend, who exclaimed exasperatedly, "Jane, you are not accident-prone. If people are not able to feel, or process their feelings, then they may well be accident-prone, but you don't fall into that category, and you aren't."

Even in one of my spiritual group meetings, someone said,"When you and Philip were there the last time we met, you were asking for healing and prayers, and I couldn't give the healing because I knew Philip wasn't going to make it." In my journal, I wrote:

> *God! Who in their right minds thinks that is a useful or sensible thing to say to someone newly bereaved? For goodness' sake! People are so weird. So weird.*

Moral of the story: When you meet someone whose loved one has died, do acknowledge it, but keep it simple. You have no idea how that person is going to be processing what is going on. Simple words, or a gesture is fine. Even saying "I don't know what to say," and then keeping silent worked very well for me. Just a card/email/text – any form of communication, really, will do. It's the non-acknowledgment that really hurts.

16
The Day After

Journal: 10th December 2011

I've just come back from taking Mum and Dad to Inverness train station, on their way back to France. I felt so sad on the way home, and now it feels like my heart is actually breaking. Philip! I want you by my side.

In the car on the way home, I felt so keenly your presence in your red coat, your blue gloves and your bright blue peaked cap that I didn't like so much. You were such a big, tall man when you were well, and I used to berate you for having a fat tummy, and now you haven't got one at all.

Today I told the neighbour, "My husband died."

How can that be? It's not possible. You were here one minute and now, the next, you're not – and it's already been over a week.

Help. What a bloody awful week.

I'm so unhappy I just want to cry and cry and cry and cry. The ceremony etc. might all have been lovely and beautiful and heartfelt, but here is the rawness of the human body and emotions, and it is not nice. Not nice.

My darling. Where are you? Will you come to me, please? Will you guide me? I really want your help. I promise to try and Listen, more and more, but it has been so difficult to get past my emotions.

I know you would encourage me to cry. You were always good at that. Let it out, better out than in. I have said that to you often in the last year, when you reached the bottomless pit inside yourself, and the engulfing fear of dying. And now you are dead – but what does that mean? Where are you? How are you? Do you exist in any way at all anymore? Can I reach you? Can I see you? Can I hear you? I want to; I want to know you are okay. More than that, though, I want you here by my side. I wish the whole bloody thing had not happened. Fuck! It's not fair!

Later:

Philip, I caught sight of your blue basket, with all your nuts and things in the kitchen while I was preparing baked potatoes – the first meal I've prepared since coming home – and I burst into tears. I couldn't bear the poignancy of the efforts you had made to be kind to your poor tummy over all those months. If only I had known when you said there was a physical obstruction in your stomach, that there really was, and had hammered away at the doctors, maybe things would have been different.

That really IS suffering, though – doing the 'if only's.' Second-guessing makes everything seem worse, and certainly isn't productive. So, where am I now? Feeling closer to you because I am talking to you. Sort of talking. Still, better than nothing, and I do feel like you are closer. I like it that my friends talk about you all the time. I think about you all the time. Or at least much of the time.

Darling, I love you. I wish you were here with me. I wish we could cuddle up like we used to. Have the companionship of doing our puzzles together. At least I have nice thoughts like that to remember you by.

And guess what! I got the car in the garage today! I was so pleased with that. No more scraping off snow and waiting for the car to warm up. I felt inordinately proud of myself; silly perhaps, but I did. A bit like when I managed to mow the lawn in Banbury when you were away that time.

Darling, I'm going to sleep now. I can imagine you beside me, doing your puzzle, and me turning over and going to sleep, snuggled up to your arm. It's not a recent memory, but it's better than the very recent ones of you being so bony, and us being apart at night times. Yuck. Never for one minute did I think we would not come back here and snuggle up together on the bed. I guess it simply was not that important in the end. What was important was that we were together, no matter where, held in love, and being loving. You were so courageous, so brave, so open-hearted. Look at all those people last night in the hall expressing their admiration for you. It was amazing! Oh, my love. I do so love you. Good-night, sweetie.

Journal: 11th December 2011

I was awake in the wee hours a lot last night, and at one point, lying on my back, lots of thoughts going round in my head. Suddenly, I was so peaceful. It was as if the thoughts just dropped away. In fact, peaceful doesn't describe it really; more a taste of something bigger. It happened three times, with the first the most intense and lasting the longest. I think this was P, communicating to me how it is for him. It was very, very beautiful, like a step into another world that I think he's in all the time. It really was as if the thoughts just suddenly dropped away. There, underneath, was this deep, deep, deep peace, unlike anything else I've ever experienced. Indescribable, of course. I am sure this is the realm where he is now.

I continued to write about and to Philip, just as if he were physically here; telling him about my day, about the challenges, about my feelings. Nothing different, except he couldn't reply and I couldn't hear him with my ears. I was used to writing in my journal, having done it since I was in my late teens, so it was relatively easy, if tearful. Just chatting out loud seems to work for some people, which I also did. As I used to remind myself, "just because you are not in a body, doesn't mean to say I can't talk to you."

Still, it wasn't as good as him being here. I rang a friend one day, who in the course of our conversation uttered the words: "I was just talking to John…" I didn't hear what she said next. My heart twanged; I was consumed with rage and jealousy because she could talk to her husband, and I couldn't talk to mine. In moments like this, I didn't care if he was in a peaceful place or not; I just wanted him back, full stop.

Journal: Friday 16th December 2011

Two weeks and one day since Philip died. Died! Fuck! NO! Those two words still don't go together. It is NOT OK! not want to be left alone and I am. Shit!

Journal: Sunday 18th December 2011

I suppose I will just have to get used to being alone. May it'll get worse. Or maybe not. Today I booked to go to Anna my sister, in England in February, just for 4 or 5 days. Real

> *ised I might need to have someone waiting for me when I come home, late at night. Especially after coming home the other night from a meeting, back to an empty house. I was wailing, wailing. I cannot understand why I cannot understand, and somehow don't believe it has happened. I suppose this is the nature of grief. We could have had another twenty years, easily.*
>
> *People say I have lost him, but he is out there somewhere. It's me that is lost.*

I received some Listening that same night:

> *Ah, dear one. You are not lost either. For I am guiding you and watching over you, showing you the way; the way of grief right now, as your heart breaks. Yet also know I am upholding you.*
>
> **Question: But why did he have to die?**
>
> *The body crumbled, and the soul completed its journey within that body. Now the soul chooses to merge, and perhaps to re-emerge later on.*
>
> **Question: I feel so bereft without him**
>
> *Yes, dear one, and it is natural.*

It really was a matter of getting used to a myriad of emotions. Just before Christmas, I was out walking in the pine woods at the back of the house one day. Bright sunshine, cold wind, blue sky: stunningly beautiful. My heart was open and I felt totally happy. At the same time, I was amazed I could feel like that, knowing Philip was no longer there at home, ready to welcome me back from my walk. How could I possibly be feeling this joy one moment, and then floods of tears the next? Not to mention the sudden bouts of rage. I was learning about the journey of grief.

17
The First Christmas

How on earth did I get through that first Christmas, when everyone else was celebrating, and that was the last thing I wanted to do? In the run up to it, I was all over the place, with intense feelings of many different kinds, trying to make sense of everything.

Journal: 23rd December 2011

A widow. Shit. I do not want to be a widow. What a horrible expression. I just hate that word. How can you be dead? How can this word apply to you? How can the word 'widow' apply to me? I cannot understand it. And then other times it appears to be okay. Help!

I want to know if you have found the connection you wanted with the Divine. Would that make it all worthwhile? Not sure. I want to know if you are happy, though, and doing all right on your own. I don't know how I am doing, I really don't. I feel all over the place.

I find it really hard to bear that I don't know what is happening to you, what is going on for you. Are you just a particle of dust? Shit. I hate it.

The Tibetan Book of Living and Dying says you might be looking around, able to see me, but not able to understand why I can't hear you, or see you. I hate that thought too. I'm sorry if you are there and I can't connect with you. I hope I'll be able to one day.

Fortunately or unfortunately, depending on your point of view, we had never been traditional celebrants of Christmas. In fact, I broke the tradition of going to family members' homes very early on in my life before I met Philip, as while travelling aged 31 throughout Southeast Asia, I ended up with a friend on Koh Phi Phi island in Thailand for Christmas one year.

It had been my first taste of Christmas in hot weather, spent with some delightfully friendly Thai people, swimming in warm waters, and experiencing the deluge of a short, but extremely heavy, burst of rain, with everything steaming afterwards. A pattern of always seeing family had been interrupted with only a short, very expensive phone call back home on Christmas Day itself. Hence, it was easy for Philip and me to often spend Christmas alone, or go to friends', and only occasionally see members of my family; his children always went to their mother's.

So there was no pattern for me regarding this first Christmas alone. I couldn't send any Christmas cards, or respond to any we received, because the thought of signing only my name was too painful. All I knew was I didn't want to leave Forres; the thought of travelling so soon was horrible.

"What are you doing for Christmas, Jane?" my friend Tree asked over the phone one day. Tree – short for Theresa – was a good friend of us both, from when I had very first known Philip.

"Don't know; haven't got that far yet."

"Well, what do you think of me flying up and us having Christmas together?"

"I'd love it!" I sighed with relief. I must have been wondering about what to do at Christmas more than I realised.

Although Tree and I hadn't seen each other for ages, and had certainly never spent any length of time together alone, she came for the ten days over Christmas and New Year. Being with her was wonderful. It helped I was with someone who had known Philip when he was really healthy, many years previously.

Journal: Christmas Eve

Tree and I went to a very soothing mindfulness meditation this morning in the Main Sanctuary at the Foundation. Sitting and walking meditation, followed by a short video of Thich Nhat Hanh and his community chanting. It was just spectacular, although I was overcome with sadness at the end, because I so wanted to share it with you; not anyone else, not even Tree. Just you.

I don't feel like I know anything anymore. I do know that we loved each other well. I do know that I loved well, and now I am grieving well. By well, I mean fully. Probably there is always room for more, but, still, I don't feel regrets about anything – a bit sad sometimes that we didn't manage to get much into the Cairngorm mountains together, or John O'Groats – but not real regrets.

Nor do I feel guilty much, either – a bit about my continual criticism about you having a fat tummy – but I am choosing to forgive myself when I can, and realise it is just my ego trying to make me feel bad. This is what I mean by grieving well.

Maybe this is not a Diary of a Widow. Maybe it's a Diary of a Window – a window of opportunity. Not yet, though.

On Christmas Day itself, we had a very quiet time. Walks, a nice meal of roast chicken and vegetables. Fire blazing; good, nourishing conversation, and little input from anyone else. Not that I was short of offers to spend Christmas with other friends; I felt utterly blessed in that way. However, I just knew it was important for me to keep it simple, to wait and see what we felt like doing at any one time, and to keep the pressure off. At the end of the day, I wrote:

I long for you sometimes, darling. I long for our simple conversations, our complex ones, your loving company, your arm round me, making love. I long for a snuggle up in bed together, and a sharing of our days; but I'm glad we had what we had, so glad. I'm so happy we loved as well as we did, and shared it a lot with others. It means a lot, that. Goodnight, my darling, my love. Goodnight. I love you.

Tree slept in Philip's bedroom, while I stayed in mine. During our lives together, we'd always had our own bedrooms. In fact, we had 'our' bedroom, and then I had 'mine.' I, in particular, needed the space, and I loved having the choice to sleep together or not, despite the fact we most often did. So it was quite normal for me to be sleeping in my own bed, and not in 'ours,' and it meant I didn't particularly miss him in my own bed.

I did, however, sleep alongside one of Philip's T-shirts, with his smell on it. Cuddling that at night was both heavenly and distressing in equal measure, until eventually the smell wore off, I washed it, and started wearing it instead.

Getting used to Tree being in Philip's bed instead of him was a bit weird; but then, we'd been nearly eight weeks away in the hospital, and everything was weird about him not being home.

*

I woke one morning and announced, "I need to go and get his ashes." Having previously stated I wasn't interested, and that the undertakers could do what they liked with the ashes, this was a turnaround. Still, I was beginning to trust my instincts more and more, hence the announcement.

It was a beautiful, typically winter's day: blue sky, sunshine, cold and crisp. We took the shore road to Lossiemouth, and knocked at the funeral home door.

"Here they are, then," said the undertaker. How I managed to keep a straight face until we got outside, I don't know.

"Oh, this is hilarious!" I laughed. The ashes were in a brown plastic tub, shaped like an old glass sweetie jar. It was decidedly tacky.

"Philip will be laughing, too," giggled Tree, and he would have been. Just another piece of ridiculousness in the whole episode of unreality surrounding his death.

Down near the beach, I unscrewed the lid, being curious. It was full to the brim with a powdery grey dust.

"There's an awful lot of ashes, isn't there?" I looked at Tree in amazement.

"Yes, isn't it incredible?"

"I'll be able to scatter them in other places as well as Dumfries and Galloway, where he said he wanted them scattered; why don't we go right now and put some into the sea from the beach?"

Which is how we discovered that you have to throw ashes in the path of the wind, not against it.

Later, ashes brushed off my jacket, and sitting drinking hot chocolate in the cafe overlooking the harbour, I spoke sadly.

"I wish Philip and I had come here to Lossiemouth harbour; I'd no idea it was so lovely. He would have adored looking at the boats and pottering around." I was going back and forth between "I wish...", the "if only's..." and feeling grateful for what we had had together.

Back home I placed the 'urn' on the mantelpiece, and stood back to look at it.

"No, all wrong."

I decanted the ashes into a large glass jar – two actually – and put one of them on the hearth, and hid the other away. I Skyped Barbara in Los Angeles to share the silliness of brown plastic urns, the large amount of ashes, and my tears.

"Send me some of the ashes," she smiled. "I'll scatter them in his favourite places over here." That became the first conversation in many that resulted in small amounts of his ashes being scattered all over the world. It was only later I found out that sending ashes through the post had been made illegal.

In my journal that night I wrote:

The things that are okay about you not being here are only a few: being able to watch whatever I want, when I want, on the TV; eating anything and not worrying about what it is; not having to worry about you and your health; being able to go for a long walk without thinking about whether you can manage it or not; being able to have candles burning without you complaining; being able to have the smell of the hyacinths without you having a coughing fit.

There's a lot more NOT good things – like you just simply are not here in your body anymore, and I don't like that. Your poor old body; just couldn't do it here on this earth anymore.

It's not that I can't believe it; rather that it all seems not quite right somehow, like something is missing, or out of place or . . . something. I don't know.

And it was true. I really did not know. I had long been someone who believed in the afterlife, who was fairly psychic and thought you could definitely communicate with the dead. I was finding that not knowing how Philip was, or where he was, was difficult to bear.

I was completely unprepared for what happened next.

18
More Visitations

Around this time, I went for a walk in the woods. I was so, so furious with Philip for dying on me. Angry that he hadn't taken care of his body well enough, when he had chronic fatigue syndrome; angry that he'd been so stubborn about wanting to address it at a physical level only. Especially when for years he'd been encouraging others to address their issues at all levels: physical, emotional, spiritual, mental. And just plain angry that he had gone and left me alone.

Stomping through the woods, I was alternately shouting and sobbing.

"Show me you are still here!" I screamed. "Tell me without any shadow of a doubt that you are hearing me! I can't bear it otherwise!" My pain and sorrow was so great I couldn't have cared who heard me.

Eventually, the storm of emotion passed through and I continued walking, still feeling very sad, but calmer. I passed a copse of trees I'd walked by many, many times before, and felt a pull to wade through the long grasses to the centre. I'd never done that before; why now? Did I really want to wade through the long grasses and uneven ground? However, the pull was so strong I found myself making my way to the centre, where I saw a dead tree trunk lying on the grass. Sitting on it, I looked around, and burst into tears again, this time tears of joy.

In front of me was another rotten tree, still standing, with numerous woodpecker holes. This was highly significant, as on our camper van trip in America, we'd spent a heavenly, star-lit night in a pine forest in Southern California. The bark of the trees with their indented woodpecker holes was particularly beautiful. We'd explored and talked about the patterns of the bark, and brought back a small piece of it with us. In fact, I've still got it. So when I saw this tree, I felt strongly this was a message from Philip.

"It's you, isn't it? You ARE here, you've heard me." I cried again, full of emotion, thinking that whoever he was now was hearing me, that I wasn't as alone as I often felt. This was undoubtedly a sign, as no one else in the whole world would have known of the significance of this tree.

That became a precious spot for me in the months to come, somewhere where I went to contemplate, to feel close to Philip, to simply sit and remember good times.

Later, I buried some of the ashes there too.

Another moment of awareness took place during Tree's visit, when we visited some mutual friends. We were talking about the idea of separation and non-duality, non-duality being the spiritual tradition that says all is one. Saying 'all is one' implies there is something other than 'oneness', hence the term 'non-duality.'

"If there really is only 'oneness,' then we are all one – you and me, that table, this chair, and even Philip, who is not in a body anymore. There really must be no separation, then," said one of my friends.

Right at that moment, I sensed Philip's presence behind my chair, towards the back of the room, shouting out, "Yes, yes, yes!" Ooh, weird. Consoling, too, though. Later I wrote in my journal:

> *In which case, although it looks like I'm separate from you, and I'm at the earthly body level, I'm not. We are not separate, we are in essence still together, which was what lots of our latter relating was about, wasn't it? Oh, we were so lucky having all that last year together for healing and growth – and LOVE :)*

Our explorations into the meaning of life, which had taken a huge leap when he'd been diagnosed, had led me to eventually read what he'd been reading, *Enlightenment Is Not What You Think,* and to this kind of discussion with others who were also interested. However, I would get an intellectual insight like what I wrote in my journal that felt right. Then before I knew it, I would have forgotten it, and be back in wondering where he was, how he was, and what he was doing. Lots of going back and forth, and I finally became obsessed with going to a medium, to see if she would receive a message from Philip that would finally put my mind at rest. I arranged an appointment for 30th December, but in fact, the biggest message came in an entirely different way.

Tree came into the kitchen that morning, just before I was leaving to drive 45 minutes to the medium's house.

"You'll never guess what happened last night!" She looked astonished, and continued, "I was just getting into bed, and I saw Philip standing at the bottom of it in front of the wardrobes. He looked quite normal and healthy, and I asked him, "What are you doing here?" He said, "Tell Jane I'll be there for her tomorrow." And then he disappeared. It was amazing!"

Tears burst forth once again; I was so touched by this. Especially coming from Tree, who wasn't really into this kind of thing at all.

So off I went to have my reading, with huge hope in my heart. Funnily enough, the session with the medium wasn't as great as the message from Tree. Perhaps because I trusted Tree more; perhaps because it was such a very clear visitation. Or, more likely, because everything the medium voiced could have come from anyone, not Philip in particular. My heart, though, on remembering the visitation to Tree, was consoled. At least for a time.

About a month later, another visit from the 'other world' happened. The good feelings associated with Tree's visitation had evaporated, and I was clamouring for more from Philip. I woke one morning wanting to ask our friend Delcia, a well-known and highly respected therapist, healer and channeller, if she could receive some consoling words for me.

What had happened to my own Listening? I'd been thrown upside down so dramatically by Philip's death that it felt like I knew nothing, couldn't believe the Listening even if I could hear it, and needed other's support instead. To be honest, it didn't even occur to me do any Listening. I opened my inbox to email Del, and saw an email there from her instead.

"I was woken this morning at 5:30 a.m. with a strong urge to channel," she wrote, "and to my amazement, what came through was a message from Philip. I'm concerned about it, though, as I don't want this to impede the process of your grieving. Would you like me to send what he said to you?"

Would I? Of course! And here it is:

Channelling for Jane, from Delcia's spirit guide.

6:00 a.m. January 3rd 2012

Jane, the time has come now for you to find a strength within that you didn't know was there. Your beloved Philip is safe and free from pain and suffering. He wishes that for you, too. He knows the struggle within your heart, and he appreciates that for, as you know, he struggled with his own heart issues throughout his life.

He now wishes for you to come into your true strength, which he has always supported you to do, and continues to do so. He is close to you and loves you dearly.

He wants you to know that being dead is all right, really. Although he feared it greatly when he was alive, it is in fact a very normal condition. There is a peace at not being in a physical body.

He wants to reassure you, once more, that your vulnerability is also your strength, and that he will support you in all you choose to do, including allowing others closely into your heart. That's all for now.

I sobbed and sobbed. 'Your vulnerability is also your strength' was one of his sayings. So beautiful, and yet it just made me want to be with him more and more.

Later on in January, I attended a silent satsang retreat, being held at Newbold House, where Philip and I had lived together previously. This meant I could stay at home, and just walk there through the woods for each day of the retreat. Satsang is a Sanskrit word, meaning 'gathering together for the truth,' and both of us had signed up to it. Of course it was only me going now. It was about non-duality, the same subject we had been reading about in the book *Enlightenment Is Not What You Think*. The teacher was a woman named Jac O'Keeffe.

With Jac's form of satsang, the inquirer comes to sit opposite the teacher to ask a question, with everyone else watching. This way the individual gets the attention focused on them, but the rest all benefit. There is no conversation other than that between the teacher and this person, with the others in the room witnessing this. The rest of the retreat was in silence, all the time, this to facilitate 'going within' and pondering what was being learnt, without being distracted by the social interaction that normally occurs.

On the second day, I sat in front of her. Tears streamed down my face as I explained what had happened just six weeks hence, and I asked her what it was that had been flowing through Philip's body.

"Just life force." She looked at me with compassion.

"I know that, but what IS that, really?" I was confused; clearly, this was an intellectual understanding my mind was trying to grapple with, and not succeeding very well. I don't remember the answer, if there was one. I do remember she leaned forward at one point, and spoke very warmly and lovingly:

"You just have to go through it." I felt accepted, loved, and witnessed. It was very beautiful, despite the painful feelings. Mind you, I didn't always feel like this, by any means.

Journal: Monday 9th January 2012

> *This process is horrible. Horrible. Just got back from my Pilates class, and in floods of tears as soon as I walked in the door. It's too empty. You're not here. And I want you to be here to share breakfast with me at the sunroom table, as usual. For God's sake! It's just not okay!*

And yet, that is the very problem: I am resisting against what is. Better, much better, to just accept it. Even in this acknowledgment, I feel something shifting.

Better get on with it, then.

19
Who is God?

Although I'm Scottish by birth, my family lived in Northern Ireland at the height of the troubles when I was a child. It was normal to have army men running around the city of Belfast with guns and rifles, shooting, doing their jobs. It was normal to have bombs going off every night; it was normal for all kinds of atrocities to take place.

Not that I ever actually saw much of any of this, although I felt the effects of it. For example, it was impossible to go shopping in the centre of Belfast without being frisked by the army and, later, to have your bags searched. This was so normal, that when I left home for a place at the United World College of the Atlantic in Wales, aged just 17, and first went into a department store where I wasn't searched, I couldn't believe it. I walked through the entrance, held out my open bag – and there was no one there to search it! It was then I felt a sense of freedom, the like of which I'd never experienced before. I understood, in that moment, that what I'd previously experienced as normal just wasn't.

It was while I was still at home, though, that I began questioning the concept of God. As I'd been brought up in a country where there were two sides killing and maiming in the name of God, I was perhaps more acutely aware and conscious of the hypocrisy of it all. What I knew for sure at that time – and it happened while standing in a church, ironically – was that I was God. What? Not how it sounds; rather, that 'I am God, you are God, we are God. All is God.' ('God' meaning Universal Energy, the Field, Divine Light, Love – any of those kinds of names).

Aged 14, I simply knew, deep down inside, this was true. I just had a feeling about it, as I was standing there in the church. I didn't dare say it to anyone, of course. That really would have been sacrilegious, especially in a country where there was so much emphasis on religion. In any case, I had no evidence to back it up. However, I somehow just felt the truth of it: I was God, everyone else was also God, and I couldn't see how it could be any other way. Even the killers. It became my secret. I tucked this knowledge away, and got on with my life, not fully understanding how thinking such a thing could have an impact other than a negative one, as the idea was so very different from the commonly held beliefs by both Catholics and Protestants.

Then, as a college student in South Wales, one bright Sunday afternoon, while walking with a friend along the high cliff tops looking out to the sparkling sea down below, something spectacular happened. Our conversation was going along the lines of:

"You've just got to be honest; just be honest with yourself, " said Pete.

"What? What do you mean?" I stopped and turned to look at him.

"Just be honest," he repeated, looking deeply into my eyes. "My Dad told me about it. You just have to be honest with yourself."

I didn't really understand at all what he was on about, and was getting frustrated, but I saw in his eyes something I badly wanted, some understanding he had that I hadn't.

Suddenly, I was suffused with a knowledge of what he meant. I was literally struck down by it. Knees collapsing under me I fell to the grass, rolling around, laughing; laughing in delight because I suddenly now knew, in my whole body, what the point of being alive was. I knew without a shadow of a doubt that this blissful state of love was what was normal. *This* was what being human was about, *this* was life itself! I wanted to jump off the cliff top with joy, because I knew if I did, I would soar. Not that my body would, because of gravity, but that who I really was would soar upwards. In that moment, I just wanted to reach out and hug the whole world, so they too could have this experience, which felt to me like heaven on earth itself.

I looked at my friend, and saw that he knew what I was going through. Eventually, we carried on walking, companionably, together in a completely different way from before.

The intensity of those moments wore off after a few hours, and I felt bereft that evening. I spoke to only one or two people about it, and they just didn't get what I was going on about. This was not surprising, as I had no context within which to explain it, or even find the right words to talk about it. I'd no clue what had happened, just a knowledge that it was profound and had changed my life for ever. Searching for a way to replicate this experience led me to meditation and spirituality, and my interest in what makes people the way they are. Ironically, it was probably this very searching that got in the way of being able to have this experience again, but I wasn't to know that for many years.

It also completely shaped the practicalities of my life. I studied psychology, and chose a career in human resource management. I gave up the career to join a rather cult-like spiritual community, where the emphasis was on the meaning of being alive. This was all the top layer of what was actually going on underneath, which was a deep desire to re-experience what I was privately calling my 'cliff-top moment', for want of a better description. I term it now an experience of God. An experience of Who I Really Am. An experience of Heaven on Earth, of the Kingdom of God lying within. Just deep bliss.

Over the years, many other moments like this happened, always without any effort being applied, although never quite the same as the cliff-top one. For instance, working in Greece one year, I was lying on my bed, looking outside the door to a clear blue sky, and the pine tree woods just outside. Suddenly, I knew, again absolutely clearly, that I was the tree nearest to me, and it was me. A blinding flash of deep knowledge, it had a feeling of 'of course' ordinariness to it.

Then, in the summer of 2009, while sitting in my parents' garden in France and reading Joe Vitale's *Beyond Manifestation*, some words on the page popped out at me.

I am God.

My heart felt like it nearly stopped. For the first time ever, I was reading words which I'd always known. And here was the truth of the matter: there was nothing for me to do but remember. Remember the truth of this statement, and be willing to stay in touch with it, more often than not. Not all the time, not perfectly, not brilliantly, just more often than not.

Wonderful words indeed, and yet, that experience slowly disappeared, just like the cliff-top happening. I wrote a blogpost about it, although I didn't have the courage to publish it. However, it helped me feel less unusual; there really were others in the world who thought like I did. And now, with Philip having died, my explorations into 'who was he?' and 'who am I?' were getting more intense.

Journal: Friday 13th January 2012

This morning as I was getting up, this thought presented itself:

If it was so obvious that Philip was not his body when he died, then 'he' was 'something else.' Not sure that 'something else' is a thing; well, it isn't a thing. What is it? It's not an 'it,' either. How do you describe it in words? Don't know. Anyway, who he was has left behind the body as an empty bag.

So that means the body I am inhabiting right now is also a bag. A filled one, at the moment. So what is it filled with? And if I am not my body (quite clearly not, as per P's death), then what am 'I'? Or who? What is it that is filling this bag that is writing this?

These thoughts stayed with me while walking through the woods to the Taize singing group. Clearly, it is just the body that does the singing, but sometimes, the singing is infused with this 'something else', which seems to be the same 'thing' that people respond to when they speak of the magic of music, or the flow, the zone, God, the Universe.

In the meditation after the singing, my body felt very warm and tingly, a very pleasant experience, which had never happened before. I had thoughts coming and going but nothing that distracted me from the sensations in my body. Am I just observing this? Doesn't feel like it, it feels like – well, it

> *doesn't feel. Apparently, there is no emotion associated with this.*
>
> *Now, here, this same body is physically typing, breathing, using its brain to think and question. It must be the 'life force' that enables all this. Therefore, 'I' am not the body: 'I' am the life force.*
>
> *The life force is everything, though. It's all the things that can be seen with the eyes of this body, and all the things that can be smelled, felt, touched, tasted, experienced through this body, and all the things the body can't experience through its senses, too. So what is this life force? And who is it that wants to know what it is, anyway?*

I was to return many times over the following months to this idea of the 'empty or filled bag.' Philip's moment of death had been so profound – such stark evidence that 'he' was not there any longer – that it began to affect everything I did, as I questioned who was the 'I' that was doing anything.

In the meantime, I was dealing with some very strong emotions. An example of this was when I was queuing one night for fish and chips (I never have fish and chips; what on earth was I doing there? Trying to do things differently, I suppose), I scowled at a man ahead of me, waiting for his order. Overweight, fiddling with his cigarette packet, aged about mid-50s maybe, and much worse than all this, he was alive! I was consumed with rage. How dare he! How dare HE be alive, he who eats food that is bad for you, smokes and is overweight, who is so obviously a waste of space – and Philip, who made such a contribution to the world, is dead? It's NOT FAIR! I had to leave the fish and chip shop without my supper. I just wanted to rage and rage at the world.

*

Talking of food, eating alone was another difficult time, particularly breakfasts, around which we'd had a sort of ritual. I often would get up earlier than Philip, go walking for an hour or so, and then come back to join him at breakfast. This obviously had been somewhat interrupted when he couldn't eat very well, but now the impact of eating alone – and facing the prospect of doing that for the rest of my life – was utterly misery-making.

I took to eating a very strict diet for a month or so, the one thing I felt I could control in a world turned upside down. As with all diets, it didn't last; but I did lose some of the weight that had gone on over the weeks in Aberdeen, when I'd been eating lots of extra chocolate, my comfort food of choice. Of course, it didn't last, and eventually I had to face up to eating alone. So I bought myself a colourful and beautiful table mat, making sure I sat at the table most of the time when I was eating, even if it was lonely. I just switched BBC Radio 4 on a lot; voices, even those just coming from the radio, were better than nothing.

20
More Effects of Grief

Being left alone after so many years of sharing our lives together brought some very practical challenges almost immediately. Like most couples, we had our different roles in the relationship. I liked doing ironing, and Philip had a thing about cleaning the draining board in the kitchen. He also cared more about our car than I did; he had really loved the latest one, a Toyota Prius, half electric, half petrol, and bought in 2005 in Belfast with money from the earlier sale of our business. Now I was left with something that had largely been Philip's priority. I had the List relating to the car, and thank goodness, as a visit to the garage did take place, sooner than expected.

Journal: early January 2012

Today I learnt a lot about the car. Got tearful about it though; didn't want to have to do it – at all. Eventually I booked it in at the garage for a full service. I imagine it will cost at least £500 which is an expense I hadn't budgeted for. Blimey. I started crying in front of the receptionist, because I just didn't want to be doing it. Cars are not my thing! And it bloody well does need new brake pads; I don't know what you were going on about, Philip, it not needing anything.

Anyway. Anyway. It is 4 weeks since you died. 4 weeks... is that long or short? It feels like AGES. Ten days of shock, and organising the services; ten days of being on my own, more or less, and being taken out for coffee by friends; and ten days of being with Tree. I am quite afraid of her leaving. I like someone being here.

I just cannot get over the shock of those words, 'death' and 'Philip,' being used in relation to each other, even though I cleared out your wardrobe today, with Tree's help. I couldn't let go of everything, though. Just too difficult. I kept your lovely pink linen shirt, your white one, and your wedding waistcoat. I took everything else to the Macmillan Charity Shop, it was nice to be supporting them after the Macmillan Nurse has been so supportive and loving.

The fact I no longer thought of Philip as a body helped enormously with clearing out his clothes. When my brothers were here from England for the funeral, I took advantage of this.

"Simon, would you like any of Philip's clothes? You were more or less the same size. I've sorted them out and there's a lot will just be going to the charity shop if you can't use them."

"Wonderful!" exclaimed Simon, and eventually took quite a large pile.

"Alastair, I bought these chinos for Philip after he'd lost a lot of weight; they're practically new. I know they'll be too long, but do you want to try them and see if they fit all right around the waist? They can always be taken up." I was in practical mode once more, and I particularly wanted to get rid of the chinos, which were only a reminder of how very ill he had been. How did I decide about what to keep and what not? I listened to my intuition, which I was paying a lot more attention to. It was as if I'd given myself permission to act from that place, without the usual thoughts about what others would think. In fact, I'd learnt not to care very much about what others thought while we were in the hospital, and it was incredibly freeing. And so it continued, with small things, which made a big difference.

For example, when I took Tree on the 30-minute drive to Inverness airport on her way home, my head was saying, 'It would be very sensible to go on into Inverness to Marks and Spencer and change that jumper; an excellent use of time and money.' But my heart said, 'No, I want to go home and be with Philip', even though he wasn't there in bodily form. I obeyed my heart, and was glad later when I realised that M & S would have been closed on that particular day. As I acted on my intuitive impulses more and more, a small seed of confidence began to grow.

I was, however, completely blown over by the exhaustion I felt. It took the form of being unable to concentrate on conversations; getting throbbing headaches that didn't respond to any painkillers, only to lying or sitting quietly watching silly TV programmes; or reading a light-hearted novel. For ages all the novels I picked – however randomly – seemed to have a theme of death. At the same time, I was not sleeping well at all; having been early to bed and early to rise all my life, suddenly I was wide awake at midnight, not knowing what to do. It was all very strange.

On 22nd January, I wrote:

At home this afternoon I could hardly do anything. Just sat and watched TV. Messed about a bit on computer, too. Finally went for a walk when it was beginning to get dark, and tears started to flow again in the woods. So many, many tears. Hugged a tree; did it help? I do not know.

Rang F and told him I was very weepy today and was that all right with them (they had invited me for supper before the Course in Miracles meeting). I went and managed okay. Feeling washed out now, but still not sleepy.

Of course, I had loads of time to spare. Empty hours, empty space, the sound of silence to get used to. I quickly cottoned onto the fact I needed to make sure I was seeing someone each day. The bungalow which had been so perfect for us just a short while ago now felt enormous. The garden seemed bigger when I knew it was just for me. Plus there was no point in doing anything in it anyway – no one to share it with.

Journal:

I used to complain I had no time. Well, I've got loads and loads of it now. Reaching way into the future, near and far. Just masses of it. And no desire to do anything much. Good thing I had arranged to take E to Taize singing this morning; otherwise I might not have got there. Because of that arrangement, I debated about going for a fast walk for half an hour to see if I could change my energy. It worked.

The singing was great, though I felt very tearful. A friend put her hand on my knee; it made such a difference. Afterwards, I collapsed in her arms and just sobbed and sobbed. I am so very lucky to have these people around me; they just held me while I cried. I am really very grateful, but oh, my God, I wish I didn't have to be going through this.

The silence and being alone took a lot of getting used to. Coming home to an empty house was particularly difficult.

Journal: mid-January

Oh dear. Very wobbly start today at 5 a.m. Felt so alone. I so hated it last night after Lisa left. We had a lovely relaxed evening, cooking together and then watching the film 'What the Bleep.' I even nodded off. After she had gone, God, I felt so bloody miserable. Ate a whole bar of Swiss chocolate in one go. Haven't done that for weeks.

I began to discover what it was like to enter into places on my own. Even going to the local cafe alone, which I'd been used to doing for years, now felt highly intimidating. As for groups of people – even when I knew everyone, I found it very difficult, and avoided them for ages. My whole impulse was to be small, to hide, to retreat into a burrow, and I simply couldn't cope with the energy of a group. And yet I knew I needed to stay in touch with people, too, so I managed this by arranging to meet with just one person at a time.

When I re-started seeing the few clients I had, after the first one left, I walked out of the office and called, "Philip, I'm done!" and fell to my knees, crying. House empty. No one to share with any more. The heartache was awful, really awful. For years, we'd supported each other in our work, and even when he was so ill with chronic fatigue and then the cancer, he was still interested in what I was up to, until the last few weeks in hospital. I so wanted to share what I was doing with him, and now he wasn't there anymore. I began to understand fully the meaning of the word 'bereft.'

Another effect of grief was vulnerability. About two months after the death, an email from my friend Pedro dropped into my inbox. *"Hi Jane, I'm stranded in Barcelona, can you help me? I've been robbed and now have nothing to get home with, they took all my credit cards, cash, passport, everything. Is there any chance you can send me some money to help me get a ticket and live until I get home? £1500 would do it probably. Love Pedro."*

My heart went out to him; poor Pedro. Even though I hadn't known he was abroad, he was always coming and going. I replied sympathetically. Thus began a long thread of emails going back and forth, with me making useful suggestions. About 16 emails in all, ending up with me agreeing to transfer some money. I didn't have much, and yet for a friend I was willing to lend it, as I trusted him when he said he would pay it back. I made sure he really did know that I couldn't afford to give it to him, as I did need it back. He was of course reassuring. In the end the bank wouldn't let me transfer more than £400, which I did.

4 a.m. the following day: awake and suddenly upright, thinking, "What if this is a scam?" It had never occurred to me before, but it was right in the forefront of my mind now.

8 a.m: Phone call to Pedro's wife.

"Hi Lucy, it's Jane here. I'm just wondering: is Pedro in Spain right now? Only I received an email from him saying he's been robbed."

"Oh, no! Don't do anything!" exclaimed Lucy. "It's a scam. His email has been hacked into, and lots of his friends have received the same message."

My heart dropped. I'd hoped against hope, in the wee hours, but I kind of knew already. "Oh dear. I've already sent some, £400."

"Oh no! I'm so sorry."

We ended the call. I put the phone down and burst into tears.

This would not have happened if Philip had been alive. I would have checked with him, and he would have known immediately it was a scam. I'd been naive and gullible again, one of the traits that people tend to like in me. It can trip me up, though, and had done so big time now. Fortunately, I realised quite quickly that the very last thing I needed to do was beat myself up about this. Instead, I needed to accept I was in a very vulnerable place; otherwise I might not have fallen for it. Habits of a lifetime die hard, though, and I didn't yet have a proper support system in place with a friend I could call about these kinds of things.

Another practicality I'd taken for granted showed itself the first time I needed to go to the airport, just three months later. In tears, I asked a friend,

"Would you drive me to the airport – and is there any chance you could pick me up too?" She hugged me.

"Of course. Tell me the dates." When you're part of a couple, you just assume the other will drive you, do errands, be intimately involved in the details of your life; and you only ask a friend on the odd occasion when that can't happen. When you're on your own, a different system is required. Eventually, a friend who was also living on her own agreed we would deliver and meet each other on our way back from various travels, and also give each other a meal on that night. This way, we were both taking care of ourselves, and it made up considerably for the difficulty I had in coming home to an empty house.

Then there was the letting other people down, when I cancelled things at the last minute. The walking out of gatherings when I couldn't stand being there any longer. The forgetting of arrangements made with friends. Fortunately, I knew this was grief expressing itself, and I didn't judge myself.

21
On and On

Slowly, I began to face up to the fact that my worst fear had come true: a widow without children, being of an age where having children was no longer possible, and living on my own. One morning I googled 'widows without children'. I didn't find much but I did sign up to Way Up, a group for widows and widowers over 50. Over 50! I was only just 54; what on earth was I doing being part of a group where so many were such a lot older than I was? No, no, no! It felt all wrong. I was still young, wasn't I? I very quickly came off that forum; it just didn't feel right.

Journal: 11th January 2012

> *I went to the supermarket today. Felt awful buying just two carrots and a small bit of broccoli. There is so little food now that needs to be bought. And then I saw the Philadelphia cream cheese you ate so much of in the last months, and I just went blank inside. Couldn't think at all of what else I might want. Had to just leave. Horrible. Horrible. Tears flooding my eyes as I drove home. What a ghastly, dreadful situation.*

Later, the first time of going into a department store and having no need to look at the men's section was equally devastating.

Tears spilled over again. By this time I was used to them coming at all kinds of odd moments, and of not stopping them. Most people don't notice if there are tears streaming down your face, not unless you're screaming and wailing too. That part I did keep for at home, or with close friends.

Journal: 26th January 2012

> *Just left my dear friend R off at Inverness train station. Immediately felt very down – nothing to go home for, no reason to do anything. I want to be at home more than anything, and yet it's the last thing I want, too.*
>
> *I came in the door and burst into tears. Sobbing, sobbing, sobbing. This is so horrible. I am alone. He is not here. When I feel like this, my limbs are heavy; I have no energy, I want to do nothing. I cannot do anything, anyway. So I am honouring that, having to, and am now watching TV again. It is ironic that I'm now viewing so many programmes, relatively speaking, when it was one of the things that caused so much trouble between me and P.*

An argument we'd often had over the previous 10 years since he had first been diagnosed with chronic fatigue, was about how much he liked to watch sport on the TV, none of which I was particularly interested in. We'd tried to be respectful to each other about this, but underneath we were both cross – him because he couldn't feel relaxed in his own house when he wanted to watch the telly, and me because I couldn't stand the telly on so much. We'd become more free from this after an amusing couples therapy session some years previously.

"We need some help," I said to Philip. "We're going round and round with this at the moment, getting nowhere, neither of us happy. I want to try and find someone to work with, a couples therapist or somebody."

"All right," he replied, "but it needs to be someone highly experienced. And I don't want anything long term." I agreed with that; we did know of the huge positive benefits of long term therapy, having both been on the receiving end as well as the giving of it ourselves, but this felt much more like we just needed a nudge in the right direction. We ended up seeing someone highly experienced for just three sessions.

My memory of the first one is that we both stated our case about whatever it was, including the TV arguing. It all felt awkward, but also relieving to get our thoughts and feelings about each other out into the fresh air, and heard by someone other than ourselves. By the end of that initial session, I'd decided I would ignore Philip for the next two weeks. That sounds a bit odd, I realise, but remember I'd had to look after him pretty much full time for a couple of years when he had been so debilitated when chronic fatigue first took hold of his body. In some ways I was still trying to look after him, even though he was better to some degree.

What ignoring him actually meant in reality was I had to stop doing things for him due to him having such low energy. It meant I had to keep my mouth firmly shut when he was watching TV all afternoon, every afternoon, and sometimes in the evenings too. And it meant I had to stop offering my opinions on what he could do that would help him heal from this illness, and just let him be. Not easy, but I did it.

The second session arrived a fortnight later.

"I'm fine," I replied in response to the therapist's enquiry. "I decided to ignore Philip and I've managed it really well." A huge burst of laughter came from the corner where Philip was sitting.

"And I've been feeling appreciated!" he exclaimed. Whereupon more laughter erupted from all of us.

That was the essence of those sessions, really – no wonder we had been getting on better. Me stopping 'interfering' in his life, letting him get on with it, and not being so judgmental about what I thought was best for him, had worked. And although initially I had felt guilty about ignoring him, I was determined to behave differently. Philip had begun to feel that, at long last, I was getting 'out of his head,' as he put it, and that he had room to breathe again. I was beginning to enjoy putting my attention back onto myself, and my own needs and wants. That experience of properly understanding each others needs and wants allowed us to concentrate on loving each other again.

But now, here I was with the TV on, alone, watching inane programmes, like a zombie, in the chair in which he used to sit. Oh, the irony of it! If it hadn't been so bloody awful, I would have laughed. And actually, many times I did manage that, for I realised Philip would also have found it funny too, and that helped.

Journal: Sun eve 26th January 2012

> *I am lonely. Still haven't quite got it into my head that every evening is going to be like this now. Never have P here again. Always alone unless I go out somewhere or organise something. Yuck.*
>
> *So, he has died. Is never coming back in his body. That's just the way it is. And I begin a new kind of life. Whether I like it or not. Without him. Without children. Just me.*

began to read book after book about grieving; I needed to know what was going on. Did the books help? Some of them, yes, some of the time. It certainly helped to realise that others were going, and had gone through, what was happening to me. It helped to know they had come out the other end, especially on the days when I simply felt I could not bear the pain any longer. What I couldn't bear was the thought of self-help books: I did not *want* to be made to feel better! I just wanted to read others' stories about how they had managed, get some inspiration and hope, and feel less alone with it all.

Journal 12th February 2012

Philip! I miss you! God, I miss you. How on earth could this happen to us. It IS NOT FAIR! I feel cheated somehow. I just wish you were here again.

We had such a lovely Taize singing practice this evening at Newbold. I thought of you, and you maybe were there joining in somehow. It brought tears to my eyes, and then I got exhausted and finally managed to leave, and I JUST MISS YOU! Shit.

It's going to go on a long time, this situation. Actually, forever. How the hell did that happen? It wasn't meant to. I feel so, so sad. Need to nourish myself. Going to watch TV and knit. I find knitting very soothing. It's good. I love you, darling, and I wish, so wish, you hadn't had to leave so early. Nor in that awful way in hospital. Do people really realise that the dying process can be so physically awful? I doubt it. I need to prepare for mine. And hope it is not like yours. Or worse. It could be worse if you had no friends or family that you loved with you. At least you had that. You poor old thing, in that body of yours. What a dreadful end.

This was probably the first time I seriously began to think about my own death. I hadn't been frightened of it, particularly; but faced with the run up to the death that Philip had, it made me stop and really think about what actually does happen when the body becomes old or ill. This motivated me to compile my own List, although I didn't do that until much later on.

22
Work and Money

I needed to start work again, as soon as possible. The unexpected costs of the funeral were to some degree offset by a gift from the government of £2,000, and bereavement benefit for the first year of about £50 per week. I was once again immensely grateful for the country I lived in, with the National Health Service and other benefits. I hadn't even known this kind of support was available before. Even so, more money was required for day-to-day living.

Philip and I hadn't taken care of ourselves very well financially. This was due to a mixture of him fundamentally disbelieving in the whole concept of insurance, and therefore refusing to have any kind of extra insurance, unless he was bound to by law. I sympathised with him, but was unable to stand up for myself regarding this. So we didn't have life insurance, and rarely had any travel insurance; nor did we have mortgage insurance on our own home, or on the two rental properties we owned. All three mortgages I was now fully responsible for.

Basically, we never really thought it through properly. No wonder this had been one of his regrets. To be honest, it would have made a huge difference to me financially if we had both life insurance and the mortgages insured against something like this.

As it was, we had lived in blissful ignorance, never considering that an event like early death might happen. And now I was faced with living with the consequences.

Looking back, I realised I had often gone along with Philip in making decisions of a financial nature. I was only able to stand up to him in a major way when it came to setting up my own coaching practice in 2008. I'd had to pluck up my courage.

"Philip," I bravely said to him one evening as we were chatting after dinner, "what I'd really like to do is operate this new coaching business myself, as a sole trader, not as a partnership. What do you think?" He looked a bit affronted.

"Why?"

"I think it's essential for me, as a woman, to somehow be responsible for my own financial matters. And as it is going to be me doing the coaching, this makes more sense."

"Yes. Well, okay, but I'm sure I will be helping you a lot."

"I know, but, honestly, darling, I feel really strongly about this. I want to have it in my own name only, and not feel like I am sharing it, although of course any money will be shared. And I'll still want to talk to you about everything, like we always do."

"Well, why can't it be a partnership, then?" he retorted. That back and forth conversation went on for quite a while. I did feel strongly, though, had grown in confidence, and needed to take my stand. Eventually, reluctantly, he agreed. Knowing I was fully responsible made me take a different attitude to my work which was very healthy for me. It's a bit ironic that now I don't have an option *but* to be fully responsible, and for all the debts we had taken on from a position of two incomes..

The bereavement benefit helped, however, because I discovered I was completely unable to do the kind of work I was doing before, which involved running group tele-classes and conference calls. Grief had put an end to that now; the thought of doing anything with a group of people, let alone leading a group, was impossible. I just could not do it. What was unexpected though, was my strong compulsion to offer one-to-one counselling again, just in the local area.

As I saw just one or two clients, I began to understand I was returning to something I felt very comfortable with. In that sense, it fed my soul as well as supported the clients. I could only work with one client for one hour per day maximum, and I had to let go of the efficiency involved in putting clients back to back, and focusing in that way. I just didn't have the energy; after seeing a client, I would have to do nothing much else for the rest of the day. It got better, but very, very slowly.

Of course, I laid down boundaries. I didn't see anyone who was going through any kind of loss, and I only had a handful of clients on the books at any one time. It was very good indeed for me to feel I could put my attention out onto someone else's challenges, and help them with that, when much of the rest of the time I was feeling helpless in the face of my own grief.

Was the quality of the sessions good enough at that time? I hoped so. I was aware this was a strange thing to do – probably not something I would have advised myself – but acting on this strong intuition, I felt I would be given only what I could easily manage. Which is what happened, and after several months, the counselling clients dropped off and I returned to purely coaching.

Journal: 13th February 2012

This has been a really awful day. Started crying in the 8 a.m. Pilates class, and then couldn't stop when I got home. On and

> *off all morning. Spoke to a policewoman about the scam; she called me 'my lovely' and I burst into tears again. God. Then, eventually, I rang Joanna and went over there and had a big sob on her shoulders. Came home and ate some chocolate.*
>
> *Went to Universal Hall for a story evening but left early. Home again in more tears. God, this is relentless. Will it ever get any better? I rang my sister; she is so lovely, suggested we spoke to each other every day. That started me crying yet again.*
>
> *Oh, God, Philip. I so wish this hadn't happened. It is very, very painful. I suppose some good will come out of it eventually, but right now it is very hard indeed.*

One thing that did come out of it was a resolution of some of the money challenges. In spring that year, a legal situation that had been dragging on for over five years resolved, possibly helped by Philip dying. Who knows? For whatever reason, the other side finally stopped battling against the inevitable and paid up. After enormous legal fees, and a low exchange rate between the euro and the pound, this was still enough to pay off nearly £15,000 of debts (not mortgages), make a donation towards Mistletoe for Cancer (which we had agreed on before Philip died) and still provide some towards my living costs for a while. Phew! So many times I had wished for this legal situation to be resolved; so many times I'd thought it would be the perfect time to receive a lump sum of cash, and now here it was, and of course, the timing was, indeed, perfect.

I also sold many of Philip's things on eBay. This took ages, too, mostly in the amount of time it took thinking about how difficult it would be. I had access to all our accounts and passwords, so it was relatively easy from that point of view. From an emotional sense,

I was able to make clear decisions about what to sell and what not. But the thought of the technical side of things was alarming. However, when I did actually get round to it, the process was actually quite simple, and I felt a sense of achievement at the end. I sold his expensive leather shoes he wore at our wedding, and had only worn a couple of times since. I discovered he'd brought back a spare boat pump from New Zealand – what on earth for? – so that went too; and then there were a few other things as well. Overall, I banked about £1,000; I felt proud I'd done it.

Fortunately, Philip had made a will. It was one of the things on The List, after all, and my ex-lawyer friend Lisa had made sure it was all fine. Everything was to be left to me, and I set about very slowly discovering the financial situation of everything we had owned so I could complete the necessary paperwork. Even so, it was a challenge, as once again, I could only do a little bit at a time.

Eventually, I had everything together. Lisa came with me to the Sheriff's office to lodge the documentation, and I nervously approached the counter where the clerk was working. She looked at the documents.

"You don't need to lodge this," announced the clerk, "not unless a bank or other institution has asked for anything other than the death certificate. Have they?"

"No", I replied.

"Well, you've got a will made in your favour, so there's nothing you need to do then."

"Really?" I couldn't believe it.

"I know; it's not exactly clear in that pamphlet you were given, but look at it this way: you've saved yourself £200," she smiled broadly at me.

Lisa and I had a coffee to celebrate, and she commiserated with me over the huge amount of unnecessary work I'd done. "Still, at least you know the exact state of your affairs now." She smiled at me. True. I had said I wanted to be totally responsible, and now I was.

Just wasn't so sure I wanted to be any longer.

23
More Changes

It is said you are not supposed to make any big, life-changing decisions too soon after the death of a loved one. However, what about when the changes happen *to* you, and there's nothing you can do about it?

On the 4th of February, just two months after Philip's death, I received a phone call from the letting agent.

"Hallo, Jane. First of all, let me say how sorry I am for your loss."

"Thank you."

"I need to tell you that your landlady is wanting to sell the house."

"What!" Tears welled up. "She can't! She knows Philip's just died. What on earth am I going to do? Where am I going to go?" I was really shocked, and panicking as a result. We had been reassured when we moved in that we could have a long-term tenancy, even though in Scotland it's usually done on a 6 month agreed short hold tenancy, and then a rolling two months of notice on either side after that. Not great for the tenant's sense of security at all.

"It won't happen that fast," responded the agent, "and we'll make sure you have somewhere suitable for you to go before it's sold. You won't be homeless."

I was very shaken by this. Even though I was rattling around in a big empty bungalow and it's correspondingly large garden, it didn't mean I wanted to move. And I definitely did *not* want to. I felt helpless, furious, and utterly bereft.

That evening I wrote in my journal:

> *I sank to the office floor tonight in tears, suddenly. All this insecurity about a house. That's the problem with renting: the landlords can just chuck you out when they want. So I need to buy a house outright, and build a business that shows 3 years of profit to do that. Simple. A bit overwhelming, though, to put it mildly. I so miss P to discuss all this with. We were so good on houses together. I will have to learn on my own. This is a long, hard slog.*

I turned to everything I knew to help me with this. I had begun to be able to Listen again. This is what I heard:

> *"You are about to step over a threshold, symbolised by the moving of your home. However, this is simply an outer expression of the move of your inner home, from the apparent world of form, to the real world of essence. That is why this is happening now, in your time: for though it appears to be hard to have another change so soon after Philip has left his body, in truth this is just another step home. He has gone home in a particular way and you are to come home, too... while still inhabiting the body."*

However, despite knowing all this, it took me two weeks of alternating rage, tears, and fear, while I desperately tried to find a way to stay in the bungalow. Then I remembered a phrase I'd originally heard way back in the summer:

"You cannot know this is not the next step in your liberation." This phrase had helped us both in the run up to Philip's death, and it finally came to the fore again in a burst of insight and clarity. It was true; it was simply my attachment to the place which we had loved so much that was getting in the way. It really could be that another place might be better for me, even though it was hard for my mind to imagine that.

So I started looking for other accommodation. The first place I went to was nice, very nice, but tears erupted again when the agent asked if I was interested. I simply could not comprehend making this kind of big decision without Philip. As it turned out, that flat had just been taken by someone else anyway. Everything else I looked at was just depressing. It was incredible, the differing standards of what was available for the same amount of money. Then one day, an acquaintance rang and told me about the flat underneath hers.

"It's empty at the moment; I know the owner, she's rented it before and she might be willing to rent it again."

"I'm coming round," I responded, and went to peek through the windows. Reluctantly, I could see it might be a possibility.

"The owner's away at the moment, but here's her number; give her a ring and see what happens." Suffice to say, everyone said yes, and I arranged to move in mid-May. Another awful thing happened, though, before I barely had my head around packing up the house.

Journal: 9th March 2012

Oh, God. Becky (Philip's eldest grand-daughter) died in the early hours of yesterday morning. Becky! Died? How can that be? Only 16. For God's sake, what is going on?

Here I am again, in a place of disbelief and shock. I hope Philip is there with her, so she's not alone.

Later, I talked to Jackie, her aunt, to find out what had happened to Becky, poor darling. She got very upset when she heard what was happening regarding me having to move out. So many losses for her.

This is so grim. I still get a twinge when I buy a paper, and he is not here to read the sports page; but that is minor compared to not being able to talk to him regarding Becky. This is very, very hard indeed.

Thank God, though, that Philip didn't know of this. Thank God. Becky had been having a bone marrow transplant at the time he died, meaning her dad Matt had been with her, rather than by his dying father's side, having visited a week or so previously. Hopes had been high that Becky's transplant would be successful, and initially it had seemed like this might be the case.

When someone dies towards the end of their life, it's relatively acceptable. Even I could see that: Philip dying at just 66 was very different to Becky dying at 16. Not only do you have death itself to deal with, but the horror of it happening to one so young, who has only just embarked on life's journey. Death in the young is just out of the natural order of things.

Even though we had not been greatly involved in Matt's family life, especially in later years when living so far away, Becky's death still made a huge impact, and one I could hardly take in. I debated about going to the funeral.

"What shall I do?" I asked a good friend. "If I think about going to the funeral, where all Philip's family will be – to which I feel mostly connected through him, and yet he isn't there – I just feel like it's too much. I feel so bad, though, at the thought of not going. I don't know what to do."

"Jane, you absolutely need to take care of yourself first. That's what is most important."

It was an awful decision to make, but in the end I didn't go, not least because of the trouble I was still having being around groups of people. My own pain was so very raw still, like an open wound, and I felt that attending this particular funeral, at this particular time, would have been like rubbing salt into that wound. Not very self-loving, and one of the more major decisions I had to make in a new life that involved putting myself first instead of others.

Not an easy thing to do at all.

Becky's parents were amazing about this; also Jackie, the person in Philip's family I am closest to.

"It's fine, Jane. It's completely understandable," they all agreed. I've no idea if they were telling the truth or not, but I didn't want to find out. I just could not play the game of being all right if I wasn't.

Later, I heard the funeral had been amazing; attended by hundreds of people, of course. On hearing that, I knew I'd made the right decision, albeit a difficult one.

24
Ash Scattering

One of the things we had covered on The List was where Philip wanted his ashes to be scattered: off the diving rock at the beach in front of my family's holiday cottage in Dumfries and Galloway, Scotland. We hadn't got any further than that, though, so it was down to me to think who else to involve, and what exactly to do.

"Jackie? Hi, it's Jane." I was calling Philip's eldest daughter.

"Hi, how are you?"

"Oh, I'm okay at the moment." This was my standard answer at that time. "I'm calling because I want to know whether you and whoever else would like to come with me to scatter Philip's ashes at High Tide? He wanted them put there because we've had so many heavenly holidays in the hut, as you know."

"What a lovely idea. I'd love to come and I'm sure Dan would, too." And so in April, I arrived there, on my own in this lovely place for the first time ever. I'd been quite ambivalent about it; I didn't want to spend time there on my own, and yet I realised I needed to, in order to be able to be there at all. So I'd arrived a day and a night before the others.

Journal: 19th April 2012

Hi, Philip. It's the 21st anniversary of our first date today. Remember that lovely meal in that vegetarian restaurant in Hampstead Heath in London? And me asking you what you were interested in, and you replying, quick as anything, "Hill walking and making love." I got so embarrassed! I can even remember it now: I spluttered and blushed – typical – and didn't know what to do. But it was so exciting, too! Oh, my goodness, we have had some good times.

Anyway, here I am on my own at High Tide. It was dreadful arriving today. I really did not like it much. Driving over the hill on the A75 after so many years of doing so together. Then coming in to the hut itself. Just cried and cried. You probably know that – do you? I asked in the end for a message that you were here, and when I went outside to sit in the sun by the front door, I suddenly heard an unusual amount of birdsong. I knew that was your message: it brought me into the present moment again. Thank you for that.

Of course, I released the tears and then felt washed through. Had a lovely walk down past Ardwall Beach – even dared going through the field with the cows in! Very impressed with myself. Climbed to Knockbrex viewpoint: it is so, so beautiful here. We have been incredibly lucky having all those great holidays here. Remember when we used to come for three weeks at a time, and I used to get bored in the third one?

We had some great times exploring the area here when you were healthy, too. Remember our walk up Ben John, and what happened at the top? And those delicious long days, with the sun setting so late in the evening?

Keri rang. She wants to bring their cat, but Dan is bringing their dog, so that won't work. God, it might be a bit of a madhouse when they are all here. Oh, dear. I am so glad I came early though. I knew I needed to do that.

I love you, Philip. So inadequate, those words.

Deborah just texted me, and Randi called later. They are concerned about me being here alone. My wonderful friends. Oh well, off to bed, I suppose. I'm going to sleep on your side, I think; I'll see how I feel. Even though I know you're here without form, I still would like you to be here IN form, your healthy form that is, hence I might have to leave a space for you in the bed.

I just couldn't bear to see you in pain and distress any longer, it was so awful. However, I have been practicing my Course in Miracles lessons and also the quote: "I am the Peace and Presence of God." It's very good and they both work. It is true that I can be reminding myself of that truth even when in the midst of strong emotion. It is just the body having the emotion, that is all – not me.

Oh! Just heard a squeak of a curlew; and the oyster catchers on the beach were amazing earlier on. Lovely. Good night, my sweetheart. Goodnight. I love you.

The following evening, some of Philip's family arrived: his grandson Dan, with his family; Jackie; and his son Matt and wife Keri, very sadly indeed without beautiful Becky, but with the three others, Ben, Sitha and Adam.

During that week, before the scattering took place, I had a wander round the beach with Sitha, aged 9, looking for interesting shells and stones.

"What do you think happens when someone dies, Sitha?"

"Oh," she replied easily, "they go up into a kind of floating garden, and Becky has a mansion there with a swimming pool, and Grandpa Philip is beside her, and Michael Jackson is living opposite, and everyone from the Titanic are there too. And they're all really happy." [6]

Tears sprung to my eyes as my heart filled with love, and a smile came to my face. She was so clear. It was just beautiful to hear how she had explained her sister's death alongside all the other tragedies that were important to her, in her own world. Later, she drew a lovely picture for me which I pasted into the Memories Book.

We were at the mercy of nature for doing the actual scattering: the tide had to be high enough to be around the diving rock, and it had to be a time during the day, so all of us could easily be there, even the youngest. We gathered on the beach in front of the hut, in gentle sunshine, and with the tide high. Each of us who wanted, took turns to say something about the ashes being scattered, no longer just Philip's, but now those of his grand-daughter, too. It was very emotional, lots of tears; we all sat on the rock, or on the beach beside, and were quiet. Sadness was present, too, sitting alongside us all. Quietly I spoke to Matt, perched on the rock next to me.

"It's nice to see both lots of ashes mingling together there. I like to think of them looking after each other."

He looked at me with pain-filled, tearful eyes. "How could it happen, Jane? How could it?" I held his arm. No words to explain, or even comfort, in the face of the death of a child. And so soon after his Dad's death, too.

*

6 You can see Sitha's drawing at www.giftedbygrief.com/the-book/photos

The next day, we planted a beautiful yellow rambling rose by the hedge, where it would grow through the leaves and branches and provide splashes of colour all summer. Philip would have liked that; Becky too, probably. Later I heard that the family planted a tree for Becky near their home.

In the end, there was so much of Philip's ashes to scatter, that small deposits have been left all over the world, in some of our favourite places. The driveway of my parent's house in France; around Loch An Eilean in the Highlands; in the woods out the back of my home in Forres; in The Joshua Tree National Park, California; a beach on Hawaii; and in the ocean off North Island, New Zealand. That felt good, him still somehow being a citizen of the world, just as he'd always been. No one place to go to, to remember him – just the knowledge he had been in many places, and still was, in a way.

25

Moving

I kept being amazed at how shocked I was. Probably this was the most surprising thing about this whole process. My mind simply could not understand why it could not understand, if you see what I mean. I had been there; I had seen him die; I had said all that needed to be said. I knew death was approaching. Yet still the shock permeated my life months later.

Journal: 2nd May 2012

It's complete rubbish that I've begun to understand that he is not here anymore. Today I found myself thinking he was just away for a long time. Shit!

He is dead Jane, D-E-A-D. Never, NEVER coming back.

That's hard to take in. I need simply to focus on what I CAN have of him, which this morning I realised was to keep opening to being loved. In all instances, and particularly by him 'coming through' in a different way. Just because he has no body any longer doesn't mean to say his energy and his love is not here, when I want to receive it.

And then, a week later:

> *As I am watching Britain's Got Talent, Philip's photo looks down at me from the mantelpiece. No one has ever said how relentless this is. It goes on and on and on. I just don't get it; I'm somehow not really taking it in that he is not here; not only not here but never coming back. And yet, at the same time, I get on with my life.*
>
> *Will it be different in the new place? Will I still have all the memories? What on earth will it be like? I haven't got a clue. I will be living the life of a single woman. A widow. A widow! Ha. Fuck it. This was my biggest fear; P leaving me and not having any children. And here it is, come true. So what now? What on earth do you do when your biggest fear actually happens? You just get on with life – no other option.*

And so it was – I did just get on with life, which in mid-May took the form of moving out of the bungalow and into the flat, accomplished with plenty of wonderful help from some good friends. It was a long, long time before I really began to feel like it was all right being there, even though I could see its benefits much earlier on: less garden to maintain – a lot less, as it was a communal garden; just two bedrooms; only one living room; easier to maintain; and of course, cheaper. Lots of practical benefits, and I cared not a jot about any of them.

On the evening before moving, late that night, I was Listening:

> *"Into the open heart flows a love of such proportions that it almost cannot be experienced. The open heart allows its presence, which in turn allows for healing of wounds to occur. The healing of wounds is essential to a daily progress of simplicity, wholeness and insistence upon the way of Spirit.*

> *You are at a new stage in your life. Enfolded, by material needs having been met, a challenge is now issued to ignore these still further, and embark even more on your inner path."*

The enfolding of material needs was referring to the sum of money I now had in the bank. Earlier I'd been reflecting on this, and how it didn't make a blind bit of difference! How ironic. It is so easy to attach to the idea that having plenty of money will make one feel safe, and yet here I was, with plenty of money, and still feeling distraught, upset, in mourning and completely understanding of those who say they would forgo any sum of money, in order to have their loved ones back. Not that I wasn't grateful; on the contrary, but I was once again being reminded of a conversation that had happened with Philip some years previously:

"Darling, look. We have £5,000 in the current account," I exclaimed.

"That's wonderful!" he replied. "Nice to have that amount for a change."

"Yes, I feel rich!" I enthused.

Next day, I looked at the same account, same amount of money.

"Philip, I feel utterly terrified. We haven't got nearly enough for the future. What on earth are we going to do? I really don't want to be a bag lady on the street. I can't see a way forward, and I'm scared!"

"Jane, calm down." He gave me a big hug. "The amount of money hasn't changed. It's you that feels different inside about it. Yesterday you were feeling rich; today you're feeling poor. It's about you, not the money."

Wise man. So very true. Of course, if your basic needs are not taken care of, then the focus will be entirely on taking care of them, and for that, in our current economic system, money is very helpful indeed. However, no matter how much money is at hand, whether one feels rich or poor is entirely down to how one thinks about it.

That night, 11th May 2012, I wrote in my journal:

> *My last night in our lovely home, Philip. It has been such a good place for us, so loving and nurturing at a time when we really needed it. I suppose, in the future, I'll look back and see that being given notice was a good thing, but right now it feels like I'm being kicked out before I'm ready. Actually, I am. I ate two chocolate bars and a small tub of ice-cream tonight for dinner. I don't feel like I'm coping very well.*

I was still wanting to hide away on my own quite a lot, and yet too much of that could lead to a very depressing spiral. Thank God, yet again, for friends.

One of them called me. "Jane, you must make a list of whom you can call when you feel the need. Pin it up somewhere where it's easy to see, and then you won't have to think of, or search for, numbers when you're feeling awful."

"Good idea," I replied. This appealed to the side of me that likes to be organised. "You can be at the top of it."

She smiled. "I think you'll find that there will be the exact right person for however you are feeling at that particular time; it won't be about who is at the top or not."

Of course, she was right. I trusted completely when I viewed it, and could tell immediately who would be right to reach out to. Even though reaching out in itself was very hard; it was easier just to respond to offers. Most people don't offer specifics, though. Usually an offer is along the lines of 'Let me know if I can help you', which is fine, but not that easy to act on. So what I most appreciated in the first month or so after Philip dying were the practical offers of help, like someone saying "I'll cut your grass," or "Let me make that meal for you," or "I'll take whatever you want to the Post Office." It helped, because often I was incapable of thinking straight about practical things that needed to be done – and even if I did think straight, I often didn't have the energy or the inclination to ask for help.

I still have that list. It's up on the inside of a kitchen cupboard door. I don't need it now so much in the same way, but I like to look and feel the warm smile that comes as I feel grateful for these wonderful people. No wonder one of the top regrets of the dying is that they wish they had spent more time with friends and family. There is nothing more important, really.

Not that it was all plain sailing with friends and family.

Journal 20th May 2012:

> *Oh, dear. Lost the plot with Mum today when she told me how exhausted they were. I shouted at her on the phone, but after, I couldn't stop crying, and realised how exhausted I am, too. Eventually I went to see Joanna, instead of going to the Course in Miracles evening meeting. I just really miss Philip! It is awful. Awful, awful, awful.*

Given I'd just moved house, perhaps it wasn't surprising I was exhausted.

In the new flat, I took great pleasure in being surrounded by things Philip had made or given me. Several years earlier, he had created a beautiful desk from a piece of wooden kitchen worktop found in a skip. It was a lovely colour, and I was so delighted it fitted perfectly in its new location. As I organised furniture and settled in, I saw the paua earrings he'd made to welcome me to New Zealand, when I first arrived to join him; the board he'd made to display my earrings on; his Moroccan belt which he'd bargained for so successfully on our holiday. And one other thing that I just adore.

"You're 54 today, darling," he'd said on my birthday the previous year. "I really wanted to mark the occasion, as it's been quite a year." He handed me a wrapped box. For many years in our marriage, I was nervous about him remembering my birthday, or anyone else's, for that matter. He had no time for Valentine's Day at all – that was fortunate now, because it had passed by without me noticing; nothing unusual in that. I'd got less uptight and more trusting about this more recently, but it was still pretty remarkable to me that this gift he was giving me now was a complete surprise. I opened the wrapping paper, excitedly.

"It's a Kindle!" I shouted, "and it's got a pink leather cover!" I burst into tears. This was far more than we usually spent on presents for each other.

"How did you know I wanted one?"

He looked at me with a mischievous grin and a twinkle in his eyes. "Well, I just thought you'd be able to use it, especially when you're travelling; and I know you like pink these days, though I can't quite see why myself."

I hugged him, overcome with love. I also love my Kindle, which I've still got, but most of all I love the pink leather cover. After he died, and I was clearing out the cupboards in the bungalow, I came across the empty delivery box. In it was a label he'd forgotten about, with some beautiful words on.

"With all my love. May you spend many happy hours with this new friend :) Philip."

I've still got that too.

26

Disbelieving Still

Journal: 26th May 2012

I remember the feel of his arms around me as they sometimes were; and the feel of my own arm draped across him as we snuggled in sleep together. The memory might have been upsetting but, in fact, it was comforting. I can still hardly believe this has happened.

I thought, after 6 months, I might've got used to it, but no: it doesn't seem to have made any difference at all. It is so strange, how I can seem to be doing all right one minute, and am utterly devastated the next.

And here I am now, living on my own, in this new flat. Never in a million years did I imagine this. Not even when he was ill. I suppose there was no time to think about that. Perhaps I'm feeling all this because I now do have time. Perhaps I need to be grateful I have some money, and can go off and visit people and not worry about it. Perhaps I just need to be kind to myself. Life is strange, to say the least.

Someone had suggested I read Anita Moorjani's book, *Dying to Be Me*, quite soon after he died. I'd got a Kindle copy and looked at it, and just felt furious that she had lived and Philip hadn't. I knew I couldn't read it then, had to trust that if it was right, I would read it when I felt ready. And sure enough, after I'd moved into the flat, I was open enough to take another peek, especially after two other people had suggested it to me in one week.

Journal: Monday 28th May 2012

Reading Dying to be Me. Now I understand that it was Philip giving me the opportunity to read this, through those people mentioning it to me. Felt it as an absolute certainty in my bones, which is a way of knowing something I'm becoming more and more familiar with.

I'm also reminded of the vision experience I had when he was in hospital, when I described it as a warm glow, and realised there was no separation between what he was walking into, and where I was. We were both in that golden light, and he was walking away from me. AND IT WAS PERFECT! Remember that perfection. Oh, God, it was such a relief, and so utterly, indescribably beautiful! And so much LOVE!

So this morning I am realising that this golden light is here, now. Right here, right now. All the time. Never goes away. There is nowhere for it to go away to. It is always available for me and for everyone. It is only when I forget that it exists and is here, right now, that I get worried, anxious or bothered about anything.

I'm sure Philip has delivered this book to me through these two people, and found me receptive because he knows, too. He, himself, now KNOWS about the golden light. Oh, God. What a lovely, lovely thought. In fact, I can share that with him, by living my life in that place whilst here in this body on earth. It is not dependent on me doing anything, or being any particular way. It is not available only for some, and not others. It is not judgmental. It is not critical or withholding. It is simply expansive: wide, open, loving, cherishing, nurturing and healing LOVE LOVE LOVE.

Did you have an inkling of this, Philip, before you died? I think you did; why else would you have called your star, 'Love is the Answer'?

I hope you knew. Perhaps you did. Perhaps you have been having experiences like Anita's – oh, yes, you have; of course. Thank you: this is your way of telling me. Oh, that is so lovely. That means Becky must be, too. I wonder, are you together? You told me she was with you, so I guess that must have happened; there is no separation. No time exists where you are, for anything to happen other than in the moment. No 'where' for anything to happen, and no 'thing' to happen. No delineation of experiences or history or facts or words or linear anything. Just the LOVE. Love love love. Just that. I feel I can get a small taste of it from time to time, but the golden light was quite a big taste. Yummy. Very yummy.

A week earlier, I'd been walking in the woods out the back of the house, and while crossing a small bridge over the river, found myself wondering about Becky: was she really in the floating garden Sitha had talked about? In other words, was she really okay? In that moment, I heard a voice saying, "She is with me; I'm looking after her." It wasn't Philip's voice, nor any voice that I knew; just words, really. I took them to be him, though, and again felt very comforted.

Did it matter if I didn't 'know' that these words were from him, or if he had actually 'brought' me to read the book? I just decided to think this, as it was a lot nicer than staying in the place of wondering, of not knowing. Given I would never know, this seemed quite sensible, and definitely a way to reduce suffering. It's so easy in this world to live a life of suffering; more people do it than not, even with things they actually *could* do something about, if they chose to. It's mad, completely mad, when our actions are so often determined by our thoughts and our feelings. Surely, it makes complete sense to deliberately choose to think in such a way that will make you feel better.

Back on practical matters again; I had a checkup with the dentist.

"I suggest you have that tooth out, the one that's been causing a bit of a problem," the dentist spoke in a rather offhand manner.

"Oh, all right then." I made an appointment to have that done. Then, at home, as the enormity of that began to sink in, I wailed out loud.

"Philip! I need to speak to you! What should I do? Shall I have my tooth out or not? Could something else be done? I don't know what to do and I want to TALK with you about it!" The impact of there being no one, not even a friend, who would care about my tooth the way I would have done was very hard-hitting. Nor was there anyone who really cared whether I got a new smart phone or not. Of course, I could discuss these things with friends, but there just was no one now who would be impacted by me having a new phone, or no tooth, in the same way that Philip would have been.

Another practical dilemma was what to do with tools and technology. I kept Philip's basic toolbox, with everything in it. I knew how to use a screwdriver and some of the other things in there, so that was fine. I had to pay someone to come and tell me about the computer, and then there were the three (yes, three!) times I paid another person to come out to fix the TV, only to discover that each time it was a plug that simply wasn't in properly. A bit embarrassing, to say the least.

"Next time I ring you up, will you please ask me if I've checked every single plug before you come out?" I laughed. Fortunately, I *was* able to laugh at this – and then have a good cry about it later, too.

These incidences were similar to leaving the house to travel somewhere, knowing that no one else in the whole world really knows what you are doing at that precise moment, not like a husband or partner would. When you live alone, there just is no one else involved in your life to that degree. Painful to get used to, when you've lived for so long with someone there alongside you, who cares about your teeth, who cares whether you change your phone or not, or cares what time you leave the house and what time you'll be arriving back.

27
Explorations in Non-Duality

In June, I went to my parents in France for a holiday, to be followed by a week at another satsang retreat with Jac O'Keeffe, further south in France. Having first met her on the silent retreat back in January in Newbold House, I continued to feel obsessed with finding out what had been going on when Philip died; what it was that had left his body, but was still in mine.

In the few days before my friend Lisa arrived to join me, I wrote:

Journal: 1st June 2012

Reading the book, Love Money, It Loves You, and suddenly I felt a strong, energetic visitation from Philip. In fact, an immense sense of being loved and feeling loved, and basking in love alongside him – together. Because – there is no separation! In fact, all there is to do is to open up to LOVE – open and expand into it, to what is already there, and then enjoy. Nothing else. Just bliss.

He is now leading me through a door, the same way he led me into the village hall for our wedding reception in that photo we loved so much. This door is opening out of the

> *human realm into the true realm of reality, where I and we truly belong, because we are LOVE itself. There is nothing to be done other than be in this Love and act from here. Simple. Thank you, Philip, thank you. All this, six months from the death of your body.*

This was one of several 'visitations', which I only recognised as such after the first few. My sceptical mind could often take over and argue it was just my imagination, but after this loving sense happened a few times, accompanied by thoughts out of the blue about Philip, I was a bit more trusting.

Lisa and I enjoyed a lovely couple of days sitting in my parent's garden in the sunshine, reading, eating good food, and being looked after by my Mum and Dad, then off we went to the retreat.

Around forty of us gathered in a gorgeous chateau and conference centre, La Domaine du Fan, near Limoges, a complex of buildings that used to be an Osho meditation centre. I loved the synchronicity of this. I was getting a tiny taste of what it might have been like for Philip when he was in the ashram in Poona, India.

The extensive and beautiful grounds were dotted with small wooden one-room cabins for individual retreats. However, Lisa and I were in a shared bedroom in the main building, while attending the actual satsang sessions in a stunningly simple, huge white room, reaching up into the eaves of the roof. It was carpeted – rashly – in an off-white colour, with no furniture other than folding chairs and meditation cushions. We gathered there twice each day to pose questions to Jac, to listen to and respond to answers, and simply to be.

In the car on the way to the retreat, my Mum had asked,

"Do you really think you'll be able to be in silence all that time?"

I looked at Lisa. "Yes," I announced airily. "We've both done it before; we're used to it, and we know the benefits. I'm quite looking forward to it, actually."

Just after the start, I wrote in my journal:

9.45pm 2nd June 2012

Jac said something like "allow yourself to drop within and have movement happen from the consciousness flowing through this body, as opposed to 'you' deciding to 'do' something."

That is what has been happening more and more for me since P died. How? Listening to and following my inner impulses. How? Offering counselling sessions again, even though it appeared completely mad; trusting more and more regarding money; not working more than 1:1; finding a new house to live in; watching my life work out (so long as I'm not attached to what I think that ought to look like).

Perhaps I would not have described it as Jac did, but I did resonate with it. Later, I wrote:

Grief, which I'm not too keen on, knocks on the front door of my house. If I open the door and say hallo, and then I also open the back door, so it can pass through on its visit as quickly as possible, that helps. Then surely I have to let that happen when an emotion I LIKE knocks on the front door, too. I don't want to, though! I want to keep the nice feeling inside the house forever!

Does the feeling of love and joy come visiting too? Or is it always there? Maybe it IS the house and sometimes 'I' am just not in to experience it.

Because I'd been slowly acknowledging the experience I'd had in my teens, which had morphed at this time into the statement, 'I am the Peace and Presence of God,' I liked this idea of the house itself being the love and joy, but I wasn't inside it. It meant that all that had to happen was to fully inhabit the house. Easier said than done, of course.

I'd bought Jac's book in CD format at her last retreat, and I'd been listening to it every time I drove anywhere. I read the book again on this retreat. By now, I'd worked out that, although I'd previously been thinking 'she has something I want', it was in fact the other way round: I had something she hadn't. I didn't know exactly what that was, but I wanted to let go of it, because whatever it was she didn't have, I wanted not to have it, too! Bit backwards, but it made sense to me.

What didn't make sense was the feeling I kept having of bewilderment regarding my marriage with Philip. Some months previously, I'd posted on Facebook that it almost felt like being married had never happened, and several people replied, very lovingly, to reassure me that I *had* been married, that it had fundamentally been a very good marriage, and to trust that. The trouble was, in a strange way, I wasn't at all sure that the marriage had, indeed, happened. I asked Jac about this.

"This is being in the present moment," she replied. "When you are in the present moment – which you always are – then there is no sense of past or future. Of course, at one level, you have been married; you have that history. However, when you are fully here, fully present, there is only this moment."

I was intrigued by this. Something in it rang true, and I just had to trust that and go with it. On the one hand, it made no sense at all, and on the other, I could feel the truth in it. In fact, lots of that retreat made no sense at all to my mind . . . and yet something in me was not only responding to it, but lapping it up. It was as if I was desperately thirsty, and was finally being given a long, cool, drink of water. I began even more seriously questioning who 'I' was and, more so, who I *thought* I was.

"Who am I?" is the well-known question posed by sages such as Ramana Maharishi, and other teachers from this tradition. I'd been aware of it for years, but had never focused on it in the way I was now doing. While Philip had cancer, we'd both come to the conclusion that asking the 'Why?' question, as in 'Why am I doing this?' or 'Why is that happening?' was not always helpful. For two ex-psychotherapists who had spent most of their adult lives pondering this question – both in their own lives and helping others to do the same – realising the futility of 'Why?' was a bit humbling, to say the least. In the face of cancer, though, it just hadn't worked. Now, instead of asking 'Why?' I was asking 'Who am I?' and 'What is this?' All in line with 'Who, or what, is inhabiting this bag?'

Journal: 4th June 2012

> *Defending your position, having strong opinions, judging a lot, are all attachments to who you THINK you are. So my judgments do this: keep me stuck in who I THINK I am. It all maintains the belief in the personality and character of this being labelled 'Jane.'*
>
> *I judge everyone else, too. I judge myself negatively, and positively, and therefore keep myself stuck in the vicious circle. Stuck, stuck, stuck! How mad is that!*
>
> *Can I resign from the Judgment Club? Can I resign as President of the Judgment Club of the whole world? If I resign, I will not exist anymore!*

Help! (says my mind) How can I live without judgment? Or is it the attachment and meaning put on judgment that is the real problem? Yes; maybe the problem is I think the positive and/or negative judgments of myself or others mean something.

So you can see the style of inquiry: many questions, and not many answers. Just more of being in the place of not knowing, the place of uncertainty. We had both had a baptism of fire in that when cancer descended on us, and it was continuing for me now.

Journal: Tuesday 5th June: Day 3 of the Retreat

Philip, I am missing you tonight. I don't care about anything Jac has said about everything not existing; I just miss you. Particularly in the Gayatri mantra chanting, you came to mind and I had the idea you were there somewhere, and yet you're not here. At least, not in your body. And even if it is all a bloody illusion, and it's made up, I bloody well miss you! Fuck it.

Four days in, and Lisa and I were whispering and giggling in the bedroom, the wonders of total silence having worn off.

"We've been brilliant at this, haven't we?" grinned Lisa.

"Yes! But shall we decide consciously to go for a walk tomorrow and talk? That way, we don't have to whisper, and we can catch up properly on what's been happening."

I think we did remarkably well, lasting this long.

28
Accepting What Is

A large part of non-duality teaching is about accepting what is. In the context of death, that meant accepting it had actually happened. Indeed, much has been written on this subject, not least with the 5 stages of loss, as originally outlined by Elisabeth Kubler Ross, and now challenged from many directions.

At the time, I didn't know anything about these challenges; all I knew about the 5 stages was that they didn't happen in any order, and that any, all or none of them can be experienced. In fact, this was what I found helpful: that DABDA, as I called the stages (denial, anger, bargaining, depression, acceptance) could take many forms, and in fact I experienced all of these stages other than bargaining, but I experienced them in moments. So a day could go by thus:

"Oh, no. No energy. Feeling very low. Not interested in anything or anyone. Just want to hide." (depression). Then "What? Has he died? How could that have happened?" (denial). And later, "I'm so bloody angry with you, Philip! How could you let this happen? How DARE you die on me!" (anger – rage, actually!) And then, tiny moments of acceptance before another emotion whooshed through, or denial visited again.

For quite a while, though, one emotion really did puzzle me. I'd gone for a walk alone in the woods: it was a beautiful day, sun shining, blue cloudless sky, cold but thrilling to the senses. No one else around as I walked along the edge of the woods, farmland spreading out to my right, pine trees with dappled sunlight filtering through on my left, the path ahead of me opening up. I felt totally, deeply happy. There it was: simple happiness at a very deep level. I watched my mind say, "How on earth can this be happening? Philip has just died! How can you be happy?" but I couldn't deny it. I was deeply happy and, what's more, at peace.

Was that a moment of acceptance? At a mental level, it could be described as a moment of denial. However, I didn't care about concepts; I just knew the truth in the moment, and that moment was happiness. It passed, as all moments do, but it has remained in my memory as an amazing experience. Clearly, just because someone has died doesn't mean to say you'll never feel happiness, peace and joy.

In the first retreat with Jac, I'd understood something about pain and suffering.

"I know about pain: it feels raw and sore; it's wide-open agony, there, in the moment. If I'm feeling it fully, though, which I've done a lot, I've noticed there is a cleanliness about it," I told a friend afterwards. "It's almost as if it's okay, like it really *has* just come to visit, and if it's allowed to visit, then it will go again."

"That sounds great, except that most people most of the time don't want a visit at all, as you put it, from any emotion they don't like," my friend replied.

"Yes, well, neither do I, really, but apparently I don't have much say in the matter; the feelings are so strong." This experience of pain coming and going had happened so often, especially in the first few weeks, that I was very familiar with it.

"The real trouble is when, for whatever reason, I don't want to – or can't – feel it, and then it kind of gets stuck somehow." This is a familiar notion in therapeutic circles, that emotions and feelings need to be fully felt in order for them to go. Unfortunately, the emphasis is often on the 'going' bit, rather than the 'feeling' bit.

What I found, though, even in those early days, was that if I didn't censor any of the feelings, they didn't last that long. They morphed into something else, even if it was just a dull ache. It was often that, which I didn't like much either, but just got on with life anyway. That's when the quotation 'This too shall pass' sometimes helped; it had been pinned on a noticeboard on the wall of Philip's room in hospital, and it was stuck up on the wardrobe door in my bedroom now.

"Suffering, though, that's another matter," I carried on speaking to my friend, and referred to something I'd learnt from reading *Enlightenment is Not What You Think.*

"Suffering is about when I'm saying, "I wish..." or "If only we had..." It's about something in the past or the future, and it goes on and on and on. In fact, it never stops, unless I choose to stop it. To do that, I have to direct my mind to something else, very deliberately. In fact, suffering is the result of not accepting what is."

A lot easier said than done. I was learning a huge lesson about this. For much of my life, I'd lived according to the premise that I could affect where my life was going. In fact, much of my life had been lived improving myself, reading self-help books, trying to understand why I was the way I was, and why others were the way they were. I'd had the idea that, along with the understanding, would come some kind of freedom. Sometimes this happened, but often it didn't. Occasionally, an insight into my behaviour would affect that behaviour for a while – but not necessarily.

I'd begun to question the notion of being able to affect my life around the time of not being able to have children easily. Because of the vasectomy, it would take lots of medical interference and support to create the conditions for a baby, and the effort and commitment this meant would be enormous. I did explore IVF treatment by joining a local group of women at the nearby hospital, all of whom wanted a child but were finding it difficult for various reasons. Hearing about the amount of drugs taken, the invasive procedures to the body, and the emotional impact, I realised this was not going to be an option for someone who was still ambivalent. Nor was adoption, invasive in another way. Not that I disrespect anyone for wanting to go down either of these pathways, but for me, I became more and more enamoured with the idea of 'stopping trying to make things happen.' This would mean I had to accept not having children, not being part of 'The Mothers Club,' and having an immediate family life of just two of us.

'Trying to make things happen' came up again around the cancer treatment, although of course it was Philip's decision regarding his body, not mine. I often wondered, though, whether I would have chemotherapy at all if I was diagnosed with cancer. You can never know, of course, until or if it happens, exactly how you will respond. I did question this for myself, though, while fully supporting and backing his decision. Now, with this visit from death, it was here again in a big way. Nothing I could do, nothing at all, would make what I wanted to happen, happen: for Philip to be alive again, and healthy. It was very sobering.

Whether I liked it or not, I was going to have to get used to this idea that he was dead, even if I didn't accept it. So out of the window went the self-help books. The ones on grief that had exercises to do I shunned. I was only interested in reading stories of others and how it had been for them, and gaining what solace and insight I could that way. I'd already become a bit fed up with the self-improvement movement; considering that if perhaps we are fine just the way we are, deep down, then there is no need for self-improvement. The idea of 'accepting what is' was by now actually very appealing to me. Even if I didn't like the 'what is' much.

Journal: Sometime in June 2012

> *Where IS Philip, anyway? I don't want him to disappear off the radar completely! I haven't felt the love for days now. If I don't feel that, then where is he? Being the ocean is fine, but I'd like to bump up against some of that love occasionally, please. Being a wave myself should allow me to do this.*

The idea of the wave and the ocean was something we had first been introduced to in Wayne's book. We are all the ocean, just showing up as apparently individual waves, with a particular shape and form for however long that wave lasts. When it is finished being a wave, it is still the ocean. It never stopped being the ocean, in fact.

As Eckhart Tolle says: "The person is the ripple, the deeper being is the ocean – the person loses its identity as the ripple, and realises its true identity is the ocean. Then fear is lost and replaced by trust."

This really appealed to both Philip and me; it struck a chord, and also emphasised the idea of there being no separation. It only *appears* that there is separation; the wave only *appears* to be separate from the ocean. So you, as a person, only *appear* to be separate from everyone and everything else. For now, though, I was experiencing this as just a comforting idea: sometimes it worked, sometimes it didn't.

29
A Revelation

On the outside, it probably seemed like I was coping fine, and I was, often. But at home, alone, I'd fall apart regularly. A few good friends were aware of this, as well as my sister, who had taken to ringing me every day for a good few months. It had made a huge difference; not that I felt any less awful but, in the awfulness, there was someone else out there, just being there, not asking anything of me. Sometimes I'd be sobbing on the phone to her, other times cheerily talking of what I'd done that day. I suppose that is what grief is like.

A colleague who had been giving therapeutic help to Philip in his last year offered to support me too. I felt incredibly blessed by this; it was so helpful.

Journal: Early June 2012

She (the therapist) pointed out I was not whole. This so resonated with me, and I cried and cried. I do not know what is happening. I do not understand, really. Even though I do intellectually, emotionally it's a very different ball game. I do know I have to be much more patient and kind to myself, and that I have no way of knowing when I will be able to do certain things, until the moment when it feels right.

I must have thought that, after six months, I would be okay. But I don't feel like that, and the only answer is to honour this and trust it, and in the meantime, take care of myself as much as I possibly can.

Trusting myself became absolutely crucial. It took the form of leaving meetings early, of changing appointments at the last moment, of arriving at a gathering only to have to leave again immediately. Very good at doing this on the whole, I actually felt I had no choice. It was either that or be putting on a front, pretending, and I wasn't willing to do that. That way lay a prolonged agony as another layer would be put on top of the grief and I did not want that. So I learnt to listen to the subtleties of my intuition more and more, and was willing to act on them.

Eileen Caddy, one of the founders of the Findhorn Foundation, used to say it was not only important to listen to your 'still, small voice within,' but then you had to obey it, too. She and her husband, Peter, and friend Dorothy MacLean (the three founders of the community) were all expert in 'obeying', whereas I had been just reasonably good. Now, though, I simply was not willing to pay the price any longer for not obeying, which was what led me to sign up to my next workshop, *The Elusive Obvious,* with a man called Roger Linden. It turned out to be life-changing.

Journal: 27th July 2012

My darling Philip

I so wish you were here right now for me to tell you what has been happening this week. I am in tears as I type this, at the end of the Roger Linden week in Cluny. There is only one person in the world I would want to tell this to, and that is you. I suppose it is better than nothing to write it but, oh, God, I wish you were still here for me to share with and feel your hugs, my head on your shoulder, just as we used to. I miss you. I miss you.

Let me try and tell you, though. Maybe you already know. Maybe when I heard the woodpecker this morning in the woods, it really was you trying to tell me you can hear me, and that you are all right, and knowing what I now know. But I don't know for sure and, anyway, I still just badly miss you. Miss your physical presence.

One morning, not understanding what Roger was talking about at all, and feeling a bit disturbed by that, I was soothing myself by imagining peaceful white light surrounding me, and saying to myself the words 'All is well; all is well,' over and over. And then it happened.

Suddenly there was a shift, and I realised that this experience of the light I was imagining was in fact me. THAT was who I am: there is no 'me' being soothed by words and peaceful light. There is just this peace, which IS who I really am. It was sort of like a glow. So I was not the me I usually think I am, in this body; and the other bodies I could see in the group were also just other forms of this 'glow' showing up.

It was like I always had viewed this 'God' thing as out there, viewed from me over here. When in fact it's the other way round, if anything. I am this 'God' thing, or glow, seeing lots of bodies who think they are separate from godness. Such an ordinary revelation, and yet, so amazing all at the same time.

If that essence IS who I am, then this body through which it flows is NOT who I am. It just seems to be. Rather, it's that the behaviour and conditioning through socialisation and repeating thought/ feeling patterns over 'my lifetime' to date has meant that it seems 'I' am this body/mind. When it is not.

This is very odd. It's as if this body breathes, tenses, and relaxes regardless of 'me,' which is constant. The sensations belong to the body, not to the glow.

So what is the glow? It watches the body making movements, writing, partly listening to people talking. It is not the glow that does this; the body apparently 'does' it. The glow simply glows, and the glow is actually 'me' (except there is no 'me,' as the glow is universal).

So that's what happened. It was extremely odd, going to tea break and talking about 'I' when I had just experienced knowing that the 'I' others were referring to, however spiritual, was not the same 'I' as I was talking about. And to think, just an hour or so previously I'd been talking about the same one as them. Very odd indeed. It's even odder writing it down . . . it sounds a bit mad when I read it back!

The next morning, I thought whatever this glow was might have gone, but no. In the early morning Taize singing, I watched the other human beings – including this apparent me – singing 'In manus tuas pater, commendo spiritum meum,' (Into your hands God I commend my spirit) which was all very odd because I was seeing and feeling and experiencing and knowing that 'I am God' – and they are, too – already! So why do they ask for what is already theirs? Strange, to say the least.

Then I had another realisation. The Quakers say, 'There is that of God in everyone,' but, actually, it's the wrong way round. (That is what humans do: they get it the wrong way round completely.) Rather, it is that God is everything and everyone, all of the time, and humans are just a manifestation of that. WE are God, or this Is-ness, or I AM, or glow, or whatever you want to call it. That is the point!

This is definitely not a feeling, nor a thought, nor a sensation, nor an emotion or experience, nor an image, although I can think about it like images. It's not like what happened in that moment of insight in the garden in France when I realised the truth of the statement, 'I am God.' What is it, then?

Well, darling, I don't actually know. It is impossible to describe, and I can only hope that where you are you know what I am talking about!

Telling Roger about this in a private session, he said it can take some time to come to terms with it when this sort of thing happens. True; I mean, it has been such a very long time I have assumed and thought this being sitting here typing was me, even when I knew intellectually it wasn't. And now it's just a body doing typing, and 'me' is just this still, peaceful, never-ending presence. I'm understanding some of the non-duality phrases I've been reading in a completely different way now; it is so odd. Like 'THIS is it.' When I hear this phrase now, from this other place, the words are true in a very different way. How? Hard to explain. Impossible, maybe. It's just different. I don't know if I'm making sense here, am I? I just know I so wanted to share it with you.

I'm off to bed now. Wish you were there to cuddle up to. I miss that such a lot. Goodnight, my sweetheart.

The following day, I told Roger about all the deaths of Philip and Becky, and moving house. As I spoke of it all aloud, I realised this was a lot of loss in a short space of time. I wrote in my journal to Philip:

> *We spoke of these many losses, including the loss of the sense of an 'I' inside, which is the essence of the sense of separation. Yes, that's another loss too. It's the loss of the need to have meaning, that need which exists to compensate for the false sense of separation that is perceived. I appear to be going through a reinterpretation of how the world has been assumed to be.*
>
> *It was good, talking to Roger. I feel better about it all. Somehow, in the context of all the other losses, there is a place for the huge disorientation I'm now feeling.*
>
> *So back to watching terrible TV. Not even the Olympics – and, by the way, how did you, who loved sport so much, manage to die before experiencing Andy Murray winning Wimbledon, a British guy winning the Tour de France, and the Olympics in London?*
>
> *I love you, Philip. I have a sense your death may have given me true life. Maybe I am closer to you than I know.*

And then the fog rolled in.

30
Effects of the Fog

Down at Findhorn Village on the Moray coastline, a grey misty haar regularly rolls in from the sea. It's then impossible to see even a few feet in front of you, as the fog seeps in over the land, slowly and steadily occluding everything. That's exactly what it was like with the glow. I tried to stop it – ha! Then I had to laugh at who it was that was doing the trying.

Two days, this glimpse had lasted. Just two days. I chose to feel glad about this, rather than upset it was *only* two days. At least I wasn't frantically trying to recapture the experience, as I'd done with my previous great revelation on the cliff tops at college.

Some things had changed permanently, though. I found I could no longer go to Taize singing; the words which had previously been so soothing now just made me feel awkward and uncomfortable, like I was singing nonsense. I also began to have an aversion to anything 'deep and meaningful,' and that felt like another bereavement, along with the loss of the 'glow.' So, in spite of having had an incredible revelation, I was experiencing loss all over again, and feeling bereft about the death of all I had known myself to be.

Journal: end of June 2012

It is quite distressing, this, at least on a surface level. In periods of still silence, there is peace; a different kind of peace from before this shift. I felt that in meditation this morning. Is there anything to be done? No. Just stay still. Watch the mind's process as the thoughts come and go. Just as all the meditators say: don't pick up a thought and think it means something. It doesn't. It's just arriving, and if there is no engaging with it, it disappears again.

Philip, love was present; we acknowledged that. Love IS present still. That is what is available to me, and there I find you. Well . . . in those moments of overwhelming ordinariness and obviousness, there is no I, and no you either. However, there is a sense of peace and stillness. It is very lovely. And 'I' still wish 'you' were here for us to explore this together.

It's a bugger, darling, in spite of what has just happened. It's just a bugger.

I was getting used to the flat by now; it was clear to my practical side that it was much better than our bungalow, which had been so big just for me. My friend living above was great solace; hearing the occasional creak of the floorboards above made me feel less lonely. I wasn't keen on the loneliness: having always been someone who enjoys my own company, discovering I could have too much of it was a challenge. I went out a lot, particularly in the evenings, which could be very long otherwise, mostly just to meet one of my many friends. Sometimes, I'd get what I called grief headaches, just like earlier on in the year; I'd have no choice but to stay in, being a zombie in front of the telly. Finding the balance wasn't easy.

Journal: 17th August 2012

Philip, I do wish you were here for me to talk to. I really miss that. A lot. My initial concern about you dying last year, when I thought "Who would I talk to?" is correct. I am utterly bereft of anyone to talk to like I talked to you. It is sad. Very sad. I suppose writing is better than nothing.

I love you. I still do. I guess I always will. I am so very, very glad we met and grew in the way we did together, in what turned out to be our last year. It is a source of enormous consolation to me, that. So thank you, sweetheart, for your courageousness in turning your thoughts around. You big, sweet, lovely man. Even though I am still very angry sometimes with you, I also still love you. Nothing changes that.

In early October I wrote:

I'm astonished at how intense my feelings still are. There are days now when I think about P less. No doubt about that, but the days when I miss him, and that is often, the feelings are no less intense than ten months ago. It's horrible. In many ways, it's worse, because I now have the grief of realising I am moving on, and there is definitely no way he is coming, too.

My birthday was approaching fast, and I knew instinctively I needed to take care of myself properly that day. Two girlfriends I didn't see that often joined me for a delicious meal one evening at a local restaurant in Findhorn village. We dressed up, we ate and drank well, and I managed.

Then one Sunday morning in early October, 2012, I woke and realised I had to take off my wedding ring. I no longer felt married. This was somewhat astonishing, but it felt very strong, and so I removed the ring completely, and then put my engagement ring on the ring finger of my other hand. Sitting up in bed, reading something on my laptop – my new bedtime companion – a Skype call came in: my friend from Cape Town, South Africa.

"Cat! How wonderful to hear from you!" We chatted for a while, and as I told her about taking off the rings, I burst into tears.

"I thought I was fine with it, but obviously I'm not!" I wailed. Dear Cat, she knows me well, so was able to be there for me, even on the other side of the computer screen.

"What are you doing over the first year anniversary?"

"Oh dear," I sniffed, "a few days before it would have been his 67th birthday. I thought I would go away alone on that day, and then on the anniversary I'll have a few friends round. It'll be all right, probably."

"Why don't you come out and see us? You can stay in the spare room; it's got its own bathroom, the weather will be hot and sunny, and you can just relax and let us look after you. We'd love to see you!" More tears.

I arranged to go. No reason why not. I had some money. I had some time. Not before a very important event, though.

Having awoken to the need to take off my wedding ring, I decided to have a ritual to mark the occasion. I went to the woodpecker tree in the woods, and at the base of that tree, laid out a photograph of Philip, a special box in which I still had a small amount of his ashes, the ring, a picture that had meant a lot to us, and a candle.

Sitting on a fallen log amongst the copse of pine trees, I looked lovingly at his photo, and lit the candle.

"Philip, I want you to know I haven't taken off this ring because I don't love you, but because I do. I know you'd want me to be moving on. It's important I move on in this life, just like you have done in yours. I'm here today to acknowledge our love and what it has brought me, and to bury some of your ashes here, at the base of this special tree."

I'd like to report I heard his voice, or sensed his presence. None of that happened, though – just a deep sense of rightness of what I was doing. Cleaning out the small, jewel-encrusted pot that had held the ashes, I put in some clean white tissue paper, and placed the wedding ring in there. I took a photo of my left hand, showing it empty of a ring for the first time in 20 years. At home, I posted on Facebook about this, and was overwhelmed at the loving response I received in the likes and comments. Tears flowed once again.

The trip to South Africa brought many 'firsts', and they started with the night before I was due to catch the early morning flight from Edinburgh to Amsterdam, where I would connect with the flight to Cape Town. I wrote:

> *Sitting in the Edinburgh Airport hotel room, where I am for a night before going out to Cape Town tomorrow. It is HORRIBLE! I didn't realise I would feel so alone here in a place like this. Just had a big, big cry, biggest for ages.*
>
> *It is pretty horrible being alone. I don't look forward now to the return journey, but maybe it will be okay. I feel a bit better having cried so much; tried calling my sister, and a couple of other friends, but no one in. So I'm going down to the café to get online, see what is on TV later on, and occupy myself that way.*

Later, back in the bedroom, I did some Listening:

> *"Yes, you see, remembering is just underneath the surface, so close, and yet when you forget, so far. I am always here. Accessible at all times. A deep, deep peace into which you sink, for this IS you. My dear one, here YOU are. And all really IS well. The truth you read in your journal from last year is still here now: peace and fear and all other kinds of emotions can exist together, for peace never leaves, ever. So keeping the mind calm enough to remember is important, and you have done that. True and utter beauty is unfolding in front of you now, in more and more waves of honesty and humbling truthfulness."*

And so I got through yet another 'first.'

It made sense to do something very different over the first year anniversary and what might have been a difficult time. Although I'd never met Cat's new husband Brian before, I knew her well and trusted we would all get on fine, which we did.

I had a most glorious two weeks with them, being sensitively taken care of, driven around everywhere, viewing the most famous landmarks – Table Mountain, Robben Island, and various other places – in between simply hanging out with them in their lovely new home. I most certainly was blessed.

Plus something magical happened, too.

31

Dancing!

Sitting in the back garden in the warm evening sun in Cape Town. Relaxing. Drinking wine. Chatting.

"We thought we'd go to a dinner-dance venue on Friday; it's a stunning location in the city, and we can ask my good friend Dawie to come with us. What do you think, Jane?" Cat smiled at me.

"Oooh," I replied nervously. "A man – eeek! Is he nice?"

"Yes, he's charming. I wouldn't invite someone whom I didn't think you would get on with."

It felt far too soon for me to contemplate any other relationships, but I did hope he would be someone I could like and have some fun with.

Cat and I had a great time that evening, getting ready. It was an occasion for long dresses; I hadn't worn one of those for years, and she lent me a beauty, tight-fitting yet comfortable.

"I would never wear this at home; I'd feel too exposed." I was nervous.

"Well, you're a different person here, so you can!" We went the whole hog: nails painted, make-up, hair, the lot, and it was great fun. Brian wore a white shirt and smart black trousers, more formal than I'd seen him yet. We made a great trio. Dawie then arrived, similarly attired, and whew! He seemed very pleasant. Maybe this was going to be all right after all.

Here's what I wrote in my journal after that evening:

Philip, I've just come back from Pigalle, a dinner-dance venue in an old but very well-appointed warehouse, full of people in casual and smart clothes. LOVELY food, great ambience, live band, fantastic music and I DANCED! And danced and danced and danced. It was with Dawie, their friend, who is charming.

It was a bit odd, at first, to have a man hold me so close – the first after you – but I liked it! And I LOVED it when we danced the last dances together, and he held me in front of him. LOVED it.

I could have gone on for ages, but it is now 1:30 a.m., and I hadn't even noticed time passing. Amazing. I feel extremely grateful to Dawie for 'breaking me in' to being with someone else, and to enjoying myself.

IT WAS JUST PLAIN FUN, FUN, FUN! I feel I just haven't had that for AGES –years in fact. God.

The next morning, 5 a.m., 25th November, 2012.

I feel like a rocket that has just had its touch-paper lit! I am FULL of excitement, purpose, destiny, passion, fizzle, fun, sparkle and poise.

Oh my God! I can't write about it even! What has happened?

It's a combination of that dress, the nails, the willingness and openness to embrace my feminine power, to adore my body as it is, the opulent atmosphere, the music, the food, the being taken care of, Dawie's hand upon my back, and being held in the arms of a strong man. Gosh, that felt good again. How was it different from Philip? A long time since I had felt him really strong. And Dawie was confident, confident! It's very appealing. Being guided on the dance floor, knowing this is all a game and enjoying it for that, not taking myself so seriously as a consequence, ENJOYING THE FRILLS AND FLOUNCES OF BEING A WOMAN!

Being a woman! A WOMAN! My God, is THIS what being a woman is like? If so, I LIKE IT! I feel I can hardly contain myself. I don't want to contain myself!

I just know now I'm going to be financially fine in the future; I'm going to be doing work I love and am well-respected for; I will be paid well for it; I will receive invitations and opportunities of amazing influence. In demand as a great speaker, here I come! Published best-seller, here I come! Deep joy, happiness and peace – doesn't need to be here I come, because HERE IT IS! ALREADY! Everything else in the material is simply a matter of catching up or not. Gosh, this is heady. And yet it also feels whole. Despite my excitement – or perhaps because of it – there is still a strong core of peace flowing through me that this feeling has nothing to do with. Woooo!

I think it can charitably be said that I did indeed enjoy myself!

When it would have been Philip's 67th birthday, we were in Addo Elephant Park.

"What do you most want to experience, Jane?" Cat had asked before I left the UK.

"I want to see elephants in the wild. It would be nice to see other animals, too, but elephants are the most important." Hence Cat organised two nights for all three of us at Addo, at the end of a beautiful road trip that took us through the rocky and wild semi-desert of the Karoo region. On the way, we stayed one night at Mymering, a magnificent guest house on a wine estate. That night at dinner, there were two other couples as well as the three of us, all sitting at the same table. The usual conversational talk was happening:

"Where are you from?" "Do you have children?" "What do they do?" I began to feel increasingly uncomfortable about being alone amongst couples, and yet I wasn't just single. I needed to mention Philip, something I was now acting on more and more.

"I just want to say, this trip is something my husband would have loved. He died a year ago, and it's coming up to what would have been his 67th birthday. We'll be in Addo Elephant Park when it happens, but I just wanted to include him here; he would have loved this place so much." All the other couples were respectful, and one of the ladies asked something about Philip. Then Cat mentioned Brian's previous wife Lorraine, and it was then the table felt complete to me. Both of the dead spouses had been acknowledged, respected and included.

Journal: 27th November 2012

Philip's birthday. What could be a more fitting experience for me to have, on this first anniversary of his birthday without him here, than for me to be in the African bush, in the middle of wild animals? We'd always thought it would be nice, someday, to do a safari. So I'm now doing something he would love; that feels very good. I didn't hear any lions roar last night, but the birdsong this morning is fantastic.

I don't feel very close to him anymore. Perhaps I don't need to. Yesterday, I read over a tiny bit of what I had written last January. The grief was so, so raw. And it does change. I am not so raw now. I am getting used to it.

That morning I also Listened:

> *"The quiet depth of sustained Love is what feeds you now. It has always fed you and continues to do so, if you will allow it. There is nothing else important at all. Learning to live in that place more and more is your only challenge right now. That is what you call the flow, or the zone, or whatever. It is just this. This peace – and even that is a label.*
>
> *This is where Philip is too. You can no longer relate to him as a body – that is just a memory – but who he REALLY was is still in (and of) the etheric world and, as such, is continuing to take pleasure in your pleasure. Fear not the struggling ties that wish you to look back and cling on. They are withering away more and more and allowing you to be present to now; and then, from there, into a future which holds you know not what. All that matters is here, now, in your heart, your soul, your love, and the presence of Love itself, shining through your friends, and all other elements in this world of yours."*

Something I experienced while being with Cat and Brian was how wonderful it was being around them. It's so easy, when you're single, to feel out of it when around couples, but even when they were cuddling up together in the evening as we watched their favourite half-hour soap opera together, it was fine. All three of us lined up on the sofa, they had a way of including me that made it all okay. I suppose they were not at all embarrassed about expressing their affection for each other, and I felt part of that that somehow. And yet, they'd only been married a year. Amazing! I don't suppose I could have stayed with them for as long if it had been otherwise.

On the first year anniversary of Philip's death, the day after we'd returned from Addo, we marked the occasion in an unusual way. I wasn't looking forward to this day, but being with friends helped. We'd had all sorts of plans, but in the end, I didn't want to go anywhere special, just wanted to mark the occasion.

1st December 2012: A year since you died.

Hi, Philip. We went to the garden centre for me to buy them a lemon tree, to plant as a symbol of the growth that occurs when someone you love dies.

We dug a hole together in their back garden; quite hard, clay earth and very hot sun, even though it was 6 p.m. Then we all settled around it: I cut up the 'Life Is Good' T-shirt we had bought together in the Anza Borrego desert in California all those years ago. That felt good, seeing those words lying in the bottom. We wrote words to represent your qualities on pieces of paper, and put them in the hole, too. It was lovely. We had John Lennon's 'Imagine' and 'Love' playing in the background – your favourites. Cat scattered some dead and living leaves into the hole, to represent life and death. We planted the tree on top of all this, and that was that. It felt lovely.

And then, at 8:19 p.m., I stood briefly outside the front door, just remembering the point of your death, darling. It didn't last long because James (their two year old grandson) came scampering out behind me, and so I got distracted, but that was fine. He is a symbol of life, for sure!

Now, I get to move on. Properly. I wonder what will happen this next year?

Journal: 3rd December 2012 (*1 year and 2 days since Philip died.)*

I woke this morning and, for the first time, I felt different: nothing horrible to remember from last year. It was wonderful.

I feel ready to go home again. Mind you, not until after visiting Robben Island, which is tomorrow. I have a make-up and hair session to have, too, before I go, and perhaps a dress to buy. Otherwise I'm looking forward to going home. That feels very good indeed.

Ultimate Jane-ness is here and ready to flourish, being honest, authentic, straightforward, bold and clear in my communication, and congruent in my appearance.

I had met up with Dawie again, and we'd had a lovely day exploring the Paarl Monument, with a tasty barbecue with Cat and Brian in the evening, quite a few glasses of red wine, and a corresponding amount of kissing. Kissing! And I enjoyed it!

That evening I looked very briefly at a dating site for the first time. It was alarmingly scary, but it was a sign my heart and body were opening up – very healthy.

Then I came home, and it all changed again.

Part 3: Rebirth

Introduction to Part 3

At the very end of that first year, I was feeling low. I had really thought I'd feel so much better than I did, and I didn't know why that wasn't happening. I was coping on many levels, but why wasn't I feeling better?

Many changes had happened, and not just moving house and managing my work differently, but also within myself. I'd become a different person, I could feel it: more assertive, more independent, more confident in my abilities and thoughts. I'd developed new ways of managing being alone, too. Although I'd feared the trip home from Cape Town, it was in fact fine. No lonely night in a hotel, for a start, and I'd arranged to have a meal with my friend on the first night home – very sensible.

My strategy of coping by keeping busy continued, and before I'd hardly had time to land from the South African adventure, I was off again to France to spend Christmas with my parents. On the train to Stansted airport, I reflected on the last few months.

Journal: 16th December 2012

I think I'm running away from feeling lonely and unhappy without Philip around. Even though there are some benefits to him not being around, I really don't like being lonely. It is horrible. The contrast between being with C and B in Cape Town and sharing their space, and my wee flat all on my own is huge. Ugh! Just keep busy, Jane, just keep busy.

It was relatively easy, spending Christmas with just my Mum and Dad, as I'd often spent time with them by myself in France. I couldn't ignore, though, that this second Christmas, there was no one to ring up at home for a chat.

Journal: 26th December 2012

I couldn't go to drinks with their friends. Mum asked me how I was and then offered me a lifeline by saying I didn't need to go, which caused me to burst into tears. It was the kindness. She hugged me and held me while I cried. Then, after they left, I bawled again for a few minutes. Will this ever leave me?

I've felt tearful all day. God, I miss you Philip. I so miss you. There are no other words for it, I suppose. I just miss you. Miss you, miss you, miss you. I miss so much our conversations, and our cuddles. I miss your company, your quiet presence. I'm so glad we had our last year together but, my God, I miss you now. I may like the idea of dates and kisses, but the thought of anything else is pretty ghastly. Although I'd like it to happen sometime. Maybe. None of it makes any difference really. I just feel bereft, in the true and only meaning of the word.

I was still being amazed at the after-effects of his death. I would never have guessed the feelings could last what I was terming 'this long,' even while knowing that just over a year is hardly any length of time at all.

32

Reaching Out To Others

At the beginning of January, 2013, Sally and Andy, old friends from England, paid me a surprise visit. It was a relief to be able to tell the whole story to people who wanted to know the full details of what had happened to Philip, which they hadn't heard.

Journal: 4th January 2013

In telling them the story, I felt very nourished by remembering all the amazing messages and gifts that happened in the last year. Sally said she'd received various messages from her father after he died, and for some reason, that helped me realise that you, Philip, perhaps guided them to me here, today, at this particular time.

So, I hear you. I will turn your blog into an e-book or something like that; I will edit it; I will get it published and out there to as many people as I can.

Philip had felt inspired to write his blog in an attempt to help others on a similar journey, and to address the idea of 'beating cancer' and treating it as the enemy in a war that had a winner and a loser. I also felt very strongly about sharing what we'd been through. Many people had told me I was coping very well with the grief; I knew intuitively that one reason for this was being able to allow the feelings, and I also knew that many people simply cannot do this, or don't know how. So I was moved to help others; it was an extension of the kind of work I'd been doing most of my adult life.

I'd been shocked when I discovered, about this time, that in the little cul-de-sac where I now lived, there were at least three deaths I hadn't known about. I occasionally used to say hallo to the man in the garden opposite, but I hadn't seen him for ages, and never thought anything about it. It never occurred to me that a death might have happened, so I was quite taken aback when a friend told me he'd died several months ago.

"You mean his wife is in there, living all alone now?" I asked.

"Yes, I suppose so. I never see her, she never seems to come out. Occasionally, I see a car in the drive." I was horrified. I knew I had to do something. My own aunt, who now lived alone in southern Scotland, had found it difficult after her husband died, especially as she hadn't had many friends. I couldn't visit her regularly, but I could visit my neighbour. I knocked on the front door of her bungalow one day in January 2013.

"Hallo, I'm Jane. I live in the flats over there, and I was told your husband died in the summer?" She nodded, looking a bit surprised. "I'm in a similar situation as you. My husband died a year ago, and I just wondered how you are, because it's all so different for me, and it must be for you, too."

Fiona did the polite thing and invited me in. It turned out she was 75, had problems with diabetes, couldn't easily walk, and had never learnt to drive. Very different from my own Mum, who was older but had a full life, and whom I thought would manage much better if she was widowed. Fiona had two daughters who visited once a week, and a cousin who also visited regularly. Otherwise she was rattling around in a huge house, alone. As my own coping strategy was keeping busy, I couldn't bear to think of her being alone, day after day, nothing to do, with hardly anyone visiting her.

"Is it all right if I come and visit again, sometime? I know it must be really lonely for you without your husband here. I'd just come once a week or so."

"Yes," she nodded, again looking slightly surprised. I guess not many people had reached out to her in that way.

It wasn't easy. She couldn't go out, because of her various illnesses, so my idea of taking her for a coffee somewhere was a non-starter. She wasn't a great conversationalist; fortunately, I could make up for that. She didn't want to know about books to read; instead, she relied on the doctor who had diagnosed depression, and given her some pills. Depression! Aren't you supposed to be depressed when your husband dies? It sounded mad to me, to be given pills for this, but it did seem good to be able to talk about our husbands. Eventually, she got an assisted living place in a nearby town where one of her daughters lived, and just over a year later she moved.

Still, I was appalled. How many men and women are left to deal with the death of their loved one, their companion, all on their own? I'd no idea, but I knew I needed, and wanted, to do something about helping people deal with death and grief in a healthier way. So in February, when I heard about an afternoon workshop in a nearby town about living and dying well, I arranged to go.

My heart sank when I saw the house where it was to be held; full of new-agey things in the garden and the room. A lovely house, but now I'd completely gone off anything 'deep and meaningful', it wasn't a great sign. Nine others sat in a circle, all women, all with their own stories of why they were interested in death and dying.

As the afternoon wore on it was obvious it was far too soon for me. Feeling utterly furious I had to be there at all, near to tears and in danger of taking it out on these well-intentioned women, none of whom had lost their husbands, I realised it was too soon. Much too soon. I appreciated what they were trying to do – raise awareness about death and dying – and I wanted to do that too, but not now. Not yet.

I left early, to return home and pack away all the stuff for any book that might be written, and forget about it. It was just too soon. I knew I just had to wait, and when the time was right, the urge would be so overwhelming I would simply have to sit down and write. Instead, life was about to present me with a different way of engaging with others than visiting my neighbour.

33
Stepping Out

Apart from the kiss with Dawie in Cape Town, I wasn't in the slightest bit interested in men. In theory, I'd made a list of the qualities I would want in any new relationship; in practice, the very thought of being near someone was ghastly. It didn't stop me looking at all kinds of men, though, and if I found someone attractive, running them by 'The Bedroom Test' as to where I was in relationship to love, to sex, to commitment. All I had to do was imagine them lying beside me in my bed. None had passed The Bedroom Test yet, perhaps not surprisingly, and for some, just imagining them sitting in my living room was enough to put an end to any fantasies.

Did this trouble me? No. Many years earlier, Philip and I'd had one of those conversations that couples often have.

"Of course, we'll probably live long into our old age together, pipe, slippers and rocking-chair-by-the-fire kind of thing," I pondered.

"I've got the slippers already," replied Philip, "but there's no chance of a pipe, or a rocking chair if I have my way. I hate them."

"Let's hope we make it that long. How would you feel if I died before you? It's unlikely to happen because you're so much older than I am, and men usually die younger than women. If you did die before me, though, would you want to have another relationship?"

"I'd hope I would fall in love again, yes, and I'd hope that if I die first, you would, too. I'd really want that for you." So I knew I'd have Philip's blessing, which was soothing. Even if I hadn't, I just couldn't believe I might spend another thirty or even forty years alive and not have another relationship.

After being egged on by a friend, I took another look at a dating site – and another, and another, until finally, daringly, I entered a profile and arranged an initial coffee meeting with a man, at a place half way between where we both lived. This was very different from going out in a foursome with friends, as in Cape Town.

What a disaster. I was too scared to give him my mobile number, so he couldn't text to say he was going to be late. When he did arrive, it was clear he was furious; this was somewhat intimidating, him being a rather large man. He blamed me immediately, even when I apologised, and just to top it all off, I found it almost impossible to understand a very broad Scottish accent! Suffice to say, not only did we not arrange to meet again, but I took down my profile and left the world of internet dating for the time being. I wouldn't venture into it again for quite some time.

Meanwhile, having somewhat rashly accepted an invitation to speak to the local Federation of Complementary Therapists six months previously, the time had come to give the talk. I wished I hadn't offered to speak.

"What am I going to do?" I wailed to my friend. "I'm so scared!"

"You'll be fine, Jane," she reassured me. "Just focus on what you know about presenting from Toastmasters (the public speaking group I had been part of); you're already speaking about something you know a lot about, and then you can invite them to have a free Strategy Session with you at the end."

"Okay." I was a bit glum, but everything she said made sense. "I've entitled it "*Your Mind: Friend or Foe*?" which gives me lots of scope. I suppose I will have to do it, then." I hated letting people down, even though I'd had lots of practice in the past year, but to let people down professionally? That was another matter.

The night of the talk it was very dark, and snowing heavily; in fact the white lines on the main A96 towards Elgin were invisible under a thick blanket of snow. I was so scared, I might easily have given up, except I couldn't even see well enough to consider turning around in the road. Would people turn up? I couldn't imagine anyone coming out in that kind of weather, but I'd underestimated the Highland determination, and the local weather discrepancies. I did eventually arrive, to see twenty people waiting for me.

It was the first time I'd spoken to a group, online or offline, for 18 months. I was nervous, but also felt buoyed by the fact of so many years of experience. As the talk progressed, I began to relax and feel confident again, and in a different way from before: I cared much less than I had ever done about being brilliant. What a relief, and what a load of pressure off my mind. I even enjoyed myself.

More than half signed up for a complimentary Strategy Session, and I left for a relatively easy drive home, with a lot less snow around. Now I was glad I'd acted on the impulse to book myself in for this talk; it had really boosted my confidence in my ability to work. Arriving home, though, brought another horrible first:

Journal: 8th February 2013

No one at home to share all about this amazing evening with. That was sad. I did share it with Deborah via email and I will share it with our business support group tomorrow, but it's not the same. I think this is the first time I've ever done a talk and not had P. either with me, or waiting for me at home. It is sad. Very sad.

Suppose I'd better just go to bed. Sometimes I really do wonder what is the point of it all.

I'd prepared well for that talk, hadn't done any other work that day, and seemed to be able to manage it from an energy point of view, but that didn't last.

Journal: 12th February 2013

I am exhausted. Utterly exhausted. With a headache. Oh, dear. Worked with clients for 2.5 hours this afternoon, was already feeling the effects of that, and then had a Toastmasters committee meeting. Had to leave early.

I am horrified at the physical effect that grief is still having on my body and my capabilities. I had no idea whatsoever. It's a bit alarming. Especially as I've realised I'm not earning nearly enough. Still, what can I do? The best thing is to manage my mind, keep it calm and not let it go into worrying thoughts.

Grief also continued to visit at odd points, which I could never predict in advance, and which I simply learnt to live with.

Journal: 27th February 2013

I had to leave the Pilates class early tonight. Just couldn't stay there. It was all so pointless, and the tears were beginning to come again.

A colleague came out after me, gave me a hug. I was in floods of tears on the way home in the car, and in the flat. God, what is all this? It's been nearly 15 months and it still hurts so badly sometimes. I don't really understand why. Do I need to know why? Not sure.

I do know sometimes I just feel very alone, and I miss you a lot, Philip. A LOT. I guess I just have to go through it. Blast. I think about you a lot. Not always first thing in the morning anymore. Not even all the time, but a lot. Maybe today it was highlighted by having to get the MOT done and discovering I'd been driving without an MOT certificate for 9 months. (An MOT is the UK compulsory annual test for safety and exhaust emissions if your car is over a certain age). *I didn't know that, without one, you're not insured, even if you've got your insurance certificate. I've just been lucky. You would have taken care of these things. Oh, well. I suppose I just have to get on with it. Again.*

34
New Experiences

"There is no 'I' in this body", pronounced Adam, at a Course in Miracles study group evening.

"What?" my ears pricked up. This sounded like something I could relate to, even though, at the same time, it was a very odd sentence.

"Who I am is not this body. Nor am I the emotions that happen in the body, or the thoughts, the feelings, the ideas, the concepts, the language – anything."

Journal: 6th April 2013

It's true. There is no 'I' in this body; you showed me that, Philip. I am so very, very grateful for realising what that means. I'm joining you right now, right NOW, in this moment, because it is only illusory that I am 'stuck' in a body and you are not.

And . . . it's funny! It really is funny that there are so many people earnestly being spiritual seekers and all the time looking away from what they are seeking for. It's like when I got stuck in the toilets at school aged 5, screaming and wailing, terrified I would be locked in there forever, when I was just pushing against the door, instead of pulling it open.

We here on earth have got things all the wrong way round, completely back to front. Maybe we are all pushing against the door of enlightenment, instead of simply opening it towards us. It's good to have a conversation with Adam regarding that. He has been diagnosed with MS, and doesn't know how it will affect him yet. Nothing like that to encourage you to live in the moment.

I was also reading about the idea of life being a story.

Journal: mid April 2013

I'm flirting with the idea that this is just the next chapter, or even part of a chapter, in the story of 'life as it inhabits the body labelled Jane Duncan Rogers'.

If life really IS a story, with individual lives being smaller stories within the large, then everyone is participating in one great big story called The World. Then life itself forms into various different energy balls, shaping what we appear to see before us – a tree, the sky, clouds, the tarmac, a car, our friend, a mug – anything.

And if we really are life itself, and part of it is currently shaped into a human-body-energy-ball identified as Jane Duncan Rogers, then it seems obvious to me that there is understandably a lot of attachment to being this particular person.

So if a particular body, with all its characteristics, personality, and history is a novel – not like a novel, but IS a novel – then, when the body dies, it's just like coming to the end of a novel. To take this metaphor further, when I read a novel, I want to know all the ins and outs of the characters in it;

I WANT there to be drama and suspense and a plot and not knowing what is going to happen in the next chapter. It's boring otherwise. Readers actually LIKE the story: it's entertainment, it's enjoyable – it's not as much fun without the drama of the story.

Without all those ups and downs, I'd just skip to the end after reading the beginning bit, to find out what happened, but we hardly ever do that when reading a novel, because it spoils the story. However, that's exactly what I appear to be wanting to do now, in life: skip to the end, skip to the bit where everything is revealed, and I can finally relax. Just like one does at the end of an emotional journey through a novel. Mad!

Still, could it be that life is MEANT to be full of ups and downs and don't knows, that you are MEANT to be in the moment, experiencing them? Meeting those challenges as best as possible, while knowing they're just another chapter in the story? Then the point would be to enjoy the story, not just hurry through to the ending.

Oh, this is odd! I won't be able to read a novel in the same way ever again!

However, I LIKE the idea we could all be pretending, that we are all in a great, big, fantasy storyland, having convinced ourselves it is serious and meaningful, and there is meant to be a big purpose in being alive. It seems to me extremely funny that we humans are so earnest in our endeavours, that we take life so seriously, that we really believe ourselves. When it isn't like that at all!

Around this time, I also began to notice the value judgments that humans put on things in a different way. Walking through the woods one day, I noticed a thought in my mind:

"Oh, these woods are so beautiful!" The value judgment was 'beauty.' That reminded me of an experience some years previously, on a workshop.

"I'm having a bit of trouble walking around the campus," I shared one morning. "This place is known world-wide for its beauty, its dedication to love, and its expression of that in all kinds of creative ways. However, I went for a walk today and discovered some areas that are obviously just dumps for people's rubbish. That's at odds with the message you're giving out."

"Yes," acknowledged the group leader, "I know what you mean; I have trouble with that too. However, beauty really is in the eye of the beholder: what is one person's idea of beauty, is another's sore spot. What's more, it's evident that beauty is just a value judgment. We tend to prefer beauty to ugliness, but maybe that object you are looking at is neither beautiful or ugly; maybe it just is."

"Oh . . . yeah," I spoke slowly. "It's me that has the experience, of beauty – which makes me feel warm and fuzzy – and ugliness – which makes me contract a bit and feel sad. It's me that is putting this label on something that actually just simply exists."

There was silence as the group listened, and we all took this in. "I might as well label at least most of what I look at as beautiful then, as that's going to make me feel better."

It's a simple idea, and doesn't even begin to get into the value judgments of wrong and right, but I found it liberating, too, just like the idea of life being a novel. The whole theme throughout the last 18 months or so had been me exploring what being 'in a body' meant, and what is this 'I' we talk about. An expanded understanding of all this was happening.

*

Around this time, paradoxically, I also started to embrace the physical body much more. I'd joined a Body Confidence course being held locally, and was benefitting a lot from that: the course was more along the lines of accepting and appreciating my body as it is, rather than trying to lose weight, and only then liking what I saw in the mirror each morning.

I composed the 'I Love My Body' song, sung to the tune of 'Summertime,' which I sang in the shower every morning for a few months. The motivation for this had come from hearing a quote from Jac O'Keeffe: "*to let go of the idea of the body, you have to first have fully claimed it,*" and my song was part of me claiming my own body more fully. Another element was rather more physical.

"Have you heard of the 5 x 50 challenge?" asked a colleague one evening at the Body Confidence course.

"No." I spoke somewhat cautiously, not at all sure what she was talking about. It sounded like a big deal.

"I think you'd love it. I did it last year: you simply commit to running, walking or cycling for 5ks per day for 50 days."

"50 days!" I exclaimed. "Without any break, you mean?"

"No, the whole point is you do it whether you feel like it or not. After a while, you begin to really reap the benefits of exercise, and before you know it, you actually WANT to go out and exercise every day. It's a nationwide thing; lots of people will be doing it, and you can join my team if you like, meaning we can support each other."

Once again, I was surprised by my answer.

"That sounds fun. Put me down. When do we start?"

So began a period where I was enjoying the physicality of my body far more than ever before, while at the same time exploring how much more we are than just bodies.

What else was I doing that was new? Everywhere I went, there seemed to be opportunities, perhaps because I had deliberately decided to say yes to anything that showed up, and to consciously explore what I might like doing. I'd been shocked at how many times I'd said, "I don't know if I like that or not – we never did it because Philip didn't like it." Which makes him sound like a tyrant, but perhaps it was more because I just didn't feel strongly enough about whatever it was.

I was changing that now. I ventured out into the singing world; I took up the 5 x 50 challenge; I started to love my body as it is, and I also dyed my hair, for only the second time in my life. I'd had streaks put in for the first time while in Cape Town, just for a laugh. This time, though, I went the whole hog and became purple coloured overnight. Alarming! Others seemed to like it, though, and again, it was just plain, ordinary fun.

I also began silent sitting regularly. More commonly known as meditation, it was a lot easier to think of simply sitting in silence, as by now the word meditation had lots of connotations for me, not all of them positive. I'd tried various kinds over the years, practiced them more off than on for short periods of time, and always felt vaguely guilty that I 'should' be doing more.

I'm fortunate here in belonging to the New Findhorn Association – the organisation associated with the Findhorn Foundation – and that allows me to take part in various activities, one of which is meditation in their meditation sanctuaries. These are places that have been used every day for over 50 years for meditative purposes. It's only a walk of ten minutes or so through the woods to the nearest one from me, and so I began sitting at 6:30 a.m. most mornings, except Sunday, for an hour, along with a handful of others.

Again, surprisingly, I found I was loving it. Something had changed: no longer was I 'trying not to have thoughts,' or to 'meditate.' Instead, I began using my own Place of Peace meditation[7], and then simply sitting silently, finding it easier and easier to drop into a place of stillness and peace. It was a wonderful way to start my days.

Books were also having a profound impact. I've mentioned a couple of them already, but there was another one around this time, *Busting Loose from the Money Game* by Robert Scheinfeld, which seemed to be addressing the very things I'd been learning about in my non-duality studies. It was through him I first encountered the idea we are all just living a story. That who we really are is something – not even a thing – that plays The Human Game, and within that context, a series of smaller games, demonstrated by our roles in life. I was telling a friend about it.

"What, you mean you're playing a game called 'Being a Grieving Widow?'

"Yes, and a few others, too: 'Living Alone,' 'Running A Business,' and, of course, the 'Not Part of the Mothers Club' game."

"Mmm. So, then I must be playing a game called 'Being a Teacher.'

"Yes, that's the idea."

---

7 The Place of Peace meditation is available at www.giftedbygrief.com/meditation

"I'm also playing other games called 'Wondering What My Purpose Is' 'Struggling with Money,' and 'Being Positive.'

"Yes! It's amazing, isn't it? But to be honest, there's something in here that feels completely right to me." This way of thinking enabled me to feel a lot lighter about life. It's not everyone's cup of tea, this, but it did really help me, especially given the unusual experiences I'd been having. Plus, if you think like this, then it is easier to change the rules by which you play the game, simply by how you think about it.

35
Birth of Wild Wisdom

Trusting my intuition much more, I responded to a Facebook post from a business coach named Lisa Berkowitz, offering a free consultation. I was motivated by feeling I had to do something about my long-term financial situation. Despite the reprieve from the lump sum, I was still facing a large mortgage debt with no foreseeable way to pay it off, and the time for that felt ominously close. Something had to shift, otherwise repossession would be on the cards. However, this prompted some poignant thoughts:

Journal: 23rd March 2013

It'll be fun doing the coaching, but she'll ask me what I want, and what on earth is that?

I wouldn't care if I went to sleep and didn't wake up. (Of course I wouldn't, because I would be asleep and not know anything about it!) It's not because I want to die, though. Or live. It just doesn't seem to matter that much. I've already had a good life.

Is there anything to live for? Not particularly, but there's no real reason to die either. So how will I answer that question,

> *'What do you want?' Especially when the one thing I want is impossible – Philip back. A strong and healthy Philip.*

In the coaching world, you're often asked what it is you want, and encouraged to apply yourself with enthusiasm and the support of the coach to do the things necessary to achieve that. To be honest, that thought wasn't appealing at all, so why on earth did I sign up? I just knew I had to do something different, in order to begin to see change happening in my life; intuitively it felt right.

With Lisa's encouragement, I ventured into holding a group again. It was only one conference call for the people on my mailing list. It was entitled 'Bringing Spirit into Business,' and it felt highly significant; I was stepping out into the world again. It went well, and I was very pleased afterwards. I had been hugely nervous and it had taken a great deal of courage to do it despite my anxiety.

"I've been dancing to the Diana Ross song, 'I'm Coming Out!,' and I've drawn this great picture of me doing just that!"[8] I exclaimed in an early coaching session.

"That's wonderful, Jane; congratulations!" Lisa praised me, smiling.

"I feel I've been waiting and waiting, and now I want to move forward." She worked with me to do this. Then one day, almost as a throwaway line at the end of a session, she said,

"Something's just popped into my head; I wonder if it's time to change the name of your business, from RichThinkers to something else? Just a thought. Ponder on it and see what you think." I didn't need to think for any length of time at all.

---

8 You can see this picture at www.giftedbygrief.com/comingout

"You've just hit the nail on the head; I've been wondering that myself. RichThinkers is the old me, and I feel so different. I need that to be reflected in my work. Thank you!"

Sometime after that, I was awake again in the wee small hours. The words 'wild and cheeky wisdom' were floating around in my head, and I just knew in my bones these would be important somehow in my work. That's how the full rebrand of my coaching business happened: the word 'cheeky' was dropped, as it has too many different meanings in different countries, but Wild Wisdom Ltd emerged from this, and began to slowly take shape in the form of a new website during the latter part of 2013. A huge part of this was an explosion of creativity in the form of doodling.

As a kid, I'd been mad about horses. I also loved drawing, and was encouraged by my parents, who are both artists. Whenever I was sitting still, my crayons, paints, or felt pens would be with me, and I'd be drawing horses. I copied them, cartooned them, I drew them live. When I got bored with horses, I drew people's faces, mostly ones from my imagination.

At school, I had doodled patterns of one shape or another, along with horses and faces, all over my notebooks, and it continued into university. In fact, I discovered I could listen to lectures much more easily if my hands were occupied with doodling.

Occasionally, people sitting next to me would comment on what a lovely drawing I was doing. On Jac's French retreat, I'd taken to drawing profile sketches of others in the seminar, occasionally catching enough of a likeness for others to recognise who it was.

"Jane, you should be doing these to sell them. They're brilliant!" exclaimed one person.

"Why don't you do greetings cards?" asked another.

"You could use these in your new website." *That* was the comment I liked the best, once I'd got used to the idea that people liked these doodle drawings, thought they were valuable, and wanted to see more of them.

This doodling I'd been doing had been with me so long, I'd taken it completely for granted. However, it became obvious – even to me – that embracing this particular form of creativity was part of my own wild wisdom, and needed to be out there more.

Once I'd adjusted to this idea, I was delighted. It meant I got to doodle more, the general doodling developed into doodle drawings, and I had great fun creating my new website. What I really loved, though, was that because I loved them, and loved doing them, what other people said or thought mattered less. However, it still took courage to be vulnerable and 'come out to the world' in this way, all alone, without the man who had been not just my husband but also my business partner. But there was no doubt about it: I was moving on.

Journal: Tuesday 9th April 2013

> *At Anna's. I've forgotten to bring my photo of Philip. Oh, dear. Or maybe it's good. Or even just 'oh.' No judgments, Jane.*

I took this to be highly significant, despite the idea of no judgments. It meant I was moving forward into life alone without Philip. I didn't need the photo, and anyway, at home, the photos had been going up and down like yo-yos: I veered between soft feelings of love looking at him, fury I had to look at a photo of him at all, and tears of pain and sadness that it had all happened. So forgetting the photo was, indeed, perhaps a good thing.

Others might have a judgment about this. As there weren't that many people coming to visit me at home, it didn't bother me. What they thought wouldn't have bothered me anyway, as this was one of the things that clearly was changing: I cared far less what people thought of me and my actions. What a relief that was, given that I could never predict others' actions, thoughts or behaviour in any case.

I'd noticed this more and more, since being in the hospital with Philip. I'd had to take such a stand there on occasion, in order to get my way around what treatment he was having, that I'd somehow, without noticing it, begun to drop my fear and respect for authority. I could listen, instead, to my own intuition and wisdom – and then act on it. This trait had been coming out in regard to photos being displayed, hidden, and then displayed again, and it was coming out again in relation to the doodle drawings.

It also took the form of me sharing on Facebook – something I'd done little of previously – when it was the second anniversary since Philip died of when we had had our first date. We'd always celebrated this more than our wedding as it felt much more significant.

Journal: 20th April 2013

Wow, Philip. Yesterday I posted in Facebook about it being 22 years ago when we had our first date (remember?) and loads of people commented and over 60 people liked it! I feel so blessed, it's wonderful.

I'm staying with Lisa (friend Lisa) tonight; David is away, so she's on her own. It's amazing how they have invited me into their 'family' so much. They describe themselves as my brother and sister, and they do feel like that. It's very comfortable. We went to see Jane Siberry, a musician of a kind. The most amazing thing about her is she is a bit off the wall and really inhabits that! I found her so inspiring, found myself wondering how on earth I can be more ME! I'm sure you would approve.

Plus – I am now a woman who has doubled her prices. Lisa my coach has helped me. And I feel different! Very different. I think it would have been great if I'd been more financially successful when you were alive, but maybe it doesn't matter that you aren't.

Maybe nothing matters much, other than what we think matters. Because if you don't mind about something, then it doesn't matter what happens, does it? It's so simple, that. Too simple for the ego!

I do miss our conversations, though. Ah, well. It doesn't stop me loving you. That is still here, probably always will be. Perhaps the best way I can love you is to live my life as fully as possible, stepping right up and in and out to the world fully, in a way I have never done before.

Listening wasn't happening much at this time, but one day, these words came through:

> *"Come wander in the grounds of Peace. Wander without direction or intent. Wander as Love itself, simply being, and therefore being Love.*
>
> *Learning about stillness and safety is important, for your sense of safety and security comes from here and nowhere else. Resting here, the breathing becomes the breath of life itself through a body. Breathing becomes the deliverance of beauty itself.*
>
> *Simply be still. Stillness. All else comes and goes, with and around stillness, but stillness itself never falters. It cannot. For it just IS."*

A few days later, during meditation, more Listening came:

28th May, in the sanctuary.

"Death is but a passing from one form to another without fear or clinging. As easy as moving through a doorway from one room to another, and as lacking in fear. So come to this doorway when you are ready to anoint and bless your true Self. Stillness is the secret passage through which this journey is made, and indeed is what life is made of, in essence."

I began to practice remembering this idea of stillness, and then stopping and being still at odd moments during my days. This really helped whenever I felt the shock of Philip's death.

Journal: 29th May 2013

Almost every day, I still feel a bit shocked I am living alone. It was a reasonable film I watched tonight, but it wasn't reasonable having no one to talk about it with after. No wonder I don't watch that many films.

I had heard that many people find themselves dreaming of the person who has died, and I'd been hoping this would happen for me, too. In fact, it was very rare I had a dream with Philip in it, but there was one that stood out:

Journal: 1st June 2013

Dream: 19 months exactly since he died.

I was in bed somewhere, a double bed. I'd seen a friend earlier, it was a sort of community holiday place. I'd been here before and had found someone had left out my camera and something else which I must have left behind. I was in a kind of dorm and a man was on the bed beside me. I thought,

"I hope he knows this is MY bed and isn't going to try and have it for himself."

As I tried to get up, I realised he was holding me, and I struggled a bit and turned round to see it was Philip, but younger and with dark hair with single strands of red and gold. He said, "I've come back to love you" and then something about him not being able to do this in the old body. I was shocked and amazed and delighted and disbelieving all at once.

I asked him how he had managed, did he have money to buy food. Then I saw that there were lots of little stones coming out of his mouth. We kissed, and then I had a stone or two in my mouth and I had to tell him it wasn't quite right. I woke feeling buoyant, feeling loved.

It was so nice to be touched and held again. And feel loved! It felt so real, so real! I knew there was something not quite right though.

This dream sustained me for quite a time; I didn't analyse it, simply enjoyed the memory of the feeling within it, deliberately using moments of sadness that it hadn't been true as a spur to remembering times that had been wonderful.

36
More Letting Go

I'd been in touch with Wayne Liquorman, author of *Enlightenment is Not What You Think*, and invited him to come to Findhorn to give a workshop. On the Saturday evening of that weekend, I went out for dinner with him and his wife, and another couple. It was enjoyable, although I didn't talk much.

Journal: 8th June 2013

Home again and I'm feeling deflated. What causes that? It would appear, on the surface, it's because we had a nice time together, and now I'm on my own again. But actually, it's more than that.

Who is it who thinks thoughts? This thought 'I'm deflated'? What causes the thoughts to be thoughts? Who is it that is feeling deflated? It's not 'me'. The feelings just happen, and then meaning is ascribed to them. And always underneath and beyond is the peace. Which doesn't seem to have much to do with the thoughts or feelings, even.

Still, who is the author of these thoughts? I've spent my life trying to lessen the 'bad' thoughts and become more 'good.' That's self-improvement for you. However, now the sugges-

tion is that I never had the thoughts in the first place! Well, who did then? This is really doing my head in.

I had more questions than anything during this period. I'd even begun to question the validity of The Listening, which was distressing. Obviously, I was changing in other ways than just in the rebranding into Wild Wisdom, the loving of new activities, and my new living accommodation. Rather, these seemed to be the manifestation of inner changes, as I explored more and more what was actually inhabiting this 'bag' that was my body.

And then there were other activities I was forced to question, too.

Journal: 10th June 2013

I went to Knockando Woollen Mill today on my own. Beautiful day, and yet I felt sadly aware of my single status, because this was the sort of thing we would have done together. I suppose I need to find different things to do that are fun, not just doing the things we used to do.

This was in the wake of having had a day out with a male friend who was attracted to me. Although I didn't return his feelings, I did like him and we often had a good laugh together. During the summer we agreed to go out for a day, exploring along the coast. He picked me up in his car and I was excited.

"I've never driven this far along the coast before, and it's so stunningly beautiful!" I exclaimed.

"Yes, and look!" he pointed to a pile of rocks on the sandy beach.

"They're seals, not rocks!" I cried out. And indeed they were: basking in the sun, not far from the road, enjoying themselves, just as we were. We stood at the side of the road taking photos, feeling the warm sunshine on our faces, and simply enjoying the delights of a beautiful summer's day.

Later, over lunch in Cullen, I began to feel a bit odd; not physically, but just not quite as engaged. I didn't say anything, as I didn't know what was happening. Eventually, we walked down to the beach, and sat in the sand, watching families having fun; children playing in the water, teenagers messing about with a football, all just enjoying themselves in the lovely warm sunshine.

"Something isn't quite right anymore," I eventually said, in a quiet voice. "I don't know what it is, but I'm wondering, perhaps, could we go home?" I looked at my friend, feeling rather vulnerable, as it was only early afternoon. He looked disappointed, but we got our stuff together and walked slowly back along the beach to the car.

On the way home, I felt tearful and suddenly it all came out.

"You're not Philip!" I shouted, in the midst of tears, while we were driving along. "I know you're not, I know he can never come back, but it just feels all wrong doing this kind of thing with you sitting there, and not him."

My dear friend. He took all this very well. It can't have been nice to be told you were not the right person.

I felt like I'd been doing something I knew from my previous life. Philip and I loved exploring, pottering about, checking out a town here, a visitor attraction there, and exclaiming over the various discoveries. He would have sat somewhere on the beach while I paddled in the sea. There would have been an easiness and pleasure about it all, and while I had this to some degree with my friend, it just wasn't the same. While the setting looked the same on the outside, the characters on the inside were different.

I had to admit, it was too soon to be doing things Philip and I used to do together. I needed to find other ways of spending time with friends, and just let that be in the past. Hence the visit to Knockando on my own, and then, later that summer, another visit of a completely different kind to somewhere where Philip would never have gone.

"Jane, I've had the most amazing experience!" Keri, mother of Becky, sounded incredible, given she had lost her eldest daughter just over a year previously.

"Someone told me about a medium in the Cotswolds, so I went to visit her. It's a very beautiful place, she's incredible, but the best bit is I found myself able to be in touch with Becky again, and hear that she's doing well." I wasn't surprised to hear this, as Keri had always been quite psychic. Now, in the context of Philip dying, my ears really did prick up.

"How can I find out about her? Could I go too? What does she actually do?"

"She's written a couple of books, and I can send you her website address." Thus I began to explore in depth another way of being in touch with my dead husband.

I gasped as I drove into the parking area of the Cotswold Healing Retreat later in the summer. I saw a beautiful honey-coloured stone house with two magnificent cedar and beech trees on the front lawn. Huge, spreading, yet somehow very calming. As soon as I'd settled in, I went for a walk.

Stopping on the slope of a flower-filled meadow to look back over a green and lush valley, I had a very strong sense that Philip was there. Turning, I saw a big male fox, just a few feet away, trotting casually back into the woods. This was startling because I knew it was extremely unusual to see foxes at this time of day. It felt like a special visitation, a sign from Philip.

"Philip!" I cried out, "You're here!"

No answer in words, but I felt the sense of being deeply, deeply loved as I continued on up the valley.

I had prepared questions for Louisa, the healer and psychic, who had given over the family farmhouse to the needs of this Retreat Centre, while she herself lived in a converted stable block on the other side of the driveway. Although we didn't have an actual appointment time for the following day, I reminded myself to trust it would all work out perfectly. The next morning I was down in the kitchen before anyone else.

The back door opened. "Good morning. You're up bright and early!" Louisa was cheerful. "You must be Jane."

"Yes; nice to meet you," I replied, shaking her hand.

"I've just brought over these eggs from the hens; do help yourself if you'd like one."

"Thank you, how lovely! Will I be able to see you later this morning? Only I have to leave late afternoon."

"Why not meet me on the bench in front of my house at 10:30 a.m. then?" It looked as though it was going to be another beautiful day, so sitting outside was very appealing.

"There's a man just behind you, over there on your right," she said, as I sat down on the bench. I couldn't sense that specifically, but I still had this strong sense of Philip being around generally.

"He's got a lovely smile; he's tall, and with a gentle energy."

"That sounds like my husband. Is he okay?" I asked her.

"Yes; it wasn't an easy time and he's still working it all out, but he's all right. Was he involved with some kind of guru?"

"Yes!" I exclaimed. Wow. She must know her stuff. She knew nothing about me, or him. Only that I'd had a husband who'd died, and was related to one of her previous visitors.

"Well, he's trying to work it all out now; he somehow was wanting to be a guru-like figure himself after he left the ashram, except he never fully understood the idea of self and non-self. So he's still trying to sort that one out."

"Did he have a life review before he actually left his body?"

"Yes, and he's still having it; he's reeling a bit from the wrongly-directed effort he was making during his life. He's realised he wasn't as enlightened as he thought he was, and he has regrets about that."

"Oh, the poor thing." I recognised this, and it made sense to me.

"His body came to the end of its journey; he'd been holding himself back. However, your relationship can continue, unhampered by both being in a body. In fact, he wants to help you, and it's your job to receive his help now. What will assist you with that is stopping remembering the suffering in the hospital. Focus instead on the beautiful love and the other good parts of your relationship; in fact, use any memories that come up which are about pain and suffering as a signal meaning it's time to deliberately focus on a beautiful memory."

These words made a huge impact on me; I knew this truth instinctively, I'd been practicing deliberately choosing lovely memories to some degree, and now I realised the importance of thinking like this more consistently.

We talked more about my life, and she strongly emphasised doing what was right for me, and only that, and especially acting on my intuition.

In my journal, I doodled:

I can accept and embrace the gift of his death

This was the first time I referred to him dying as a gift. It sounded odd but it felt perfect. And still, I missed him.

Journal: 24th July 2013

Missing you, Philip.

Sometimes it just hits me, like a punch or a wave. Horrible.

I miss our conversations. I miss your presence. I miss the feeling of companionship. I miss the connection we had. I miss the love, I miss your body next to mine in bed. I feel so alone without you.

Alongside all of this, I was still continuing to say yes to all kinds of unexpected and delightful opportunities, and doing things I'd never done before, like skinny dipping in the Findhorn River, with a friend. Skinny dipping! I would never have done that before, even if I'd been on my own, let alone with a friend.

Journal: 3rd August 2013

Walking home from the shops, I suddenly realised again that P only ever looked like he was in a body. He is in fact still here, and I can relate to him as the truth of that, so long as I am not thinking 'I am a body', or limiting myself to thinking he was a body.

I still find myself wondering, though, if he really did die. If it all really happened. It just seems so horrific. He was too young to die and I get so angry when I see doddery old people around – how come they get to still be alive? It's not fair. I get particularly furious when I see a couple, especially an older one, walking around holding hands. That's not fair either. Fuck! I'm going round and round with the same old thoughts about this. Go slowly, Jane. Just go tenderly and slowly.

I appeared to be on a journey of feeling peace and loving connection, and at the same time feeling all the other ordinary emotions that belong to the human body, with all its physical, emotional and mental frailties.

37

Getting Used To It

Journal: 13th August 2013

I've been waiting for the grief to stop. To end.

It doesn't.

It's just there.

Sometimes coming to the forefront and sometimes not.

I've been imagining there would be an end to the sudden tears

The overwhelming rage

The wondering if it all really happened

The disbelief that it happened at all.

Apparently not.

I've been imagining I will be whole again someday.

But I've forgotten – I already am.

Whole includes rage, tears, grief.

Bewilderment, shock, hurt.

Loneliness, guilt, shame, fear, anxiety.

And all surrounded by love.

Philip, I wish you hadn't had to die.

I wish we had been able to transform our relationship in another way.
I wish you had never got cancer in the first place.
I wish it had all been different.
And it isn't.
It's just the way it is, and was the way it was.
My life now includes all this.
I cannot just put it behind me, for it did happen.
It IS part of who I am now.
Someone told me, "It never really goes, but the time between the distraught feelings expands, as you have probably noticed." Yes. That is true. I suppose that is what is called 'getting used to it'.

This was all still alongside the constant exploration of what thoughts and feelings actually are: where they come from metaphysically; who am 'I' if not a body/emotions/thoughts/feelings. Indeed, what and who was Philip? The impact of seeing that empty 'bag' that had been him, just lying on the hospital bed, was enormous and very far-reaching.

I could talk about this sort of thing with my friend, Brian.

"Brian, you know all feelings come and go?"

"Ye-e-e-s," he replied, waiting to see what was coming next.

"Well, we as human beings seem to want to hold onto the feelings that we like – such as happiness, peace, joy, laughter, all those – but we want to push away those feelings we don't like, like sadness, anger, fear and so on. However, what if we just noticed that if we do nothing with them, they *all* tend to just come and go?"

"You mean, if you're not attached to any feeling?"

"Yes. Easier said than done, I know, but it makes sense. I've been noticing that, for instance, fear seems to stick around a whole lot more when I am trying *not* to feel it. That hasn't been happening that much, actually, as I made a conscious decision early on in this process to just feel whatever was presenting itself. This has meant there's a kind of cleanliness about the feelings, like they are just being themselves, without any story or meaning attached to them. And when that happens, they can then visit fully, so to speak, and then also leave fully."

"Mmm. I see what you mean," responded Brian thoughtfully.

"Here's another thing: all thoughts come and go, too; it's not just feelings. In fact, thoughts come and go a lot! But then surely that means that both thoughts and feelings are unreliable, and don't mean anything, unless I give them meaning?"

"Okay, carry on; I think I see where you're going."

"The thing is, who is it that gives them meaning? It must be the same 'I' as thought them. Or do thoughts not really 'belong' to anyone or anything? I don't know really, but I do know that the mind will find a satisfying meaning for anything, which is fine, except that it's always only *temporarily* satisfying. And then I'm back on the quest for wanting to find whatever 'it' is."

"Yes. And what is it you want to find?"

"True peace. Freedom from the tyranny of the mind. Permanently."

Not asking for much then.

Journal: 20th August 2013

I am terrified of stopping. Not just stopping 'doing', but stopping being who I think I am. Stopping being a woman in mourning. Stopping being on a personal growth path. Stopping being who I appear to be. Stopping exploring, stopping finding meaning, stopping finding fulfillment, and stopping seeking freedom, liberation and enlightenment.

I do not know what I am doing – and yet I know I do not want to stop not knowing what I am doing.

Later that same day:

Been to the spa with some girlfriends. What is this thing about being deflated, which means I must have been inflated? I've had a lovely day at the spa, but I've come down again now I'm home, just like that evening with Wayne. It feels like a balloon that has slowly been let down. All the air has gone out of me.

Truth: deflation belongs to mind or ego. I am not mind, I am simply peace and presence.

Therefore I am not deflated. The real 'I' cannot inflate nor deflate. The challenge here is in the use of 'I'. Language to describe these concepts is so limited! In one moment, that word 'I' is being used to describe what the mind thinks 'I' is, and in the next sentence it's being used to describe another meaning to 'I' entirely. Aaaagh!

There were other musings which helped to have me simply be here now:

Journal: 22nd August 2013

I used to think my life had meaning because of Philip, and now there's no meaning because he's not physically here. But now I think there's no meaning in life other than what you give it. So I might as well enjoy myself, as it's more fun that way. That reminds me, Philip, of that conversation we had so early on in our relationship, when I asked you what you thought the meaning of life was. You pondered and then came out with 'to enjoy yourself' – and I was furious! So angry, because it was just too simple, too easy. However, now I think that myself. What irony!

The truth is . . . 'I' am not my feelings or thoughts. 'I' am just Love itself. Better get on with expressing that, then.

Later that month, I noted a conversation with Philip in my journal.

Journal: 29th August 2013

Philip, are you trying to get through to me?

Yes, I'm here

Wow. How do I know it's you?

You know, Jane, you just know. And there's no need to question it.

All right, all right! That sounds like you! Why have you come?

Because you need my support at the moment, to keep you calm and on track, so you don't wander off into too much 'doing.' Specifically, it is important – very important – to listen and respond to your body. Trust it. It knows what is needed. It's good you can hear me.

Well, I feel supported. Were you around when I was having lunch with Deborah earlier?

Yes, and you sensed me, and you were right about the love. She and I were siblings in a previous life, and you our close cousin. That is why the connection was so easy in this one. There is a wealth of energetic history between us.

Wow. It IS lovely with her.

Yes. Now I want you to listen. You are, indeed, stepping into a different lifestyle. This is a very good thing, and I

can help you in it. Trusting the moments when you sense I am around is important. For I will be bringing a connective thread of energy that will prove useful. You've been practicing with acting on your impulses and intuitions and this is also good.

Oh. He has gone again. I suppose that's okay. Did it all happen though?

This conversation began an extraordinary month of movement and change. I joined Jac O'Keeffe's new online satsang forum, meaning I had a place to ask all my questions about thoughts, feelings and who 'I' was. Much of the inspiration for my work as the Wild Wisdom coach came to me, along with new clients and new ideas for programmes.

Listening played a part, too:

3rd September 2013

"Into the peace you enter, and therefore enter into the flow itself. This flow is, indeed, that which you are. This flow takes the body called Jane along with it, and your only job is to allow this to happen, without hanging onto branches, trying to cling onto stones, or stop the flow in any way. Know that these are metaphors for both life and business. Be the flow now. No love, no nothing, no feeling. Simply flow."

Still, I was affected by shock:

Journal: 17th September 2013

I was unpacking this evening and suddenly was overwhelmed with tears when I realised I would never see P again. The shock! And I completely forgot any notion of peace, stillness, whatever. I am criticising myself for still feeling like this after nearly two years.

I had expected, initially, to feel better after the first six months since he died. Why was I giving myself deadlines? It was very difficult to discover that I actually felt worse in some respects, as the reality of what happened began to sink in, and others just got on with their lives. My friend who lived in the flat above mine was a great resource at this time: her husband had died some seven years previously.

"Jane, six months is nothing! It'll take perhaps two years before you begin to feel on an even keel again. It took me at least that long." Secretly, I thought that couldn't possibly be true – even while knowing she could be right. At that stage, I simply couldn't bear the idea that the agonising pain I sometimes found myself in would continue for so long.

The one-year anniversary came and went and I felt . . . not better, but different. And here it was now, nearly two years since he died, and I was still being shocked. In fact, I was shocked that I was shocked. However, it wasn't helpful to be criticising myself. By this time, although there were moments of overwhelming grief, they were much, much less frequent. Perhaps this shock was a precursor to what was to happen next.

38
Who Manifests?

Worry about money had grabbed me again. The inner voice in my head spoke in a very convincing manner.

"Jane, what are you going to do? It's just not working that well. You can use the affirmation 'I've always had enough, I have enough right now, I will have enough' as much as you like, and you can even believe the first two bits, but that last one, 'I will have enough' – how do you know that? Better get clear about what to do. Come on, you know how to do that, just get on with it!"

The perennial problem of solo professionals is that if you can't or don't work, the money stops coming in. Not that this had ever been a problem before; in fact there *had* always been enough money. The after-effects of grief, coming in such a way that I was forced to stop working in my normal manner, made me fully realise the value of having systems in place that can be operated by anyone.

The normal business world says, 'Make a plan. Execute it. Work hard and consistently, and you will get where you want to go.' For a large portion of my life, I had tried to live it like this. But my whole being was now revolting against that. Over the course of my life, I had achieved goals, but also had numerous goals which had not been fulfilled for various reasons. The 'traditional business philosophy' also brought into question the idea of the Law of Attraction.

This had been a huge point of debate over the years between myself and Philip. We simply could not agree. The Law of Attraction was famously described in a best-selling book called The Secret. I'd been very much a proponent of this kind of 'like attracts like' thinking, whereby directing your thoughts and feelings, you can affect the outcome of events around you. The vibrational energy of those thoughts and feelings attracts corresponding events and circumstances that are a match at that level of frequency.

For instance, if you consistently think fearful thoughts, and feel afraid, you'll be more likely to attract what you're afraid of. Or if you're angry, and thinking angry thoughts, then you're more likely to attract events and circumstances that reflect those thoughts and feelings, such as an angry neighbour, or a situation of conflict.

In *The Secret*, author Rhonda Byrne posited that desirable outcomes such as health, wealth and happiness can be attracted in this way simply by changing your thoughts and feelings. This seemed potent, given what Philip and I had been dealing with.

When *The Secret* was published, these ideas were not new to me; I'd learnt them first when I was running study groups based on Louise L. Hay's famous book *You Can Heal Your Life,*® way back in the '80s, and I'd been putting them into practice sporadically in my own life. Philip and I had argued about it. A conversation would go along these lines:

"It just seems too harsh for me," brooded Philip, "this idea that just by changing your thoughts and feelings, you can get better – then if you don't get better, it's your own fault."

"It's not just changing your thoughts and feelings, you know. Louise Hay did recover from cancer, but she did all sorts of other things as well, at all levels – physical, emotional, spiritual, mental – they are all just as important."

"That's not what the Law of Attraction says, though. It says you can change just by changing your thoughts and feelings."

"Well, what about that time when we wanted to sell the clinic? Look at all the things I did to keep my mind focused on a positive outcome. And look at what happened when I wanted to buy a saxophone and had no money!"

I was referring to an occasion when I'd drawn a life-size picture of a saxophone, created a space for it in our sitting room, put the picture up, and affirmed that one like this would come my way. A few days later I'd seen a 'for sale' ad in the local supermarket for a tenor sax. I agreed to buy it, even though I had no money. The next day, a surprise cheque from my great-aunt came through the post for more than enough to buy the saxophone. I was chuffed.

"That's evidence the Law of Attraction does work," I grinned enthusiastically.

"Yes, but what about all the times when it hasn't worked?" he came back at me strongly.

"Obviously, I didn't do it well enough," was my retort. The truth was, I didn't have a clue why sometimes this kind of positive, affirmative behaviour worked, and sometimes it didn't, even though it seemed I was doing all the same things as before. This undermined how I felt about the whole thing, but I basically ignored these times, assuming I was lacking in my application of the principles, and we continued to argue about it from time to time.

When cancer came to visit, everything was different. How could I possibly have attracted this? How could Philip? How could anyone? No one in their right mind would consciously do that, but could they really be doing it unconsciously? And how could anyone be so cruel as to say 'He created this from the way he was thinking and feeling?' No one ever mentioned anything to either of us directly along these lines, but I had heard some people say it about others. Now that kind of thinking seemed far too simplistic.

So I was stopped in my tracks with my Law of Attraction-type thinking. Full stop. I was forced to admit the truth of the matter, which was that at this point I simply did not know. Despite the explorations of quantum physics, despite scientific evidence that 'like attracts like', in this situation I found it impossible to take this path. Not knowing, even though it was a hard place to be in, seemed the only option.

Not knowing is absolute anathema to the mind, of course. The mind's job is to ensure our survival with certainty, and it will do anything it can to bring that about. This means planning, organising, thinking in advance, determining possible outcomes, trying to be in control, having a Plan B, imagining the worst case scenario and all of that. Even saying 'I am willing to know' is another example of the mind wanting to stay in charge. Simply being in a place of not knowing is very challenging, but that was what we were being required to do.

As it happened, we didn't spend an enormous amount of time wondering why he'd got cancer. It was obvious there had been something wrong, at least on a physical level, for some time. He'd always had problems with digestion, usually remedied by taking some indigestion pills. It was also obvious he'd been unhappy for quite some time, and needed to make some changes in his lifestyle. Philip fully embraced change on all the levels he possibly could in that last year. What he managed to achieve was not enough to heal his physical body, although the amount of healing done at other levels was significant.

Now, with my explorations of non-duality, I was not only questioning the Law of Attraction, I was questioning everything I'd ever thought and felt about anything. It seemed the whole of my life had been turned upside down since his death, and it was continuing to be topsy turvy. Hence, I asked for support from the Listening about plans:

Q: What to do, if anything, regarding a plan?

"It is not the plan, necessarily, that is the problem: it is how you view it. The plan will NOT take you where you want to go. It will provide some direction at a practical level, which soothes the mind and, if implemented, allows for the appearance of achievement. All of this is undermined, though, by how you come to the plan.

If you want a plan because you are attached to an outcome, then the attachment itself will interfere. If you want a plan because it is fun for you to play with and you realise this is a tool for mind to have fun with, that is different. Watch out though, as one can easily slip into the other.

It is only the mind that needs plans. Life itself happens anyway. Your real question is "Do you want to play the game called 'Doing and Implementing a Plan?'"

Thus I was directed back again to the way that the mind tries to control life. At which point, I began to wonder whether the Law of Attraction in this way was just another subtle, or not so subtle way in which the mind tries to control everything.

All of this felt incredibly scary to me. I'd noticed already my interest in all things spiritual, in personal growth and meaning, was waning considerably. I labelled it as 'having gone off anything deep and meaningful'. As someone who'd spent her life being fascinated by the deep and meaningful, this was a disconcerting departure. I felt like I was wandering around in not-knowing, in a place of emptiness, just waiting to see what would happen. This was very different from 'trying to make things happen,' 'being organised', or even 'manifesting.'

I focused instead on the creative things I was doing, like singing and doodling. Everything new I was doing had to pass the 'Am I having fun?' test. If the answer wasn't yes, then I stopped doing it. I now knew from personal experience that life really was simply too short to waste in not enjoying myself.

One of the fun things I did was attend a wonderful workshop entitled 'Soil, Soul and Sisterhood.' It wasn't normally the kind of thing I would have done, so my attendance was very much in line with me exploring different things, and while this was on the borderline of 'deep and meaningful,' there was also going to be an emphasis on fun, pleasure and creativity.

"I'd like you to sit still, close your eyes, and begin to let your body relax,' the group leader spoke quietly. Well-used to this kind of thing, I let my mind drift off.

"When you open your eyes, notice which of the cards in front of you you're most drawn to," she spoke softly. Again, I took this with not quite a pinch of salt, but very lightly. I said to myself, "Jane, remember this is all just foodstuff for the mind, which in your case happens to like deep meaning, analysis, and synchronicity."

Opening my eyes though, I did indeed feel strongly attracted to just one of these Goddess cards. The card I picked up was the representation of Sheela Na Gig, and the words read:

Sheela is a cheeky, naked, squatting Goddess. She was a symbol of good luck in pagan Ireland. She is bawdy, irreverent and totally without shame. She invites us to celebrate ourselves and our sensual wild woman self.

"Wild Woman Self!" I exclaimed inwardly, loving the synchronicity. I was seeing connections between what was happening for me on the inside and signals I was seeing on the outside.

The words continued: *Sheela challenges us to journey through her sparkling open vulva to joy and sensual pleasure. If we take up her call she promises us laughter and new ways of looking at the world. She refuses to adhere to rules and regulations which instruct women to behave in certain ways. She calls you to join her in her sensual erotic dance, celebrating your female body, whatever its shape and size.*

Finally, there was an affirmation:

"I challenge conventional ways of thinking with style and humour. I am filled with joy and fun."

This really was resonating with me, not so much on the sexual side, but with the concept of Wild Wisdom. These were the ideas with which I was working and hoping to get a new website out to the world as soon as possible. In fact, I felt like I was going through a process of giving birth.

The words Wild and Wisdom don't traditionally go together, but they did now, in my world. Many of the words from Sheela Na Gig equated to the meaning of Wild Wisdom: refusing to blindly obey rules and regulations; looking at the world in new ways and challenging conventional ways of thinking with style and humour. In other words, being willing to turn things upside down, back to front and inside out. Like Alice in Wonderland, topsy turvy indeed.[9]

---

9 You can read more about what Wild Wisdom really is here: www.wildwisdom.co.uk/manifesto

39
A Shift

That year, the annual conference at the Findhorn Foundation was about forgiveness. I knew I needed to forgive Philip for dying. I knew I needed to forgive myself for trying to stop him watching TV, criticising him for being overweight, and not spending more time with him.

Forgiveness for me is all about letting go. When I studied a Course in Miracles, I had come to realise that when true forgiveness has happened, or is happening, there simply is no issue to be forgiven. When you really *have* let go of something, you've simply let go.

It's like when you're holding onto the branch of a tree – and then you let go of it. You no longer have a relationship with that tree branch. You're still related to it generally, but you're not attached to it, physically or emotionally. That's what I believe it's like to have fully let go, even if something horrific happened in your past. Forgiveness, letting go, means it no longer bothers you. You have no investment left in it. This is how it's possible for people to forgive others for some of the cruellest acts imaginable. But was it also true for forgiving myself?

Journal: 30th September 2013

Is it true I am not forgiving myself for not 'getting over' P's death more? YES

Is it true I am still stuck with him? NOT SURE

Am I angry with him for not providing for me financially? YES

Am I angry with him for dying in the first place? YES

Am I angry with him for not attending to his souls' needs earlier? YES

Am I angry with him for abandoning me? YES!

There were all sorts of elements of our relationship that needed attention. Not only that: I had some forgiving to do in relationship to money, too.

Regarding money, I asked myself: What have I not forgiven myself for? Where do I feel guilty? What is behind my belief I need a man to look after me financially? This last one had arisen in the wake of having to provide for myself. These were questions posed to me by my coach, and she suggested I focus them around money itself, as if I had a relationship with money, just like a relationship with a person.

Bearing this point in mind, I attended some of the conference sessions.

Robert Holden, one of the conference presenters and author of many books, including *Loveability*, said in one of the sessions that when we don't forgive someone, "We put them in jail; and then we become the jailer." I resonated with that, and talked with a friend about it later.

"When someone has done something 'bad' or 'wrong,' it looks like they are the ones in the wrong. It *looks* like they are the ones who need to atone, who need to change, who need to be different. And loads of people in the world are stuck in that model, in relation to their family, friends, other situations, even countries."

"Mmm . . . yes," replied Dee. "Then we say things like, 'He shouldn't have done that,' 'She was so in the wrong,' or, 'How can it ever be okay to forgive her?' "

"Yes," I continued, "or 'My whole life has been affected! There is no way I will ever forgive, because what they did was so awful it was unforgivable.' "

I began to understand that it's this very pronouncing that keeps the person who did the deed stuck. Even more importantly, the one who is not forgiving is even more stuck. It doesn't seem that way, but when you are blaming another, *you* are the one who is stuck. The other person, whom you're not forgiving, might not even know what they did.

"The person who hasn't been forgiven, doesn't often care that much usually, unless they are also stuck in not forgiving you. And they especially don't care if they are dead! So the person who is *really* affected by not forgiving is the one doing the 'not forgiving.' "

"So are you not forgiving Philip then, for dying?" asked Dee.

"Yes – I've put him in the jail; I've got the key and he's staying there. It's in my power to unlock the cell door and let him out. However, although it looks like he's the one stuck in there, it's actually the other way round; it's *me* that's stuck. Oh, my goodness. That is a revelation."

Robert went on to talk about the difference between the interests of the ego and that of love, which I'd already been exploring for myself.

"Ego maintains itself through a process of self-judgment. So you can ask, 'Who would I be without judging?' " Robert paused for us to take this in. Given I was much more interested in love than ego, at least in theory, I asked myself who would I be if I wasn't judging Philip for dying? Who would I be if I wasn't judging money for staying away from me? It was clear: the answer was along the lines of 'a lot less stressed, a lot happier, more content, more peaceful.'

All this pointed to letting go of judging, unlocking the cell door, throwing away the key and setting myself free, even though it looked like it would be Philip and money that would be 'getting away with it'. (Even as I write this, it seems mad! What was Philip supposed to be 'getting away' with? Dying? What was money supposed to be 'getting away' with? Staying away from me? Completely bonkers!)

Journal: Late September

Because the ego's focus is all about becoming, not being, it is therefore a never-ending journey in which there is no end-point, even though you think the point of the journey IS getting to an end-point, when life will finally be all right.

This is because you say to yourself things like, 'When I've lost enough weight/got enough clients/found a partner, then I will finally be happy/at peace/loveable.' So you focus on self-improvement, which means it's very easy to have highs and lows according to whether you've matched up to what the ego is dictating. Or you inflate and deflate like the balloon mentioned earlier.

The ego thrives on being separate, and produces justifications and brilliant reasoning to illustrate why it is right. It's language is often filled with 'should, 'must,' 'ought to,' 'need to,' as in, 'Philip never should have died. He should have taken better care of himself/done more exercise/got help sooner'. The ego is a hard taskmaster, and you can never get it right. It wants, worries, wonders and wishes, and tries very hard, indeed, to 'get there'.

I'd been an expert at trying: trying so hard to be a good person; to grow and become better; to make a worthwhile contribution to the world. The trying itself had been so exhausting, though.

In addition to ego, there is what Robert called Love, which was not the kind of romantic love between people we so often think of, and which is so very limited conpared to what is actually available. Love is the present moment itself; it's always there, that silent, still, never-ending peace. It already is, with no place for becoming; it has no interest in judgment, either positive or negative. In fact, those elements simply do not exist for Love.

It shows up in the ordinary human life as acceptance of what is happening in the moment; kindness and compassion and lack of judgment. It shows up as an open-hearted engagement with life, learning, loving, and listening to others. It is about sharing fully in the experiences that are presented, without any attachment to how that experience appears.

I was absolutely willing to forgive Philip for dying, if it meant I could bask in the presence of Love like this. However, I struggled with the idea of forgiving money, even though I could embrace the concept of it being like a person.

"Dee, could it be possible I'm blaming money in some way?" I pondered out loud to my friend, who was attending this session with me.

"What would you be blaming it for?" she asked.

"For not hanging around me more; for not looking after me better; for not being a very good friend."

"Well, how have you treated it in the past? Have you respected it, given it time, wanted to hang around it, like you would with a good friend?"

"Mmm. No, not really. Maybe I'm feeling guilty about how I've treated money in the past. I've been saying I love money, but I wonder if, in actual fact, I've been demonstrating that I didn't love it? I know I've spent unwisely sometimes, and also felt ashamed about even having it in the first place, especially that lump sum that came when we sold the business all those years ago."

Had I been treating money badly? Had I been disrespecting it? Yes. That's why forgiveness was necessary. Forgiveness of myself, as well as money. As it says in Lesson 193 in the Course in Miracles: '*Forgive, and you will see this differently.*' It was a revelation to consider money in this way, and I took this new awareness into another session in the conference.

Sobonfu Some is an African teacher who specialises in facilitating others to let go of grief in a strongly ritualised manner. She works in a manner informed by the traditions from her tribe in Burkina Faso. During the profound ritual she facilitated during this conference, I not only received a blessing from money itself, but also let go of much of the anger about Philip dying that was still casting a shadow over me.

Journal: 30th September 2013: after the Grief Ritual with Sobonfu.

> *Money forgives me! Oh, my goodness. Here's a message from it, received during the ritual:*

"Yes, I am money, and I have never blamed you or done anything other than been here for you. I always am here for you, and I always will be, for you to do with as you wish.

I hear your apologies and I accept them; I love you, anyway. I welcome you into my fold, and invite you to relax and bask in my arms, allowing me to take care of you. Love abounds between us, and forgiveness no longer exists in this sphere.

Hear me: you are loved. Love is present here, for you are Love, and I am Love, and we are reunited in that.

Relax and let me be, regardless of appearances. For I am, and always will be, here for you."

Journal: Later that day

What am I being called to do?

- *Forgive Philip for dying in the first place*
- *Step fully into the place left by his physical departure*
- *Embrace all the emotions that come with these two steps*
- *Release the anxiety about survival that made me believe I needed him to look after me and provide.*
- *Put myself into the hands of the real 'I' to be guided wherever, and in whichever way.*

Can I consider I have been nothing but blessed by Philip's death?

This last sentence was a difficult one, but it was a hugely important step in a forward direction in my life.

Perhaps it wasn't coincidence that this happened at the same time I had a very ordinary, and yet far-reaching, experience.

I'd got into the daily rhythm of waking early, walking through the woods to the nearest sanctuary of the Findhorn Foundation, practicing silent sitting for an hour at the 6:30a.m. meditation, and then returning home. It was a beautiful way to start the day, truly nourishing. One morning, as I was walking back down the road to home, I found myself noticing the thought: 'I can find a peaceful place in myself.'

Immediately after this came the realisation, not that there is an 'I' able to find peace, but that 'I' *am* peace itself.

Peace itself.

This was a shift, in the exact same manner as had happened a year previously, without the white light or glow. It was a momentous occasion, but felt very ordinary, more like an 'Oh, yeah, of course' moment, than an 'Aha!' one. I wrote about it:

Journal: early October 2013

Yesterday, a realisation/experience/insight occurred: 'I' am peace. It used to be thought there was an 'I' who could dip in and out of peace, which was always there. Now, it's really clear this is the wrong way round. There IS peace – and then there are forms labelled as human, amongst many other forms, that are within that.

In retrospect, that day was momentous, because this time, no mental fog came rolling in. Months later, I wrote the following:

'How are you?' is a very common question to be asked. Whereas before the answer would be 'I'm fine' (and underneath there would be all kinds of emotions and thoughts going on), now the answer, whether I actually say it or not, is 'I'm always fine underneath. Sometimes on top there is a disturbance of feeling or attachment to thoughts, but it never affects the underlying presence of still peace'.

The underlying presence of still peace.

Perhaps the very same peace and presence that Philip wrote about on page 92.

Thus began the full embracing of the idea that I might have been the receiver of a very precious gift as a result of Philip's death, and the painful grief of the previous months.

40

Singing!

In mid-October, friends Will and Angie, interfaith ministers and marriage celebrants, were finally getting married themselves. They deliberately set out to make it a community event. Many of us helped organise it, and everyone was invited to the actual wedding ceremony, and then the dancing and fun after the meal.

Naturally, they had created a beautiful ceremony and, in honour of the occasion, I was going to wear the same dress I'd worn when dancing in Cape Town, which my friend had very generously given to me at the end of the holiday. I'd nicknamed it the Goddess Dress, as that was how I'd felt in it. Sitting watching the marriage ceremony, though, I began to feel strangely disconnected. I noticed critical thoughts in my head; I felt as if I wasn't quite there somehow. I also felt awkward being all dressed up, even though everyone else was, too.

"Hi, Jane! That was great, wasn't it?" A friend came up to me after the ceremony had finished. I looked at her and felt my face crumple up.

"Oh no, you poor thing; it must have brought back memories for you," she reached out and touched my arm. Sobbing on her shoulder, I wailed,

"It's not that, it's just that it was so beautiful to witness their love for each other, I was so touched. And I miss Philip so much."

It's amazing what simply acknowledging what is going on does for you. With the support of friends – at least four had turned up by now – the painful feelings, and the expression of them through tears, led to the storm passing and I began to feel better.

I was reminded of a quote from Jac O'Keeffe:

"Emotions are like farts, a puff of air which passes through."

A while ago I would have been offended and found this statement disrespectful, unfunny, and demonstrating what a shallow character Jac was. Not so now. Instead, it was just helpful for the times when an emotional story has taken over and life becomes all very serious.

Writing this, I'm reminded of why I loved that sentence so much. Not only did I find it funny that emotions, which we often take so seriously, were being treated somewhat irreverently, but also because I had witnessed the truth of it with my own emotions. Left to their own devices, without a story being attached, emotions really do blow through of their own accord – which is exactly what happened watching Will and Angie get married.

This understanding allowed me to emerge from the tears afresh, enjoy being in my lovely dress, sit down for dinner with good friends, eat delicious food that had been cooked and served by other community members, and then to be thrilled by the dancing afterwards. In my journal that night, I wrote:

Journal: 19th October 2013

Sobbing during actual wedding – felt so moved, it was so painful witnessing their love. Dear friends saw and held me. But then later on I found myself doing salsa and jive on the dance floor! It was just lovely.

And still – especially in the quieter moments – there is an awareness that this is all happening to a body that is not me. Strange.

So the shift that had occurred was still there, and perception of life was indeed happening from a different place entirely. As Eckhart Tolle says:

'*You are both the person that does things and also something much deeper than the person. You live like that. Identity is in the depths of being or spaciousness, and no longer trapped in the personal sense of self – and that is the shift, and then you are a human who brings peace into this world.*'

A few days later, in meditation, I wrote:

Journal: 21st October 2013 – in the sanctuary

The mind says 'I want to know this Oneness' and then veils the Oneness so that the 'I' continues to look in the opposite direction, while believing it is looking, very hard, in the right direction (i.e. inwards).

The vast/tiny, empty/full, dark/lightness is never ending, never beginning. It's just there. Where? Here? Where? No 'where', and no 'here', either. The magical paradox of heaven on earth.

Around this time, a small but significant event occurred. I came across an old colleague on an online forum, whom I hadn't been in touch with for years. I emailed her to say how nice it was to have discovered her again, told her about Philip, and what had happened in my work as a result. The reply I received was odd, in that she didn't mentioned Philip at all. I didn't need sympathy, but I was a bit taken aback that she simply complimented me on my work. She had known us both, after all. What was even more interesting, though, was my response to this:

Journal: 18th October 2013

Denise didn't mention Philip in her email; how strange is that! However, let me understand this in the light of my other explorations.

There is identification here of the ego in the role of the bereaved wife. There is a friend not behaving accordingly (at least saying she was sorry about Philip, if nothing else). Hence there is a feeling of hurt.

But it did not happen to who I really am – that is Peace or Love. However, an emotion (or a fart) passes through the body, and either gets stuck or flows – and then gets expressed accordingly. This only matters if stuckness happens because there is identification with the bodymind. Then there is an apparently separate 'I' which feels bereft, believes that her friend has caused this, and then makes a judgment and expresses that. (Making her wrong, in other words).

Memories (of both Philip and Denise) are functions of the mind, and keep the 'I' stuck in identification. No wonder I've had problems with whether our marriage actually happened: at one level it didn't! Every emotion can be attached to memories, which is why it is possible to remember an event and feel different feelings about it, which I've already noticed. Are the feelings real? They feel completely real; but, in fact, it is all mind.

None of this meant that the feelings were any less valid; none of it meant anything unless I thought it meant something, which is where the stickiness of the mind comes in again. As Louise Hay says:

"*Thoughts are just ideas that are only big and powerful if we identify with them.*" The stickiness is the identification, and the mind invites partaking in a (usually sticky) story, which then becomes so apparently real that all else is forgotten, or not even realised in the first place, and the thoughts are believed as who we are. I was in danger in relation to this email from my friend of believing I was a 'hurt widow who is bitter about her friend who didn't mention her husband's death'. Instead, I recognised what was happening and could let it go.

Journal: 22nd October 2013

> *There are still thoughts presenting themselves, as in a train of thoughts, but there is no one at the station, waiting to get on the train. Or even hi-jacking the train. There is just peacefulness.*
>
> *So meditations or visualisations are useful as aids to soothe the mind, just as they have always been, and are completely valid as that. Even though it is thought that 'you are getting in touch with essence' or 'aligning with who you really are,' you are essence, you already are who you really are, so how can you get in touch with it? This is funny, we have got it all so backward!*

Practically speaking, I was still dealing with people who didn't know Philip had died. This was fine when it was someone who had known him, even if they did respond in an unexpected way like my friend in the email. However, many assumptions were made when I met a new person who hadn't known me before.

What on earth do you say when someone asks, 'What does your husband do?' or 'Do you have children?' or 'Are you here with your family?' Understandable questions, perhaps, since most women in their mid-fifties probably do have a husband/partner, and probably do have children. The questions are difficult, though, in my situation. My response to the first has gone from a blunt, 'He's dead,' to a more sensitive, 'Well, actually he died a few years ago.' The other questions I'm much more used to, and now I just say 'no.' Either way, the conversation stops suddenly and, unless the other person is a skilled communicator, it's left to me to smooth over any awkwardness, which frankly, I haven't always done. It just depends on how I'm feeling in the moment.

However, none of these questions were asked of me when I stepped out into a completely new and exciting world around this time.

Back in the spring, I'd been to a one-off singing workshop. About 30 of us in a church hall, mainly women, learning about breathing, making all sorts of sounds, and even singing a few lines of a song now and then.

"We'll do some improvisation now," announced the leader. Normally, I'd have experienced anxiety beginning to take over at the thought of improvisation. This time, I noticed, with delight, that didn't happen. My mouth opened when it was my turn to improvise a line of song, and out popped a noise, which even to my ears sounded acceptable. Miracle of miracles, I also *felt* okay about it!

This was the beginning of me realising I might like performing. Having been scared off this at the tender age of about 10, when

I messed up my one-liner in a school play, this was a revelation. I pestered the same singing leader to join her well-known acappella women's singing group.

"I think you're great. I'd love to join – what are the chances?"

She sounded a bit hesitant. "Well, there are no spaces at the moment, and even if there were, I'd need to hear your voice, and then the others would all need to agree to you joining." I wasn't put off.

"That's all right. I can wait until there is a space." Eventually, my persistence paid off, and in the autumn of 2013 I joined *Too Many Kooks,* discovering a pleasure in singing and even performing I hadn't known existed, even though on occasion it was tinged with pain.

Journal: 22nd October 2013

> *Walked out of the Kooks practice and was hit by the thought of going home alone and no Philip there. Gosh, I miss you such a lot. It's still almost physical. I have learnt and experienced such a lot lately, and I'm so very sad I can't share it with you directly. Oh, well. I just miss you, and that's all there is to it.*

Fairly soon after I joined, *Too Many Kooks* had an open mic spot in Dougie MacLean's famous Perthshire Amber Festival. We'd been practicing the two songs we were to sing each week, which for me felt plenty; after all, my last performance had been over forty years ago. We discussed costumes, hired a mini-bus, and set off to drive down through the Highlands early one Saturday morning. My friends who lived in nearby Perth were coming to watch, and that felt wonderful, to be supported in this way, because I knew Philip would have been hugely proud of me.

I didn't have a clue what I was letting myself in for, so I simply wasn't anxious. There must have been well over 100 people in the room and the spotlights were on us. It was great fun to sing and be appreciated. Afterwards, I enjoyed the fiddling and accordion session in the bar downstairs: it reminded me of my teenage days in Northern Ireland, where pals and I would seek out the 'diddly-dee' music bars to go and sing along to.

Journal: Saturday 2nd November 2013

Philip! I've just returned from my first ever singing performance! Randi and Martin came to watch, and it was FABULOUS! I loved it!

How amazing that I should like performing at this late stage in my life! We sang 'Price Tag' and the audience loved it – they clapped a lot, and roared with laughter at our version of it. I liked it. And I love you, and felt despondent when I got home and couldn't tell you. I wasn't coming home to your loving arms, your sweet smile and warm eyes. Still, I can imagine this, and I know you would have loved me doing it.

On the run up to what was going to be the second year anniversary of Philip's death, I was getting much better at focusing on the good, as in that last sentence. What was much more important was what I wrote in the next paragraph:

But then, these words came to me: 'the deep, deep joy that is from knowing 'I am Peace itself;' that is never-ending, never-beginning and everlasting; it is incomparable to this fleeting state of happiness.' And it's true. It really is.

41
A Different Kind of Wedding

The two-year anniversary had passed. Surely now I'd be feeling better – and, of course, I was. The time between episodes of feeling dreadful had slowly and steadily been extending, and by now it was unusual to be in the tsunami of tears that had become so familiar.

What was not so familiar was a new idea that was beginning to emerge. Having taken off my wedding ring a year previously, I'd been wearing my engagement ring only on my right hand. A few weeks ago, I had taken that off too; it just felt right to have completely bare hands. Recently, though, I'd realised in a flash of inspiration that I needed to buy a new ring and marry myself.

When this idea took hold, I knew if I waited – and I've had plenty of practice in waiting these last three years – that the right ring would show itself to me, and it did. As I was walking down Forres high street one day, the perfect one winked at me from the window of our local jewellers.

In the week running up to the date I set for the marriage ceremony, I found myself singing a made-up song I entitled, 'I am letting you go.' I sang it to Philip whenever I drove anywhere for a couple of days, and felt sad, but also very free. Then, walking on Findhorn beach that same week, a beautiful stone caught my attention. Its message was, 'I represent the lines of your life flowing through you; the two halves of your life (before Philip died and after), and the crystal in the middle is your essence, who you really are'. I took it, knowing it would be important in whatever ceremony was to happen. A few days later, the perfect place for the ceremony presented itself into my mind – the spot on the Findhorn river where I went skinny-dipping in the heat of the summer, and was important as a symbol of emerging to the world from the caves of grief.

I decked myself out in some brand new pretty lingerie, just like a bride would, donned a special outfit and my walking boots, and went off to the river, via a visit to one of my favourite coffee shops. While sipping a cappuccino, I wrote in my journal some of my vows to myself. Later, down by the rushing river, much higher than it was in the summer, I had a private little ceremony, with Philip's energy in the air quietly and lovingly approving and applauding, as I put the ring on my finger. I left the stone there as a memento, and came back singing all the way along the path. A change into a beautiful dress at home, and then to my women's group meeting and a celebration with them, ending up with dinner in the Findhorn Community Centre with a special bottle of wine. I realised all of this was playing the game called 'Getting Married to Myself,' and that this character called Jane was doing this. It was fun and fine, and the deep Peace underneath, which I'd realised was the same as what Eckhart Tolle calls Presence, was still there, and didn't care whether I played this particular game, or any other, for that matter. It was very liberating.

That year brought other changes, too: I committed to surgery on my eyes, so that I wouldn't have to wear contact lenses or glasses again. It was a much bigger operation than whether or not to have a tooth out, but I now felt fine about making this decision myself. It was clearly a mark of having learnt to live on my own, make my own decisions, and be fully in the world again. I was being reborn on all kinds of levels.

In May 2014 I spent a week with some friends on the Isle of Erraid, off the west coast of Scotland, and created a mind-map of what was to become this book. I knew I had to wait until the muse took me and, sure enough, I woke one morning in July while visiting Carrie and River in Devon. Aware it was time to start writing, I set up a delightful new routine when I returned home: up early, walk through the woods to the meditation sanctuary, back home again, write for a couple of hours, and only then open emails and get down to other work. This rhythm enabled the first draft to be done. What's more, I was loving writing, even if re-visiting some of the journal and blog entries was very painful occasionally.

During this time, I became aware of a sense of Philip not being around anymore. It took the form of an image of me having been climbing a mountain with him beside me. We'd been doing this for ages, and finally had reached the top. Now I was coming down the other side and he wasn't with me anymore. It felt perfect. I don't know where he went in that image, but it wasn't down the mountainside with me. I was walking down the other side, alone, and it felt fine to be doing that.

42
Gifted By Grief?

For quite a while after Philip died, it was impossible to even begin to think there could be any gifts in his death. I was angry, tearful, and bereft, and that was what was important. However, as time went on, I began to consider the idea in theory.

"I suppose there will be a blessing in this somewhere," I remember saying tearfully to my friend, Sue, one day, some months into the first year.

"Jane, don't bother about that now. So long as you're allowing the grieving to happen naturally, which you are, any blessings will make themselves known to you when the time is right."

How wise Sue was. I'd already been baffled by the tornadoes of different feelings at different times, so why wouldn't there be a blessing too? And if there were any gifts, couldn't I accept those alongside wishing my man was still with me?

Although this book is called *Gifted By Grief,* in reality the gifts have come as a result of Philip's death. Yes, I managed the grieving process well, and part of it was writing this book. However, it was Philip's death that triggered this process, and the main focus for me during this time was discovering what this 'I' we all talk about really is. Was it the same 'thing' that is currently in my body, and in yours?

Not everyone will have this obsession to discover the answer to this question in the way I had. Not everyone will even be interested in 'Who am I?' However, death and the resulting grief changes lives, sometimes dramatically. For me, there were many ways my life changed, and many small gifts I could name, but here are the most important ones.

The First Gift: What Is, Is.

One of the realisations Philip and I had in the last few days of his life was the truth of the apparently simplistic statement, 'What is, is.' It is such an obvious and simple thing to say that it can be very irritating to the mind, which often just wants to dismiss it. However, when you're in a dilemma, there is an easing of any irritation, desperation or fear when you admit that what is happening, is what is happening.

In telling this simple truth, space arises, and often that brings illumination, clarity or insight. Other times, there is just a releasing and relaxing into what is. The main thing is, the resisting of the moment has stopped, meaning that the present moment itself can be felt. However, humans often don't want to feel the pain of whatever dilemma they are in. Ironically, though, resistance to what is happening tends to prolong any pain, which then becomes suffering. Pain comes to visit as part of the human condition, just as pleasure does, but suffering (that is, how you relate to the pain, as described on Page 215) is chosen – or not.

*

One of my favourite stories is from Krishnamurti, the famous Indian sage. At a meeting of some two thousand of his followers in California one day, he paused and leaned forward.

"Do you want to know what my secret is?" he asked the crowd.

Ears pricked up and eyes opened wider; of course everyone wanted to know. In the silence that followed, he quietly pronounced,

"You see, I don't mind what happens."

When you don't mind what happens, then it doesn't matter quite so much what happens. Before you throw this book out the window at that statement, I realise this thought is somewhat controversial in a world that is populated with many, many people who deeply care about what happens. There absolutely is a place for caring deeply, especially when some humans practice behaviour that is unacceptable. Just because you 'don't mind what happens' doesn't mean to say that all behaviour is acceptable. In fact Krishnamurti goes on to say he cares deeply, but doesn't mind what story happens.

I know this seems paradoxical, but let's just look at it a bit more. What I've realised since my dance with cancer, death and rebirth, is that *things happen anyway*, whether or not I do anything. I may not like what happens, but that's another thing entirely. They do happen. If I don't mind what happens, that is, if I'm not attached to something being right, or wrong, or have a lot invested in a particular outcome, then I just don't mind what happens as much.

It's relatively easy to see this with something you don't mind about a lot. For example, if you need to choose between drinking a glass of water or a cup of tea, and you really don't mind what you have. You don't mind, because there's nothing much invested in the outcome of having either. Or say you need to choose between travelling by plane or train – each has its pros and cons, but the end result will be you will arrive. In the bigger scheme of things, it probably doesn't matter much which way you travel, so long as you get to where you're going.

It's much harder, though, to see this with something you are very attached to, and for most people, that is their nearest and dearest. How can you possibly say you don't mind if your husband or wife or child – or any loved one – dies? Of course you can't say that, it would be unnatural if you did. However, the suffering is enormous when you push up against what life presents to you.

And suffering happens whenever you resist what is actually going on. It's quite natural to resist something awful that's happening to a loved one, but it doesn't help. Pretending it isn't happening, complaining and moaning about it, blaming others – all it really does is make *you* feel worse. By resisting what is going on, you're only adding another layer, which causes you to suffer far more. Because you now have to deal, not only with the original situation, but also with your fight against it. As Eckhart Tolle says, '*Acceptance means: For now, this is what this situation, this moment, requires me to do, and so I do it willingly.*'

The quote 'what you resist, persists', often bandied around in spiritual circles, points to a way out of the resistance through dropping it. However, many people respond to these words by judging themselves, as if they ought to know better, which in itself becomes another layer of pushing up against what is happening.

'Not resisting' means simply saying 'this is what is happening right now.' It doesn't mean you approve of it. It doesn't mean you condone it. It doesn't mean you like it. It doesn't mean it doesn't matter. It doesn't mean you don't care. It *does* mean you are willing to acknowledge the truth of what is happening in the moment.

Paradoxically, that acknowledgement means you get to 'be' with what is happening, which in itself allows a change in energy, creative ideas or simply an opening into Love. All of this is very likely to affect the situation itself, leading to something else happening.

Whatever happens next might not, of course, be what you wanted to have happen, which is why you resist it. But perhaps what actually happens might have a gift in it for you, or in some cases even be better than what you thought ought to happen. Your idea, after all, is only what your mind could come up with, and our minds, while apparently incredible, are actually very limited.

For instance, I believed the best thing for Philip was to stay alive, preferably in a healthy way. So did he. We both did all we possibly could to avoid him dying, and in the process we both learnt a lot.

And then he died.

On the surface this looked dreadful, and it was painful for quite a long time, for both of us while he was in the process of dying, and for me afterwards. However, even in the midst of this pain, there were already some gifts which we had acknowledged to each other. We realised we were grateful for the presence of this cancer, even though we knew it was killing him. This was because we had become so much closer to each other; we appreciated this new depth of being together, even though we paid a high price for it. We were able to bask in Love, and this arose from our acceptance of what is. This new awareness also helped me gradually come to terms with the shock of Philip dying, and the unfolding events afterwards. As I write this, I feel waves of gratitude once more washing through me.

The Second Gift: Sitting Silently

Silent Sitting is the term I use for what others may call meditation. Meditating itself had always been a bit of a challenge for me, more of a 'should' and a 'good idea.' I'd never actually had any desire to do so, more a sense of 'do it because it's good for you'. So I'd been practicing it on and off since first learning Transcendental Meditation at university – much more off than on, though, and it always felt like hard work. I couldn't 'drop the thoughts,' couldn't sit in the 'right' position, nor could I seem to get the benefits which other people talked about.

However, early in 2010 something happened regarding meditation that changed my attitude. We'd been going through financial challenges related to our piece of land in Ireland which had lost its value. My terror and shame about possibly being made bankrupt was so great, that I was regularly waking in the wee small hours with a painful lower back, and waves of fear going up and down my solar plexus. It was agonising.

Visiting the local Chinese doctor, I told her, "I'm waking every night with a sore back, it's been going on for ages now. I don't know what to do about it; it can only be relieved by sitting up, or stretching it out." The doctor was silent, sitting opposite me for quite a long time. Then she spoke, quietly, and looking directly into my eyes.

"You need to be meditating."

Tears sprang from my eyes, as I took in her gentle but firm words. Something in me recognised this fully, and I felt relieved in that recognition. I knew this at a deep level, but the thought hadn't yet made it to the surface of my conscious mind, so when she spoke, the words completely resonated as the truth they were.

That night, sleeping separately from Philip, I woke in terror as usual, at 4 a.m. Sitting up, huddled against the cold with the duvet wrapped around me, I began to craft the visualisation I ended up calling *The Place of Peace*[10]. After about 20 minutes or so, my back was relieved and my mind calm again, so much so that I snuggled back down and returned to sleep easily.

When Philip was diagnosed, I remembered this practice. It helped me to sit silently, and just be in that Place of Peace. Feeling the benefit of this experience led me to going regularly to the early morning meditation in one of the Foundation's sanctuaries in the summer before Philip died. Gradually, I began using Eckhart Tolle's 'inner body' technique at the beginning of the meditation. This is where you simply focus on all the inner parts of your body. It's a very pleasant sensation. I stopped judging myself for having thoughts at all, and simply noticed the ones that wanted to capture my attention, instead of engaging with them and the resulting story. I began to go 'behind' the thoughts, and beyond them.

I also often used my own mantra of *'Stop. Be Still. Listen. And Only Then Act'* during the day; it's a very short form of silent sitting. Using it regularly, I'd found my subsequent actions took on quite a different quality, even if they looked the same on the outside.

Stopping is one of the things that people find it hardest to do in our society, even if they're not dealing with the challenges grief

10 You can get a copy of The Place of Peace at www.giftedbygrief.com/meditation

brings. When all around seems to be going faster and faster, with an emphasis on achieving more and more and being better and better, then going against the grain and stopping – or even just slowing down – can seem almost impossible sometimes. So a short mantra, one that can be applied in seconds, works wonders. Then you get a chance to simply 'Be here, now'. This is a typical example of the kind of back-to-front thinking that is the essence of my coaching work with Wild Wisdom.

Mindfulness meditation, so popular right now, is all about stopping. I remember, many years ago, drawing a huge poster of a quote from Thich Nhat Hanh: *Drinking a cup of green tea, I stop the war.* Pinned up in our kitchen, it was a reminder, at one level, to be present when doing something as simple as making a cup of tea. On a broader level, it reminded me to be fully present in the moment. In this way, the warring nature of thoughts, ideas, feelings and inner arguments had a break, thus making room for the silence of the moment to burst through into consciousness.

Pema Chodron, Buddhist author of *When Things Fall Apart,* says:

'Meditation practice isn't about trying to throw ourselves away and become something better; it's about befriending who we are.'

Befriending myself was a truly enormous gift that I received as an unexpected consequence of Philip dying. I also began to feel much more familiar and at ease with what it is that inhabits this 'bag' we call a body, and which had been so spectacularly empty in the moment of Philip's death. Most of this gradual understanding came during the silent sitting, not least because I was so busy doing other things much of the time. With the sitting, and the contemplation of the 'Who am I?' question, it became easier and easier to just be present and in the moment. Not all the time, but often.

After the 'shift' happened, when it became obvious that peace is who 'I' am – or Love, consciousness, presence, God, whatever you want to call it – as opposed to there being a 'me-who-*finds*-peace', the silent sitting provided a beautiful opportunity to grow in this awareness. What a gift that was, and is. Gradually, it became more and move obvious that, in the words of Jac O'Keeffe, *'Thoughts happen. Not a problem. Believing in them – big problem!'*

The Third Gift: Wild Wisdom

About 15 months after Philip died, it became clear I was so different as a person that my work had to dramatically change, too. I'd already been successfully coaching since 2007, as an offshoot from my previous counselling and psychotherapy practice. I'd completed my coaching training, opened the doors for clients, and started running face-to-face groups in the locality. By the time Philip was diagnosed with cancer, I'd been running groups online too, plus had a healthy string of one-to-one clients, both in person and via Skype or phone. I loved the flexibility of being able to coach anyone, anywhere, and as the online world was exploding, I was learning lots about internet marketing.

But with the emphasis in my own life being much more intuitive and creative, my website needed to reflect that. I also needed to explore a new way of working with people. The quality of energy required to run groups still wasn't fully available to me. Especially online, which I'd always found challenging technically, and which Philip had always supported me with. It was at this time that the revelation appeared for me to illustrate the website with the doodle drawings that were second nature to me.

Uncovering the value of something I had previously taken for granted was like finding buried treasure. Doodling was just something I loved doing and made it easier for me to listen to anything. That the drawings themselves could have an intrinsic value was the revelation. This represented one of the outcomes of listening to, then acting on, my intuition. Another outcome was a willingness to be brave enough to state what I had really thought for quite some time.

For many years I had realized that life is not what it appears to be; I had simply never had the guts to say this in public. I believe that by altering one's perspective - looking at things upside down, back to front and the 'wrong' way round - life can make a lot more sense. This is not just wisdom, but a wild way of looking at life, quite different to the mainstream view.[11] Having the confidence to bring this wild wisdom into my coaching meant a whole new doorway opened up. I began to see the benefit in the results my clients got, when I dared to say what I was really thinking, or receiving. It was liberating, for both of us. The first time this happened was when a client sent a short video to me, asking my opinion. Because it arrived in a moment when I had little time to spend on it, I fired back an email saying rather bluntly that it just wasn't good enough, why that was, and what to do about it. She emailed back immediately, effusive in her thanks; she had been desperate to get some clear feedback and pointed in the right direction. The result of her making adjustments to the video was obtaining a new contract the next week. That gave me more confidence to say what I really thought, without dressing it up. I began to make changes for myself, streamlining the packages being

---

11 You can find a list of how wild wisdom shows up in the world at www.wildwisdom.co.uk/manifesto

offered to private clients, and feeling much more comfortable explaining what my work was about. Of course, the result was a change in the type of person who wanted to work with me, and many other positive changes in the results my clients achieved. Wild Wisdom began to attract those who were not only spiritual, but already had and wanted a quirkier view on their lives and businesses, and how to apply that view in a world which was often still dominated by goals, driven behaviour (even in spiritual communities!) or a focus on money for money's sake. Wild Wisdom has birthed a few more products and programmes since then but has retained the message of viewing life differently, and inspiring others to have the courage, confidence and wisdom to act on this.

A further transition has happened during the writing of this book, when it became obvious how *Gifted By Grief* and Wild Wisdom were linked. Now, I specialize in working with those who have been stopped by grief in some way, regardless of whether it is as a result of death or not. The impact of grief, for whatever reason, on a solo professional life or a small family business is far-reaching, and therefore being able to come through the grief well becomes important in all sorts of ways other than the obvious.

The first two gifts I received could happen for you, too. This third one is much more personal to me. However, it is simply the outward translation of the inner changes received in the first two gifts, and my whole life journey, not just the last three years. If you're interested in discovering the gifts your grief is offering you, then the practical outcome for you could be anything at all. The possibilities are unlimited. There is buried treasure waiting to be found in all of us.

Of course, my preference would be that I had these gifts as well as Philip, alive and healthy. However, perhaps I wouldn't have been able to receive the gifts without him dying. Perhaps they wouldn't have been offered. Who knows? What I do know, though, is I would rather wholeheartedly accept what *is* being offered, than reject it because I'd rather Philip hadn't died. That is the kind of thinking that would have kept me stuck. Instead, I'm freer than I could ever have imagined.

Afterword

As I write this now, I raise my eyes from my laptop, and look around me. I'm in my beautiful sitting room, sunlight flooding in through the bay window, highlighting the rich colours in the Persian rug that was one of our wedding presents. Recently, there was a leak from the flat above onto the rug, and its colours ran into the carpet underneath. But the rug itself wasn't damaged. It was soaked, as I was with tears, but it remains glowing in its vivid reds and purples. Surrounded by the sunlight, I know I am glowing too, both on the inside and out.

The experience of writing about these last years has been fun, painful, and uplifting in equal measure. I couldn't wait to get out of bed in the morning to start writing, whereupon the words just poured out of me. I had no idea the process of writing itself could be so delicately creative and fully nourishing, but so it has proved.

It's nearly three and a half years now since Philip died. The length of time between big bouts of missing him has continued to increase. My biggest fear has indeed ended up becoming true. No man and no children. All alone in the world. The ironic thing is that, looking back, there was more fear associated with the possibility of it happening than there has been in actuality. I have become used to living alone, and in the light of the gifts received, being alone is not as awful as I imagined it would be.

I still think of Philip frequently, but nothing like as much as before, and that's fine. Crafting this book has been healing in and of itself. Writing began as a bud, has gently opened up into a flower, and finally, a full and rather gorgeous bloom, which has enhanced the colours, shapes and passions in my life. However, the most important message in this whole experience has been what happened when 'the shift' took place.

This stepping out from the limited position of being a person with a body, and into being the flow of light and energy that simply manifests through a body, was indescribable. Just as no words can explain the full force and impact of what happened on the cliff tops when I was in my teens, nor are words available to me today to explain fully what happened in the first shift into the 'glow'. That's because the very nature of using words causes separation from being the glow itself, and that's just one of the limitations of being human.

When life is being lived through any bodymind, kindness is a foundation stone of daily life; all actions are infused with love. That's because when you are love itself, you extend and open towards everything and everyone. You can't help it, it's just what happens; judgment of yourself and others lessens dramatically, leaving room for love. Practically, this means old behaviour that was learned as you grew up becomes much less appropriate. That doesn't mean to say you never indulge in it, but when it does happen, you have once more entered into the separate world of suffering, believing you are separate, and therefore unable to act in any way other than a separate being. Then a spark of awareness brings you out of the darkness of separation, and back into the light of being.

Paradoxically, thoughts such as 'place yourself in the hands of the divine', or 'drop down into the well of peace', or 'protect yourself with love and light' can actually enhance the sense of separation. There isn't a separate self to be placed, dropped, or protected. Having said that, these kinds of words bring enormous soothing to the mind and are valid in and of themselves. Indeed, I use them on occasion, albeit with the knowing that what is being done is simply calming the mind.

However, when you are simply left with the truth of being – being light, being love, being peace – then laughter and joy abound at the wonder and simplicity of being, and the craziness of the mind that insists there is anything else. As wise sage Adyashanti says:

As soon as you turn away from the light in your own being you immediately start to seek it.

It is this seeking that keeps you stuck in seeking, as opposed to being the light itself, the ultimate paradox for anyone on a spiritual path.

So what's the solution, if you identify with being a seeker? A seeker would ask that, wouldn't they! One pointer, though, is to simply stop.

Just stop whatever 'doing' is happening. Breathe. Find yourself feeling grateful for 'what is'. Disengage from being the seeker, or whatever role you are taking in whichever version of the human game you are playing, and what is left instead is who you really are; light, love and peace. Laughing at yourself, especially, helps with this disengagement, and is one of the beautiful elements of being peace and love. Delighted laughter erupts at the sweet silliness of the mind intent on looking for something that was never, and can never, be lost.

All of what I have learned about this way of being is new to me, and it has arisen directly as a result of the experiences I went through in the last few years. When Philip was alive we often had long discussions about love, life and meaning – in our own ways, we were both fascinated by these topics. Just after he was diagnosed, I remember asking him in consternation, 'If you die, who am I going to talk to?'

Afterwards, I not only missed his presence but missed these conversations too. It was the pain of this loss that partly spurred me into exploring these questions. I felt as if I had lost a whole rich tapestry of conversation, threads of ideas, dialogue, whole pictures of fascinating perspectives and connections. It was a huge loss; it still is, yet the loss acted as a catalyst which took me into a whole different tapestry, a completely different dimension. It was entering into this other dimension that brought forth the gifts described in this book.

Thank you, Philip. Thank you for our life together – and thank you, too, for the amazing gifts of your death.

Appendix 1: The List

This document is the one Philip and I used to formulate our List. Consider it separate from any will you have or need to make. Maybe record any discussion you have about this topic too, even if you're making notes. It'll help clarify later questions. Some of the points are only applicable if you know you are dying; others can be done by anyone, at any time.

Practical household matters

Ensure your partner or other relevant person knows how to operate any machines you have had sole responsibility for, eg drills, TV, computers, washing machine, dishwasher, burglar alarms, WiFi, location of stopcock, heating meters, computers, phones. Location of guarantees, instruction manuals etc.

Car: if you had sole responsibility for your car, ensure you have passed on information about MOT, tax and insurance dates; tyre pressures; service details; details of garage(s) used; location of MOT certificate and registration documents; when to sell.

Financial/Legal Affairs

List all financial deals, rentals, rental agreements, money owed to whom, pensions, insurances, life policies, bank accounts, mobile phone companies.

Make access easily available to all usernames, email addresses, and passwords (if appropriate).

Identify what is in joint names, and decide whether that needs to be changed now or not. Change if necessary.

List solicitor's details - name, company, address, email, phone number.

Decide who will pay bills immediately after your death - your partner, accountant, lawyer, executor. Name who will discontinue services after your death.

Itemise what needs to be done now, if anything, and do it.

Business

If you have a business, consider a separate business survival plan if necessary. Use this document to help with that, if appropriate.

Family/ friends

Think about making a DVD for your children, grandchildren, great grand-children, or anyone else. Say what you love about them. Include words of wisdom. Keep it in present tense, maybe. Make MP3's or DVD's or write letters for special people.

Go through your papers, letters, diaries, computer files. Destroy/ erase what you do not want read after your death. Or talk about it with your spouse, partner or a special person, for example, stuff that might cause others upset. They will no longer able to talk to you about it when you're no longer here.

Clear up any mysteries that might be unearthed after you die (for example, explain any family secrets that will no longer need to be kept secret. Consider if there is anything that will be gained by telling the secrets, or if indeed they need to be kept secret)

Tell your partner or other loved one what your wishes are as per this document.

Make sure you have said all that you want to say to anyone in your life.

Create a bucket list of things you wish to accomplish.

If you are single and have dependant children, appoint a guardian for them. Ensure there is money available for their well-being in the short term.

Pets - decide what will happen to them.

Consider if there is anything that needs to be sold before death; if so, make those arrangements now.

Final Arrangements

Make sure your will is up-to-date; even a very simple one will make the life of those left behind much easier.

Decide re funeral, cremation, burial at sea or whatever other way you want the body to be taken care of; and which funeral home/parlour/crematorium.

How do you want the body to be dressed?

What kind of coffin do you want? Do you want it open or closed?

Anything to be put in the coffin alongside the body?

If cremated, what do you want done with the ashes? Scattered or interned?

If buried, where?

Last Days Wishes

Who would you ideally like to have present?

Where would you like to be?

What specific music playing, if any?

Would you like people singing for you?

What kind of atmosphere do you want created, eg candles, dim lights, flowers?

After the death

List who needs to be made aware of your death and how they can be contacted.

Decide whether you want a memorial/celebration - What? Where? When? Who? Music? Would you want a programme, and if so, what would you want on it?

Obituary – do you want to write one yourself, or have input into it? Where would you like that published, if at all? (Including on social media)

Who will deliver any eulogy?

Your own special stuff (paintings, art, clothing, anything else of value to you), who would you like to have it? Even little 'worthless' stuff can hold a memory of you for your friends and family. A friend of ours who was bald and had a hat collection gave everybody a hat of his.

Do you want a headstone/grave marker?

Is there any charity to which you want donations given?

Do you want to specify what you would like to be remembered for?

You can get further information from www.finalfling.com

Appendix 2: Example of The Listening

Journal: Saturday 13th November 2011

'In turning to Me you turn to your greatest source of nourishment. There are no two ways about it, though you wish there were. It is only I that can provide the ease, grace and peace that you so crave. For it is when you drop back into Me that you truly come home and let go of all separation ideas.

You ask how to be with Philip in the path towards death. But I ask you, what IS this path you speak of? It is as if you think you are on a separate, lonely route when in truth there are no changes, have never been, and never will be. I am ALWAYS, ALWAYS, ALWAYS here for you - but it is your job to tap into Me. Not the other way round, though I may be able to gain your attention by 'screaming'.

You are moved to read about a daily practice because that is important. A new 'day' heralds a new 'start'. But beware your ego's ideas about this too. Regular, consistent coming to Me is what is important, as I have always said.

Now, I would like you to invite Philip into the knowledge that he is already connected with Me. He maybe doesn't recognise this yet but it appears in the soft touch of his hand, the words that appear from his mouth when he gently brings you back from your ego; the gentle, sweet energy that pervades around him. This is Me coming through his body and I am always there. The body may 'die' but I cannot. It is that simple.

Love, which is another word for Me, is simply present when you call it. Familiarise yourself with it's many different faces and feel its presence. There truly is nothing else of importance."

Acknowledgements

Once I started writing this book, words just poured out of me. After that there was an enormous amount of help from many people, only some of whom are being mentioned here.

Thank you to the Isle of Erraid community, and friends the White family who invited me there, and where this book was begun.

Thanks more than I can say to Carrie and River who came up from the other end of the UK to stay and help us when Philip was in hospital; especially River who stayed for so long.

Thanks to all of Philip's family, especially Jackie and Matthew, who have been there for me when I have needed them.

Deep appreciation for the amount of editing help I have received; thank you Tom and Diana Owens, Tiffany Kay, Andrea Gardner, Kim MacLeod. You all played vital parts in the evolving of this creation. Thank you especially to Dorota Owen, who sat with me hour after hour in all kinds of lovely venues, going through the manuscript line by line. She managed to fill what would have been Philip's role remarkably well, possibly even better, as it might have been more difficult for me to hear what Philip had to contribute!

Thank you to all who read the manuscript and provided an early review – and particularly to Robert Holden for writing the foreword.

In fact, I am deeply grateful to everyone who has been there for me during this time, so many I am just going to list names, in no particular order. You know how much you helped me and how much that meant to me - and still does.

Barbara and Michael Karagosian, Kathy and Michael White, Caroline Born, River King, the BYY group (Lisa, Dorota, Joanna), David Mead, Delcia McNeil, my Mistress Mind group (Kathy, Stacie, Claire, Deborah), all those who helped me move from the bungalow to the flat, Alison Grant, Jackie and Matthew Bishop, my sister Anna Duncan, my brothers Alastair and Simon Duncan, Mum and Dad, Ellen Duncan, Tjitze de Jong, Camphill WellBeing Trust, Dr. Stefan Geider, Heather the nurse from Camphill, our Macmillan Nurse Corinne, Duncan Easter and all who organised and contributed to Philip's Celebration of Life.

Thanks also to Elly Crichton Stuart, Sara Trevelyan, Mary Cowan, Diana Grell, Kate Friendship, The Penny Brohn Cancer Care Centre, Candy Constable, Auriol de Smidt, June Rickards, Alan Massey, Hugh Andrews, Thomas Warrior, Lisa Berkovitz, Phil Taylor and Wendy Richardson, Paul Harvey, the JP App group, Rodney Knights, Chris Stepien, Jac O'Keeffe, all on Jac's forum, Wayne Liquorman, Roger Linden, Sue Miles, Kelly Jo Murphy, Jeff Shaw, Ken Stone, Mark Porteous, and everyone in the Findhorn Foundation Community who showed me such support right after Philip died, and in the years following.

Many thanks too to Wyon Stansfeld, Alisoun Mackenzie, Joey Walters, Andrea Gardner, all members of ForWords, Diane Vasarkovy, Tony Ingleby, members of Publishers Empire, and anyone who has bumped into me, saw I was needing a hug, and gave me one. I also appreciate all my clients during these years, and those who are on my mailing list.

Finally, thanks to anyone else who has offered me love and support, in any way, both practical and emotional. It has all been, and is, deeply appreciated.

Jane is currently working on further e-books and online programmes. Sign up to her mailing list to hear of future developments at www.giftedbygrief.com

Resources

www.giftedbygrief.com - full of information to inspire you to find your own gifts in whatever situation you are in. Sign up to the blog and to hear about courses, workshops and online programmes that Jane is running.

www.wildwisdom.co.uk - my coaching website, helping spiritually inclined solo professionals, small business owners and others who are struggling with loss to awaken to their gifts so they can continue to make the contribution they were born to make. Loads of great free resources here too. Sign up to receive my regular newsletter.

www.philiprogers.co.uk - the full blog that Philip wrote, unedited. Full of pathos, humour and wisdom, it's well worth reading, especially if you want the full story of his last year. Get out the box of tissues, though!

People and Organisations mentioned in the text.

Newbold House - the retreat centre where we were living when Philip was diagnosed. http://www.newboldhouse.org/

La Maison Anglaise - where we had our fabulous last holiday together, one of Lonely Planet's top 10 stays in the world for 2014. www.holidays-with-heart.co.uk

Mistletoe Therapy - for all information about mistletoe treatments, centres around the UK, and research information www.mistletoetherapy.org.uk

The Penny Brohn Cancer Care Centre - where Philip visited a few months before he died. www.pennybrohncancercare.org

Kate Friendship - the energy healer Philip saw for treatments. www.katefriendship.co.uk/

Tjitze de Jong - founder of the Energetic Cellular Healing School, and whom Philip saw for treatments. www.tjitzedejong.com/

Alan Massey – the Alexander Technique teacher and Reiki healer who worked with Philip. www.alexanderpresence.co.uk

Margie McCallum – celebrant who led the service in the funeral home. www.margiemccallum.com

Course in Miracles www.acim.org

Miracle Choice Game - developed after Philip died and a great way to experience the benefits of the book www.miraclechoice-game.com

Macmillan Nurses: specialists in cancer care in the UK www.macmillan.org.uk

Ho'opono'pono - Forgiveness process. This site is where I first heard about it, by reading the book Zero Limits. www.zerolimits.info

Jac O'Keeffe - my non-dual teacher. www.jac-okeeffe.com

Roger Linden - non dual teacher. www.rogerlinden.com

Wayne Liquorman - non dual teacher. www.advaita.org

Delcia McNeil - my friend and colleague who channelled the messages from Philip www.channellingforlife.com

La Domaine du Fan - near Limoges, France, where I went for the second non-dual retreat with Jac O'Keeffe. www.ladomainedu-fan.com

Mymering Guest House – the stunning place where I stayed with my friends on the way to Addo Elephant Park in South Africa www.mymering.com

Cotswold Healing Retreat - where I heard from the medium re Philip, and felt him so strongly there. www.cotswoldhealingretreat.co.uk

Lisa Berkovitz - the wonderful coach who helped birth Wild Wisdom. www.lisaberkovitz.com

Robert Holden - so inspirational to me when I attended his session at the Forgiveness Conference. www.robertholden.org

Sobonfu Some - holder of grief tending rituals. www.sobonfu.com

Journal Writing - there are many resources out there to help you with using a journal. For organisations, I recommend www.appreciatingpeople.co.uk

Thich Nhat Hanh - and his community at Plum Village, France: www.plumvillage.org

Angie Alexandra and Will Russell, Marriage Celebrants: the couple who had the community wedding for themselves www.gettingmarriedinscotland.org

Findhorn Foundation: spiritual community, eco-village and learning centre www.findhorn.org

Death Cafes - not mentioned in the story, but a great place to meet others who want to talk about death and dying. www.deathcafe.com

Websites I used

Way Up: one of the many forums available for those suffering from grief www.way-up.co.uk

MerryWidows: www.merrywidow.me.uk

Final Fling: www.finalfling.com - very useful for organising your list and other information re death and dying

Recommended Books:

Spirituality

A Guide to the I Ching: Carol Anthony

The Power of Now: Eckhart Tolle

Beyond Manifestation: Joe Vitale

Born to Be Free: Jac O'Keeffe

Enlightenment is Not What You Think: Wayne Liquorman

Power, Freedom and Grace: Deepak Chopra

Loveability: Robert Holden

The Diamond in Your Pocket: Gangaji

An Extraordinary Absence: Jeff Foster

When Things Fall Apart: Pema Chodron

Life Loves You: Louise Hay and Robert Holden

Clarity - Jamie Smart

Grief and Bereavement

The Truth about Grief: Ruth Davis Kongisberg

First Steps Through Bereavement: Sue Mayfield

Widow to Widow: Genevieve Davis

On Grief and Grieving: Elizabeth Kubler Ross

Me After You: Lucie Brownlee

Second Firsts: Christina Rasmussen

The After Journey: Laurie-Ann Weis

The Two of Us: Sheila Hancock

A Grief Observed: C.S. Lewis

From Chrysalis to Butterfly: Anna Delves (from the Cotswold

Healing Retreat)

A Memory Returned: Anna Delves

Resilient Heart: Gail Saunders

From Heartbreak to Happiness: Kim MacLeod & Christine MacPherson

Just Me: Sheila Hancock

Mary Had Stretch Marks: Miriam Connor

Death

Dying to Be Me: Anita Moorjani

Love Medicine and Miracles: Bernie Siegel

On Children and Death: Elizabeth Kubler Ross

Who Dies? Stephen Levine

Final Gifts: Maggie Callanan and Patricia Kelley

Death and How To Survive It: Kate Boydell

Healing Into Life and Death: Stephen Levine

Grace and Grit: Ken Wilber

How We Die: Sherwin Nuland

Death - The Last God: Anne Geraghty

Blessed with A Brain Tumour: Will Pye

Being Mortal: Atul Gawande

Money

Love Money, It Loves You: Joy Prospero

Busting Loose From the Money Game: Robert Scheinfeld

Author Biography

Jane Duncan Rogers, author of *Gifted By Grief: A True Story of Cancer, Loss and Rebirth*, believes passionately that society needs to be more open about grief, death and dying. She says, "To be sticking our heads in the sand and finding these topics difficult to mention is complete madness, given we are all going to be affected by them sooner or later. It's my intention to open up conversations about these topics and bring them out of the closet."

Having worked for over twenty five years in the personal growth industry as a counselor, psychotherapist and group leader, and owned Oxfordshire's largest complementary health clinic, author, coach and speaker Jane has helped thousands of people around the world to transform their lives and business. Since her husband's death in 2011 she also brings her unique insight to those affected by loss of any kind.

Jane is known for her honest and refreshing look at life, which combined with her wild wisdom and natural compassion and understanding, makes it easy for her clients to open up and feel deeply heard. This allows the movement forward that is being sought, and the context for miracles to happen.

Jane originally trained personally in 1990 with Louise L Hay, founder of Hay House publishers and author of the famous book, *You Can Heal Your Life*®. An award winning coach, she has worked all over the world with individuals and small organisations to help them adopt a very different way of living and working.

She published *Choose Your Thoughts, Change Your Life* in 1997, and co-authored with her husband, Philip Rogers, *60 Ways to Lose/Keep your Lover* (2001). She has been writing a blog, Wild Wisdom, since 2009.

Jane is associated with the world-renowned Findhorn Foundation; spiritual community, eco-village and learning centre in the Highlands of Scotland. She sings and performs in a local well-known womens acappella group and is often to be found on early morning walks in the woods, before her regular meditation practice in one of the sanctuaries belonging to the Foundation.

A personal note from Jane

I wonder if you would do me a favour?

If you've enjoyed this book or been moved by it, please do review it on Amazon and/or GoodReads.

I know how beneficial it is for people to be able to talk easily about dying, loss and grief, and genuine, authentic reviews really help towards this.

Plus, if you know someone who is dealing with loss of any kind, do tell them about the book, or give them details of it.

Finally, I realised I wanted to give you a thank you present for reading the book. So I compiled something that would have helped me, had it been around.

I found that simple, easy statements gave me the most relief from grief in the moment, and that's what I've created for you in my **Grief Support Statement.**

Each sentence stands alone, or they can be read together, to help you release pain, feel less alone, and more loved.

It comes as a PDF which you can print it out and keep where you can refer to it easily. Or you can use the MP3 version, where I am reading them to you.

You can get your copy by visiting: https://www.giftedbygrief.com/statement

You'll also then be on my regular email newsletter list, where you'll hear about any updates on all my future projects (including the next book) and receive useful tips, information and inspirational articles to help you in loss, life and love.

Thank you!

Jane

Lightning Source UK Ltd.
Milton Keynes UK
UKOW06f0714010915

257858UK00002B/26/P